Diversity in Mind and in Action

Diversity in Mind and in Action

Volume 1

Multiple Faces of Identity

EDITED BY JEAN LAU CHIN

Foreword by Joseph E. Trimble

Praeger Perspectives
Race and Ethnicity in Psychology

PRAEGER
An Imprint of ABC-CLIO, LLC

A B C 🌐 C L I O

Santa Barbara, California • Denver, Colorado • Oxford, England

Library of Congress Cataloging-in-Publication Data

Diversity in mind and in action / edited by Jean Lau Chin ; foreword by Joseph
E. Trimble.
    p. cm. — (Praeger perspectives race and ethnicity in psychology)
    Includes bibliographical references and index.
    ISBN 978-0-313-34709-2 (v. 1 : alk. paper) : (978-0-313-34710-8 (e-book) — ISBN
978-0-313-34711-5 (v. 2 : alk. paper) : (978-0-313-34712-2 (e-book) — ISBN 978-0-
313-34713-9 (v. 3 : alk. paper) : (978-0-313-34714-6 (e-book) — ISBN 978-0-313-
34707-8 (set) : (978-0-313-34708-5 (set e-book)
    1. Prejudices—United States. 2. Intercultural communication—United States.
3. Minorities—Mental health services—Social aspects. 4. Psychiatry, Transcul-
tural—United States. 5. Minorities—Employment—United States. 6. Minorities—Education—United States. I. Chin, Jean Lau.
HM1091.D58 2009
305—dc22   2009000516

13   12   11   10   09   1   2   3   4   5

This book is also available on the World Wide Web as an eBook.
Visit www.abc-clio.com for details.

ABC-CLIO, LLC
130 Cremona Drive, P.O. Box 1911
Santa Barbara, California 93116-1911

This book is printed on acid-free paper ∞
Manufactured in the United States of America

Contents

Foreword

Within and without the sombre veil of color vast social forces have been at work—efforts for human betterment, movements toward disintegration and despair, tragedies and comedies in social and economic life, and a swaying and lifting and sinking of human hearts which have made this land a land of mingled sorrow and joy, of change and excitement and unrest.
—W.E.B. DuBois (1903, p. 129)

The poignant, profound, and haunting words of the eminent African American scholar, W.E.B. DuBois, set the tone for the contents of these volumes with their emphasis on diversity in mind and action. Indeed, the lives of countless immigrants and those of the indigenous peoples of the Americas are filled with the "swaying and sinking of human hearts" that continue to move to and fro as the populations in the Western Hemisphere swell in number. An afternoon stroll down the busy sidewalks of major cities in North America gives attention to the multitudes of people from different nationalities and ethnocultural populations; the principal elements of diversity in all of its forms rise up when one hears the sounds and tones of various languages, becomes aware of distinctive clothing styles and dress patterns, and observes the manner in which couples stroll along arm-in-arm. The multiplicity of differences is more apparent now than it has ever been. The differences have always been there, but they were suppressed. Often, when diverse groups appeared out in the open, they drew sneers, derision, sarcasm, attacks on the dignity of the people, exclusion, harsh commentary, and outright offensive injustices.

The spectacle created by rapid sociocultural changes is no more evident than in educational institutions. In some school districts around the

United States, for example, there are countless foreign languages and dialects spoken in the homes of the youth. In the southwestern quadrant of the country, Spanish is the lingua franca in homes, communities, religious institutions, and the workplace, but not necessarily in the school systems. Similarly, Canada endorses French and English as the two primary languages of the country. Diversity, as represented by the expression and declaration of one's ethnocultural allegiance and affiliations, is no longer concealed; it's out in the open.

Survey results from the 2000 U.S. Census Bureau, for example, indicate that countless Americans opted to identify an ancestral nationality or ethnic group as significant for them. One of the survey questions in the 2000 form asks, "What is this person's ancestry or ethnic origin?" Eighty percent of the respondents specified their ancestry; 58 percent provided a single ancestry and 22 percent provided multiple ancestries (U.S. Census Bureau, 2004). The specific ancestral or ethnic groups listed reveal an interesting and illuminating pattern, as 42.8 million considered themselves to be of German ancestral background; this figure represents over 15 percent of the total responses. Groups mentioned with over 15 million reporting included Irish (30.5 million), African American (24.9 million), English (24.5 million), American (20.2 million), Mexican (18.4 million), and Italian (15.6 million). Overall, the census item generated some 92 different ancestries with 100,000 or more people belonging to them; furthermore, it generated some 500 different ancestral listings. Additionally, an inspection of the ancestral demographic distributions by U.S. county provided by the Census Bureau shows heavy concentrations of national groups in certain areas of the country; a quick glance at Minnesota, Wisconsin, and the Dakotas shows pockets of people of Nordic and German descent. County maps in Florida, Texas, New Mexico, Arizona, and California show heavy concentrations of descendants from the Caribbean, Mexico, and Central and South America.

There are other powerful influences among the populations of North America that emerge from interethnic marriages and childbearing. In the 2000 census, for example, the Census Bureau asked citizens to indicate their multiethnic affiliation by asking them to check more than one so-called racial category if this was applicable; results from the survey showed that, on average, 2.4 percent of the U.S. population identified with two or more racial groups. Use of the new multiracial item created debates and problems for all who rely on use of census outcomes. The addition of the multiracial category presents difficult tabulation and reporting problems for health care professionals, economists, demographers, social and behavioral scientists and others who use racial categories for their work. Prewitt (2002) pointed out that the addition of the multiracial category represents a "turning point in the measurement of race . . . and . . . the arrival of a multiple-race option in the census classification will so blur racial distinctions in the political and legal spheres and perhaps also in the public consciousness that race classification will gradually disappear" (p. 360).

People from similar ethnocultural heritages tend to cluster in communities; this clustering is most evident when groups migrate to North America and gravitate to an area where people reside who share a common identity, cultural lifeways, values and beliefs, that are unique from the mainstream culture. This resettlement suggests a strong sense of identity and the need for affiliation. The path to like-minded communities also implies that one will find a haven from discrimination and social ostracism, as well as a place where one can feel comfortable expressing one's traditional lifeways and thoughtways. Degrees of subjective self-identity influence the extent to which one seeks social support from peers to validate and substantiate this identity; it's a reciprocal and often negotiated progression, accompanied with rules and acceptable sources of evidence such as language use, family birthrights, physiognomic features, interaction styles, and so on. Social validation brings comfort and reinforcement of one's personal identity. Personal well being is also strengthened and, along with it, the hope that daily life will be free from the suppression of traditions, customs, and beliefs.

But as the landscape changes and culture and diversity become more obvious, people insensitive to these issues must learn to accommodate differences and understand the strengths that differences and diversity provide to society as a whole; history books and chapters tell gripping and chilling stories about what happens when insensible bigots refuse to accommodate differences and, in the process, exert and ultimately abuse their power. Change must occur if we are to avoid any further intergroup and interpersonal conflict. And one of the ways proactive change can occur is through an emphasis on the development of multicultural competence, as suggested in several chapters in these volumes. While there are numerous ways to achieve and define cultural competence, no doubt there is much greater agreement about recognizing instances of multicultural incompetence. The fallout and the untoward consequences of cultural incompetence are unprecedented in the annals of the history of our planet; the emotional, psychological, physical, ecological, and economic costs are extraordinary and often beyond comprehension. Advocating and encouraging cultural competency in every aspect of life can avoid cultural incompetence; many of the chapters in these volumes provide thoughtful guidance and orientation on this topic.

In reading the chapters in the volumes, we should be mindful of the psychosocial complexities of the melting pot theory and the strong influence of individualism in North America. In one of the classic statements on personhood in non-Western cultures, Clifford Geertz (1973), an American cultural anthropologist, reminds us that: "The Western conception of the person as a bounded, unique, more or less integrated motivational and cognitive universe, a dynamic center of awareness, emotion, judgment, and action, organized into a distinctive whole and set contrastively—both against other such wholes and against social and natural background—is however incorrigible it may seem to us, a rather peculiar idea within the context of the world's cultures" (p. 34). His observation is worthy of serious consideration and contemplation as we forge and promote intergroup relationships deriving from respectfulness and civility.

The collection of thoughtful and coherent chapters in the *Diversity in Mind and in Action* collection provides a discourse on an extensive range of topics in the rapidly emerging field of multiculturalism in the social and behavioral sciences, as well as in other academic disciplines. Readers may not agree with some of the concepts, proposals, and arguments. But there may be countless others who have waited for the contents of the volumes to come along to provide them with support and direction. Volumes like these are set out to encourage debate and discussion, especially about the growing multicultural populations of North America where, eventually, no single ethnocultural group will be dominant.

Editor Jean Lau Chin and her hand-picked collection of competent and often inspiring authors are to be heartily congratulated for their stimulating and thought-provoking contributions. Many of the contributions are based on first-hand experiences, while others provide a blend of empirical research findings with practical applications. Examples abound describing the effects of cultural incompetence; their blend with wonderful and insightful examples of how to deal with them add an important dimension to the field. Above all else, however, is the hope provided by the content and flow of the volumes and chapters that intergroup and interethnic relations will improve to eliminate discrimination, prejudice, hatred, incivilities, and the vile and venomous hatred they provoke.

Joseph E. Trimble, PhD
Professor of Psychology
Western Washington University
Bellingham, WA 98225
September 28, 2008

REFERENCES

Du Bois, W.E.B. (1903). *The souls of black folk.* Chicago: A. C. McClurg.

Geertz, C. (1973). *The interpretation of cultures: Selected essays.* New York: Basic Books.

Prewitt, K. (2002). Race in the 2000 census: A turning point. In J. Perlmann & M. C. Waters (Eds.), *The new race question: How the census counts multiracial individuals* (pp. 354–360). New York: Russell Sage Foundation.

U.S. Census Bureau. (2004). *Ancestry: 2000.* Washington, DC: U.S. Department of Commerce, Economic and Statistics Administration.

Preface

This new three-volume set is part of the Praeger Series on Race, Ethnicity, and Psychology. A previous set, *The Psychology of Prejudice and Discrimination*, also edited by Dr. Chin, was named a 2005 Choice Outstanding Academic Title (Chin, 2005b).

Diversity is a hot and contemporary issue. While the successes of the Civil Rights Movement and Women's Movement in the twentieth century led to transformations in U.S. society, diversity remains an issue in the twenty-first century as it becomes even more important for diverse people and communities to live and work together for the common good and mutual survival. Diversity has also become a global issue as advances in technology, transportation, and the Internet have narrowed our borders and made our boundaries more permeable. Internationally, many countries now share the common experiences and problems of increased mobility among its citizens and a more diverse population. We must now address the contemporary issues of diversity and move beyond the melting-pot myth of the twentieth century and the segregationist policies that legislated different paths for people based on their skin color. We are talking about tolerance and cultural competence, and these traits start in our minds. We are saying that *diversity matters!* We must *act* to create equitable work and living environments, and *advocate* to change that which perpetuates the intolerance of difference and diversity.

Diversity is complex. Whereas promoting diversity once meant simply meeting the needs of immigrants and ethnic minorities, and welcoming new and different racial/ethnic groups into our communities and institutions, promoting diversity now means much more. We must address the differences between new immigrants and those racial/ethnic minority

groups born and bred in the United States. We must expand our definitions of diversity to include not only race and ethnicity, but also gender,
sexual orientation, religion, and disability. Moreover, it has become clear
that our identities do not manifest themselves in isolation, and we must
understand the complexity of how they interact. Our attention to diversity must also grapple with the issues of multiculturalism, both within the
United States and in a global society.

Diversity must also be placed in a historical context. The melting-pot
myth in America reflects a time in which the dominant group in the
United States was white and middle class; those in positions of power
were white men; the social ideal was to call on a nation to unite. Technology, terrorism, and continued immigration changed all that. We have
become increasingly global and diverse. Even our labeling of groups has
evolved, and must be placed in a historical context. It is more difficult to
label African Americans, Latin Americans, Asian Americans, and American Indians, the four historical groups of color, as minority groups. The
individual labels changed through the preference to avoid the stigma of
marginalization and racism inherent in the labels of "Negro," "Oriental,"
and "Indian."

Diversity is both a state of mind and a stance of action. How we conduct
ourselves as responsible citizens, and how we practice as ethical professionals amid a diverse population, community, and society is central in
this conversation. This volume set, *Diversity in Mind and in Action*, intends
to address just that. How do we grapple with inequity in our institutions
and workplaces? How do we honor our multiple identities? How do we
confront the adverse consequences of privilege and power that favor
some groups while oppressing others? How do we transform the bias in
our minds and actions that lead to disparities and incompetence in the
delivery of services? How do we recognize the narrowness of our borders
and our interdependence within a global society?

This set organizes each volume by major themes related to diversity
and multiculturalism that beset today's society. Volume 1 addresses the
themes of identity and how individuals and groups identify with one
another based on race, ethnicity, country of origin, gender, sexual orientation, and religion, often cutting across geographic boundaries and professional affiliations. Volume 2 addresses disparities in health and mental
health, and how our care delivery systems are often biased in providing
differential access to care for different groups. Diversity as a matter of ethics and cultural competence is the theme. The climate and contexts of our
educational institutions and workplaces in which diverse groups learn,
work, and live will be discussed, as well as diversity and leadership. Diversity matters! Volume 3 discusses the themes of social justice, power,
and oppression, which are associated with racism, classism, and social
privilege. Social, political, and psychological challenges face us as we seek
strategies and solutions to create social institutions that honor diversity,

and are the training grounds for diverse citizens living together with differences of perspectives, origins, and persuasions. This is social change and advocacy. It is a contemporary view of diversity amid a historical context.

Contributors to this set provide a framework not only for understanding diversity, but also for acting together in transforming our society and its institutions to create equity for diverse groups. All volumes are anchored in a global perspective, attend to issues of difference, and contribute to a *vision for diversity in mind and action*—a vision to honor diversity, and of a society where all groups can co-exist while respecting differences; where our institutions will no longer be biased against any one group over another, and will be culturally competent in serving their diverse needs.

Key Questions at the end of each volume are intended to make the set useful for training by educators and professionals, as well as for further inquiry by a broader audience addressing diversity in contemporary society. Each chapter author has contributed a key question to promote discussion and challenge thinking based on the theme and key issue or main focus of the chapter. These have been compiled as a table at the end of each volume to be used as exercises.

ACKNOWLEDGMENTS

I would like to acknowledge my family, and especially my mother, an immigrant from Nanking, China, from whom I gained valuable insights about our journey in life. I documented her narrative in *Learning from My Mother's Voice* (Chin, 2005a) and learned important lessons, with her as my mentor, about the importance of resiliency and endurance. These serve as lifelong lessons for us to continue that struggle and goal toward inclusion and equity and of valuing the differences that make us human and humane.

I am also grateful to my graduate assistants who contributed to this volume set including Gideon Kim, Kirsten Petersen, and especially Jessica Shimberg, who toiled together to bring together the contributions of this diverse groups of authors.

Jean Lau Chin

REFERENCES

Chin, J. L. (2005a). *Learning from my mother's voice: Family legend and the Chinese American experience.* New York: Teacher's College Press.

Chin, J. L. (Ed.). (2005b). *The psychology of prejudice and discrimination.* Westport, CT: Praeger Publishers.

Introduction to Volume 1: Multiple Faces of Identity

Why is identity discussed in this volume on *Diversity in Mind and in Action?* Identity is how we define ourselves, how we think of ourselves, and why we seek an affinity with individuals and groups based on race, ethnicity, country of origin, gender, sexual orientation, and religion; these communities and groups with which we align ourselves often cut across geographic boundaries. Fassinger's (2008) description of diverse populations includes groups currently marginalized and disadvantaged in the U.S. workplace: women, people of color, sexual minorities, and people with disabilities.

Differences in group membership and identification matter in interpreting behavior. For example, group identification on the part of members of stigmatized groups increases recognition of unfair treatment of them (Major, 1994). Many researchers have found that highly group-identified individuals (i.e., perceiving themselves as being similar to their group members) are more likely to interpret ambiguous behavior as discrimination than are individuals who do not (Crocker & Major, 1989).

Racial and ethnic identity has been central to our definitions of self identity, especially for communities of color. The signature identity of the United States, however, is that it is a land of immigrants welcoming all to its shores symbolized by the Statue of Liberty standing at the port of entry in New York. As people of color increasingly immigrated to the United States during the nineteenth and twentieth centuries, the early images of America as a melting pot were no longer relevant; many felt marginalized by these images. As racial/ethnic differences emerged in terms of identity, the utilization of services, and social and community practices, the importance of diversity grew to the point where we, as a society, called for cultural sensitivity to these diverse population groups. Attention focused on identifying the importance of racial/ethnic identity as defining and distinguishing the experiences and needs of these groups. As awareness grew, other groups joined in their shared experience of marginalization—diversity expanded to include race, ethnicity, gender, sexual orientation, religion, ability status, and many other dimensions. Increasingly, these identities and definitions of diversity began to exceed those listed above to include professional affiliations, theoretical perspectives, age, and so on. Yet, attention to diversity has continued to focus on singular and isolated dimensions of identity.

Diversity is more complex than any singular dimension. Not only should we be attending to differences between groups, but also we should be recognizing that individuals bring multiple dimensions of their identity to bear in any situation. Moreover, these dimensions are interactive. Even our singular categorization of race and ethnicity no longer define individuals of multiracial or multiethnic backgrounds; furthermore, it does not capture the differences between immigrant groups and their counterparts from racial/ethnic minorities who have now been in the United States for more than a generation. The evolution in our understanding of racial/ethnic identity has been significant, both in our research and in our social conceptualization—from the melting-pot myth used to define immigrant identities, to marginalizing racial/ethnic minority groups through notions of the "hyphenated American" (e.g., Asian American), to our recognition of bicultural identities. We have come a long way from the time when a focus on identity was viewed as reflecting a problem and pathology, and a deficit model was used to define diverse individuals and communities who were different from the majority. We now recognize these identities as inherent in who we are, even when studying esoteric areas of research.

We now use the metaphor of a *cultural mosaic* to describe a society that honors and values the cultures of origin among our immigrant groups. We are challenged by the notion of multiple identities and how they interact with one another in any social and interpersonal context. A vision for diversity in mind and action is needed to move society and ourselves toward new models for understanding identity amidst diversity and difference. It is time to move on from singular definitions of identity. This must begin not only with our definitions of our selves, but also with those of our communities, institutions, and countries. Historians have repeatedly pointed to the changing racial and ethnic demographics in the United States; by 2050, there will be no single majority. The so-called WASP will no longer characterize our dominant culture.

This is why an experience at a forum on immigration in 2008 was so chilling. The keynote speaker, Dr. Kenneth Prewitt (2008) (former director of the U.S. Census Bureau and researcher on the use of ethnoracial classification in national statistics), gave a compelling historical overview of immigration in the United States, and the injustices we perpetrated toward new immigrant groups; he suggested that these need to be used as lessons for the present. He persuaded us on how we have legislated the criminality and illegality of our immigrants, in contrast to the message of hope and freedom for immigrants coming to America from around the world that is symbolized by the Statue of Liberty and stated by "The New Colossus," a sonnet inscribed on its pedestal:

> Not like the brazen giant of Greek fame,
> With conquering limbs astride from land to land,
> Here at our sea-washed, sunset-gates shall stand
> A mighty woman with a torch, whose flame
> Is the imprisoned lightning, and her name
> Mother of Exiles. From her beacon-hand
> Glows world-wide welcome, her mild eyes command
> The air-bridged harbor that twin-cities frame.
>
> "Keep, ancient lands, your storied pomp!" cries she,
> With silent lips. "Give me your tired, your poor,
> Your huddled masses yearning to breathe free,
> The wretched refuse of your teeming shore;
> Send these, the homeless, tempest-tost to me,
> I lift my lamp beside the golden door!"
>
> > November, 2, 1883
> > *Emma Lazarus*

The response of one member of the audience during the question-and-answer period was chilling. He argued for "one flag, one country, one language, and one America," and criticized the panel for its bias in promoting diversity. I could not help but note his Sephardic features amid his fervent cry that questioned our loyalty and pureness as Americans. Was he too blind to see that he would have been eliminated in Nazi Germany? Was he too ignorant to realize that his immigrant ancestors would have faced the very discrimination he was preaching? Was he closing the doors behind others now that he was in, claiming his supremacy against the Native Americans whom we overpowered and oppressed? These arguments calling for so-called oneness fail to appreciate the contributions of diversity and difference, and define uniformity as an artificial measure of loyalty and identity in a country built by immigrants.

Bruckner (2007) claims that "multiculturalism is racism of the antiracists: It chains people to their roots." He calls for a national community, and criticizes "the tolerance of coexisting hermetic little societies, each of which follows a different norm" (p. B4). He uses, as an example, tolerance of the cultural practice among Shiites that condone wife beating while the same behavior by a French, British, or Dutch citizen would be prosecuted. These arguments are misrepresentations of multiculturalism because they do not take into account the core value of "do no harm." There are other arguments against diversity that call for a "we are all people" notion of integration; unfortunately, this frequently results in ignoring differences that do matter, and failing to provide for differential needs where they exist.

This volume is about "self in context," multiple and intersecting identities anchored in families, communities, and social institutions. It is time to consider a broader perspective of diversity. It is a time for creating narratives so that all people can tell their stories—different stories to reflect who we are, as well as our origins, in order for all to claim an equal right to the future.

These chapters address the complexity and intersection of identities— multiple, bicultural, multiracial, and multiethnic. The chapters also address racism from different racial/ethnic perspectives as an important defining context, as well as its impact on identity. Lastly, the volume addresses strategies for dealing with the challenges of identity formation— internal and external, oppression and empowerment, ethics and values, and using narratives to capture the journey in a society that is increasingly diverse and global.

REFERENCES

Bruckner, P. (2007, March 2). European multiculturalism. *The Chronicle of Higher Education, The Chronicle Review, 53*(26), B4.

Crocker, J., & Major, B. (1989). Social stigma and self-esteem: The self-protective properties of stigma. *Psychological Review, 96,* 608–630.

Fassinger, R. (2008). Workplace diversity and public policy: Challenges and opportunities for psychology. *American Psychologist, 63*(4), 252–268.

Major, B. (1994). From social inequality to personal entitlement: The role of social comparisons, legitimacy appraisals, and group membership. In M. P. Zanna (Ed.), *Advances in experimental social psychology* (Vol. 26, pp. 293–348). San Diego, CA: Academic Press.

Prewitt, K. (2008, May 15). Keynote address presented at the Immigration on Long Island: Our Challenge, Our Responsibility forum. New York: Adelphi University. Retrieved September 30, 2008, from http://events.adelphi.edu/news/2008/20080325.php.

CHAPTER 1

The Multiracial Movement: Bridging Society's Language Barrier

Alicia M. del Prado and James Lyda

Race is a socially constructed way of grouping people, which differs among societies and over time. It has no biological basis, yet has been historically borrowed from the systematic classification of plants and animals to give this concept scientific validity. In the United States, many individuals have experienced misrepresentation because of restrictive racial labels. The U.S. Census Bureau, an important and visible institution in the United States, utilizes nomenclature that may be considered limited, imprecise, and even derogatory. For example, use of the term Hispanic has been rejected by some as connoting an identity of oppression and Spanish colonization. American Indian is a misnomer given by so-called explorers thinking they landed in India, and Pacific Islander is a term incorporating multiple countries and territories of the United States such as Samoa and Guam. Furthermore, while the first U.S. Census began in 1790, it was not until the 2000 Census that respondents had the option to check off multiple categories on the race question. When this choice became available, approximately 6.8 million individuals in the United States identified themselves as belonging to two or more races (U.S. Census Bureau, 2000), providing a voice whereby a multiracial movement declared its presence.

Multiracial is an inclusive identification term that "refers to people who are of two or more racial heritages" and refers "to people across all racial mixes" (Root, 1996, p. xi). Therefore, *multiracial* encompasses *biracial* identity, which refers to "a person whose parents are of two different socially designated racial groups" (Root, 1996, p. ix). While the limitations of the U.S. Census Bureau data have been highlighted, the invisibility, muteness, and misrepresentation of multiracial people occur in a plethora of places.

Root (1996) specified that monoracial classification systems that insist "on clean lines between groups" and force individuals "to fit into just one category" (p. 5) are oppressive to multiracial persons and are often used in schools, colleges, and universities. For example, at a 2008 symposium on student diversity held by a large public university on the West Coast, an Office of Student Research director explained that the algorithm used to assess the diversity data assigned one student to only one race even when students selected two or more racial identifications. The presenter pointed to the U.S. Census classification system as determining how the university counts students. The first author pointed out to the presenter that the statistics of students identifying as belonging to multiple races needs to be examined as such. The director acknowledged that this was a problem with the data, responded "I hear you," but offered no promise of change or action for future data analyses. This example illustrates that, even within the growing movement toward multiculturalism, diversity, and inclusion in society, more attention is needed for multiracial persons.

However, the population of multiracial, or mixed race people is growing and is expected to continue expanding, especially considering the increasing number of interracial couples. In the landmark civil rights case *Loving v. State of Virginia* (1967), the U.S. Supreme Court legalized relationships between people of different racial backgrounds. The number of interracial marriages in the United States has been on the rise: from 310,000 in 1970 (0.7% of all marriages) to 2,669,558 in 2000 (4.9% of all marriages). The number of mixed-race births is increasing at a faster rate than the number of single-race births (U.S. Census Bureau, 1992, 2000). The impact of this is being felt all over the United States where, in cities like Seattle, Sacramento, and San Antonio, one in every six newborns is multiracial (Kelley & Root, 2003). The multiracial population is young, diverse, and growing rapidly. According to Jones and Smith (2003), at the time of the 2000 Census, nearly 42 percent of the multiracial population was under the age of 18, and 68 percent were under 35. In 2000, the U.S. Census reported approximately 500,000 multiracial students enrolled in colleges or universities. As the numbers of multiracial persons increase, the need for addressing the identity and psychosocial development of multiracial individuals is critical.

The multiracial movement, which gained momentum in the late 1970s and early 1980s, has been proactively addressing the unique issues of the mixed race population in the United States. The multiracial movement is being pursued by people dedicated to the advancement of the rights and self-expression of multiracial individuals and families. The movement has taken many forms, including forming organizations where mixed race people and their families can socialize, creating magazines where mixed race issues are shared, and producing art, poetry, and compositions in which the mixed-race experience can be expressed. Advocates of the multiracial movement successfully lobbied for the "check one or more" policy in the 2000 U.S. Census forms. In the twenty-first century, we need to continue to integrate the larger community into the multiracial movement. As with other civil right issues, the participation of all communities is needed in order for multiracially affirmative change to permeate throughout society. Douglass (2003) highlighted, "If we are ever to eliminate institutional racism in America, we must look to educate not only ourselves [the mixed race community] but the government agencies that tabulate people, the social services and health departments that categorize, diagnose, and treat people, as well as the general population that attempts to define us" (p. 16). Members of society can help foster an environment where people of racially and ethnically mixed heritage feel accepted, recognized, and celebrated. In our multiple roles as family members, friends, teachers, students, helpers, workers, neighbors, church members and more, we all have the responsibility to create an open, nurturing environment for multiracial people.

Our chapter aims to advance the multiracial movement by bridging the *language barrier* that is present both within the mixed-race community and between multiracial and monoracial persons. We propose that this language barrier is the lack of a vernacular that is sufficiently reflective of the identities and existence of people of mixed heritage. The voice and authentic experiences of racially mixed people within the United States have been suppressed and silenced by a lack of inclusive terminology. Current racial conceptualizations emphasize an either/or approach that can unnecessarily dichotomize identity for people of racially mixed heritage. For example, Cynthia—whose mother is Italian American and father is Salvadorian—has felt pressure from her peers, parents, and siblings, to identify as *either* Sicilian American *or* Salvadorian (C. A. Faupusa, personal communication, June 18, 2008). We suggest that the either/or mentality should be replaced with a so-called all/and mindset that embraces identification with *all* aspects of one's racial and ethnic identity as normal and positive. Under the *all/and* approach, Cynthia can identify as Salvadorian *and* Italian, and even change her identity depending on context. There is a need for people to openly consider the multiple possibilities of mixed race individuals' heritages. The language barrier in the United States can be overcome if society as a whole is willing to adopt a multiracial-affirmative language and mindset. In this chapter, we advocate suggestions for how all individuals—both multiracial and monoracial persons—can use various mixed race identity terminology, see the world through a multiracial-affirmative lens, and implement multiracial-affirmative actions.

MULTIRACIAL IDENTITY VARIANCE: MORE THAN ONE WAY TO IDENTIFY

Race and ethnicity are primary sources of identity. According to Erikson (1963), establishing a stable sense of personal identity in U.S. society is an integral aspect of the developmental process. Racial identity is a psychological construct reflecting aspects of our membership in, and identification with, a specific racial group.

The ecological (or environmental) nature of multiracial identity demonstrates that there is more than one way for mixed race individuals to identify; this also referred to as multiracial identity variance. An *all/and* approach embraces numerous possible mixed-race categories that current census standards do not yet include as recognized groups. Accordingly, Zack (2006) has identified the following mixed race identity options: fractional, inclusive, traditional nonwhite, white, generic, and aracial. *Fractional* identification occurs when a multiracial person chooses to identify him or herself in rough fractional terms. To illustrate, recall Cynthia, whose mother is Italian American and father is Salvadorian. Cynthia's husband is Samoan, and they have a daughter, Sophia (C. A. Faupusa, personal communication, June 18, 2008). If Sophia chooses to label herself as one-third Italian, one-third Salvadorian, and one-third Samoan, she is ascribing a *fractional* identity. Or she may choose to apply fractions more literally and identify as one-half Samoan, one-quarter Italian, and one-quarter Salvadorian. *Inclusive* identification occurs when an individual identifies as all or most of his/her racial identities without choosing to divide them into parts. Sophia may see herself as Samoan *and* Italian *and* Salvadorian. *Traditional nonwhite* identification takes place when an individual chooses to identify with a singular, nonwhite aspect of her or his racial heritage. Sophia may choose to identify as a Pacific Islander, because she is active in Polynesian dancing and is surrounded by peers who all identify as Pacific Islander and accept her as a Pacific Islander. Nonwhite identification may be due to family and/or geographical context, pressure from others to choose one racial identification, as well as the extent to which an individual subscribes to societal norms about racial categorization (one-drop rule,[1] phenotypic [physical] characteristics, etc.). *White* identification is self-explanatory, but is conceptually complex because of the challenges put forth by societal norms based in the one-drop rule of racial classification. Sophia's maternal grandmother is a primary caregiver for Sophia, and Sophia spends the majority of her holidays and weekends with her Italian American family. Suppose Sophia also grew up in a predominantly white neighborhood, has no experience of Salvadorian or Samoan ancestry, is fair skinned, with long straight hair, and can pass as white. Despite Sophia's mixed heritage, she may choose to identify as white. If race has no base in biology, this should be as acceptable as Sophia (or anyone with similar racial heritage) identifying as singularly Samoan or Salvadorian. Suppose Sophia decided that she will identify simply as mixed and finds no need to specify, insisting that it is distinctly American to have the racial heritage that she does. In this case, Sophia would be choosing a *generic* identity option. If Sophia opts to consider herself simply as a human being and citizen of the world, then she adopts an *aracial* identity.

Zack's mixed race identity options parallel the identity patterns Renn (2004) identified in a qualitative study of 54 multiracial college students from a diverse selection of universities across the U.S. The identity patterns include: monoracial identity, multiple monoracial identities, multiracial identity, extraracial identity, and situational identity. *Monoracial identity* occurred when students identified with one of their monoracial heritage groups either some or all of the time. *Multiple monoracial* identities occurred when students held two or more monoracial identities. *Multiracial identity* occurred when students did not conform to the monoracial categories that exist in the United States. Instead, they expressed a new construction of identity such as hapa, biracial, multiracial, mixed, and so on. *Extraracial identity* occurred when students chose not to identify themselves by any racial classification and did not accept the construction of racial identities. Finally, *situational identity* was marked by students' identification with two or more of the four patterns described above. This was either a conscious or unconscious shift based on the situation. For them, identity was fluid and contextual.

Root (2003b) identified five types of identities that emerged from research on mixed race persons: assignment by hypodescent, monoracial fit/self assignment, blended identity, bi- or multiracial, and white with symbolic identity. *Assignment by hypodescent* is marked by assignment to a racial group based on blood quantum (i.e., the one-drop rule). Historically, assignment by hypodescent stems from the prejudicial rubric establishing any person with African ancestry as black, as well as the blood quantum for legal identification as American Indian. This identity type is often influenced by generational and/or geographical norms, as well as institutional policy. For example, for older generations, monoracial identity is often the result of assuming an assignment according to the one-drop rule and hypodescent that were the status quo during their youth. *Monoracial fit/self-assignment* exists when a multiracial person identifies him or herself with a monoracial label. This identification can be influenced by many variables, including phenotype and social context. Indeed, some multiracial persons will adopt a monoracial label of a group that is not included in their racial heritage, but with which they feel an affinity or a sense of community.

After 1967, when the last U.S. state laws against interracial marriage were repealed, more identity options for mixed race persons emerged as they increasingly affirmed multiple aspects of their heritage. Younger generations have had the option of publicly assuming a blended or multiracial identity; both of these have gained increasing social acceptance. *Blended identity* is marked by an acknowledgment of and identification with multiple ethnic or racial heritages. Much like an alloy of iron and carbon is known uniquely as steel, *bi- or multiracial* identity occurs when a person of mixed heritage considers their combination of racial or ethnic heritages as a category all together different and new—multiracial, biracial, mixed, and so on. Root's notion of "symbolic whiteness" (2003b, p. 34) reflects identification with a class lifestyle and values, or a lack of exposure to an ethnic background with which one identifies. This phenomenon is analogous to the experience of many highly acculturated children of less acculturated immigrant parents in the U.S.

In concert with Root (2003b) and Zack's (2006) racial identity options, and Renn's (2004) identity patterns, *all/and* terminology is available whereby the many contextual choices of racial identification can be articulated and understood. Society may be more likely to adopt and apply this multiracial-affirmative identity language if overlapping terms are consolidated and user-friendly. However, the comparison and integration of these identity options and patterns has not yet been proposed. Therefore, we offer a synthesis of this research, allowing the larger public to access and use this knowledge in their lives.

A synthesis of these paradigms yields four domains of multiracial identity options; we are calling these: (a) monoracial identity, (b) multiracial identity, (c) contextual identity, and (d) aracial identity.

Monoracial Identity

- Traditional nonwhite
- White
- Assignment by hypodescent
- Monoracial fit/self-assignment
- White with symbolic identity

The *monoracial identity* domain comprises the multiple ways in which multiracial individuals can identify with only one racial heritage. The ecological nature of multiracial identity presupposes that options in this category are influenced by context, both environmental and temporal. Accordingly, Root's monoracial identity options (2000, 2003b) are also subsumed under the *contextual identity* domain described later.

Multiracial Identity

- Fractional
- Inclusive
- Generic
- Multiple monoracial
- Multiracial
- Blended
- Bi- or multiracial

The *multiracial identity* domain consists of multiracial identity options that acknowledge and incorporate multiple aspects of a mixed-race person's heritage.

Contextual Identity

- Situational
- Assignment by hypodescent
- Monoracial fit/self-assignment
- White with symbolic identity

The *contextual identity* domain can be self-selected or context-selected. Self-selected contextual identity exists when an individual chooses how to identity. This choice may be influenced by context, but is not exclusively determined by it. Context-selected contextual identity exists when a mixed-race person's context (e.g., geographical location, institution, local cultural norms) dictates how they identify racially, whether consciously or unconsciously.

Aracial Identity

- Aracial
- Extraracial

The *aracial identity* domain consists of mixed race identity options that represent a mixed race person's desire to identify in a manner that transcends established racial categories. This domain is inclusive of the "colorblind," "one-race; human race," and "citizen of the world" views of identity.

IDENTITY DISCREPANCY BETWEEN SELF AND SOCIETY

Root (2000, 2003) posited that the central task for the multiracial child is to achieve a positive resolution between a sense of identity and his or her environment. Root postulated that a healthy identity resolution can occur if individuals are accepted in their chosen group, do not feel pressure to change, and are supported in their identity by their immediate environment. Unfortunately, the racial and ethnic categories and labels used by society frequently seem to conflict with the identifications used by people of racially mixed heritage.

Thus, the discrepancy in self–other perceptions of identities may be attributed to the language barrier in the mixed race identity nomenclature, as the concept of multiracial identity options challenges the conventional wisdom of the check one box paradigm.

According to Lyda (2008), 78.4 percent of the mixed race college students surveyed used self-descriptions from the multiracial identity domain, and 6 percent of the sample chose options from the monoracial identity domain to describe themselves. However, participants believed that society most often categorized them in a monoracial identity domain (64.8 percent).

As such, multiracial college students appear to perceive that strangers, peers, classmates, professors, and society in general have a narrow concept of the spectrum of multiracial identity, and believe they are being viewed inaccurately by their community. The tension caused by the discrepancy between self and others' perceptions of multiracial identity is summarized by a woman quoted in Gaskins (1999), who states, "Being biracial isn't hard because we're confused about our racial identity. It's hard because everyone else is confused. The problem isn't us—it's everyone else" (p. 15). Talitha, whose mother is Filipina American and father is African American, also described this self—other discrepancy. Growing up in Hawaii with her mother's side of the family, she had a strong identification with being Filipina during her youth, which conflicted with being "outwardly identified [by others] more as [b]lack." Many people also thought Talitha was Samoan. Talitha specified that her ethnic identity conflicts "came from [the] difference between my self identification and others' identification for me" (T. P. Easterly, personal communication, June 9, 2008).

People of racially mixed heritage have experienced invalidating responses from others regarding their identities, including exclusion; difficulty finding others who will accept them as one of "their own"; pressure to choose one aspect of their heritage over another; authenticity testing; marginalization; and oppression from multiple ethnicities/races of heritage. Being told that "You aren't really black, Latino, Asian," "You don't look Native, black, Latino," and "You don't act Latino, Asian, black" have been identified as familiar experiences for racially mixed people. Sean, whose mother is Filipina American and father is Irish American, said his Filipino classmates sometimes do not believe him when he identifies as Filipino. Sean's phenotypic features of light brown hair, fair skin, and tall stature seem to have led his peers to ascribe to Sean a white racial identity (S. C. Callahan, personal communication, June 9, 2008). Renn (2000) found that physical appearance was a marker of racial/ethnic authenticity and determined who could belong and who could not. However, students who appear phenotypically more white (based on skin color, hair texture, eye shape, etc.) may not identify as such, even though others' may identify them that way. Society must not rely solely on phenotype to ascertain the identity of racially and ethnically mixed people because this often leads to inaccurate conclusions.

Many multiracial individuals experience pressure to make a single choice regarding racial self-labeling, and this may be reinforced in identity-based space (e.g., minority student groups, church clubs). Many multiracial students, especially those who are more fluid in their identity, struggle to find a sense of belonging and support in identity-based spaces that rely on factors based on monoracial norms, such as common cultural knowledge and similar physical appearance. Peers' invalidating comments made to multiracial persons participating in monoracial groups include,

"You don't count" and "What are you doing here?" (Powell, 2005). By participating in one cultural group, individuals may feel they are affirming one aspect of their racial identity while denying another part, or parts, of it. Recall the example of Sophia. If Sophia has an inclusive multiracial identity (e.g., sees herself as Samoan *and* Salvadorian *and* Italian) and participates in a Latino Student Union, she may feel incongruent, and that she is ignoring other salient aspects of herself and her culture. Monoracial identity-based spaces are traditionally expected to foster healthy identity and adjustment for students of color, but they are not necessarily sufficient for mixed-race individuals, especially those that identify with the multiracial, contextual, and/or aracial options.

Celebrities are a visible example of how society blindly puts monoracial labels on mixed-race individuals. The physical appearances, and therefore the race and ethnicity, of celebrities are open to public speculation and scrutiny. Singer and Grammy-winner Alicia Keys, music legend Bob Marley, and Oscar-winner Halle Berry each has a black parent and a white parent, but these figures are often hallmarked as being "only" black. Actor Freddie Prinze Jr. and comedian/actor Rob Schneider often "pass" as Caucasian, although Prinze's father was half Puerto Rican and Schneider's mother is Filipina. Many other mixed-race celebrities are living among us, but little awareness and scarce education is given to their multiple racial and ethnic identities.

Root (1996) created the Bill of Rights for Racially Mixed People, a series of affirmations that encourages self-acceptance, freedom, integration of identities, and empowerment. The Bill of Rights asserts that race is not a static construct and empowers individuals to embrace their identity, however they define their identity at any given time. These affirmations include: "I have the right to change my identity over my lifetime—and more than once"; "I have the right not to keep the races separate with me"; and "I have the right to identify myself differently in different situations." Golf superstar Eldrick "Tiger" Woods has described himself as "Cablinasian," and in doing so encapsulates and embraces the entirety of his racial mix, which includes Caucasian, African American, American Indian and Asian (Thai, Chinese) ancestry. Perhaps without being aware of it, Woods exemplifies the rights of people of mixed heritage to "create a vocabulary to communicate about being multiracial" (Root, 1996, p. 12). Eckert (2007, p. 1) reported, "By providing an alternative, multiracial label—Cablinasian—Woods sent a clear message to the public and to the media: he considers himself multiracial and expects to be identified as such." Woods demonstrated how others can also create their own unique identifications that may best fit their multiracial identity. Blackanese, Mexopino, and Eurasian are other multiracial identity terms that people have used to reflect their specific racial mix.

The Bill of Rights reminds persons of racially mixed heritage that their concept of self can acceptably vary from the expectations of family, peers, and authority. These rights declare, "I have the right to identify myself differently than how my parents identify me," and "I have the right to have loyalties and identify with more than one group of people." Embracing the rights gives mixed-race persons the liberty and space to be themselves without external questioning.

President Barack Obama identified his mixed race heritage in his "A More Perfect Union" speech. He stated, "I am the son of a black man from Kenya and a white woman from Kansas. I was raised with the help of a white grandfather who survived a Depression to serve in Patton's Army during World War II and a white grandmother who worked on a bomber assembly line at Fort Leavenworth while he was overseas" (Obama, 2008, p. 3). The media deemed Obama to be the first black man to run for the U.S. presidency; yet Obama's words demonstrate one of the Rights for People of Mixed Heritage "to identify myself differently than strangers expect me to identify" (Root, 1996, p. 10). Obama described his life as "a story that has seared into my genetic makeup the idea that this nation [the United States] is more than the sum of its parts—that out of many, we are truly one" (Obama, 2008, p. 3). With eloquence and hope, Obama has articulated both some of the struggles of and pride in his racially mixed heritage.

MULTIRACIAL IDENTITY MODELS: THE INFLUENCE OF FAMILY AND COMMUNITY

Monoracial identity models are unable to accommodate the full complexity and heterogeneity of the multiracial identity processes. While monoracial models have accounted for the nonlinearity of racial identity development, they have not acknowledged a paradigm that allows for an individual to carry multiple racial identities simultaneously in a manner that is adaptive and psychosocially healthy. A paradigm shift in the way that we construct racial identity is necessary to account for the unique experience of multiracial individuals, as well as the contextual factors that influence their experience. Wardle and Cruz-Janzen (Wardle, 1992; Wardle & Cruz-Janzen, 2004) and Root (2000, 2003b) have proposed identity models specifically for multiracial persons.

The interactional components of the ecological model formulated by Wardle and Cruz-Janzen (Wardle, 1992; Wardle & Cruz-Janzen, 2004) determine the success or failure of the healthy multiracial or multiethnic identity process. The family's impact on the child's multiracial identity depends on the attitude of the family towards such an identity, discussion of the topics such as the child's identity and racism, and the means by which the family supports the child's overall identity development. Family includes biological, adoptive, foster, extended, and blended families on all sides. In a video interview, a multiracial woman, whose mother is black and father is Mexican American, shared how her parents positively impacted her racial identity through their supportive words and actions. Powell's (2005, p. 2) article discusses a female college student who reported that her Chinese mother and African American father were mutually committed to ensuring that she and her siblings got "equal exposure to both sides of their culture," for example through Chinese dance lessons, books on African American history, visiting Taiwan, and hearing her father talk frequently about Rosa Parks and Malcolm X. These examples highlight the pivotal roles that parents and family members play in the development of multiracial identity. Familial attitudes and actions of acceptance and celebration can empower racially mixed persons, while words and acts of rejection and neglect can scorn them.

After the family, the community represents the most important ecological impact on a child; according to Wardle (1992) and Wardle and Cruz-Janzen's model (2004), this includes school, church groups, immediate peers, and neighborhood groups. Talitha, whose mother is Filipina American and whose father is African American, shared how attending an elite private college on the west coast shifted her racial identity. She recalled identifying as African American on a university entrance survey, when only being allowed to check one racial box, which in turn connected her with the African American community on campus (T. P. Easterly, personal communication, June 9, 2008). According to Wardle and Cruz-Janzen, three factors demonstrate the impact of the community on healthy multiracial identity: (a) families' feeling of belonging; (b) the community's acceptance of diversity; and (c) the presence of minority representation and multiracial/multiethnic children in the community groups the child attends. Furthermore, when adults openly embrace their mixed race identities, they serve as positive role models for multiracial children. Multiracial children can benefit from seeing adults that resemble them give voice to the multiracial experience.

The level of racism that multiracial children experience largely depends on phenotype, community context, and school environment. A community's rejection of multiracial identity can take the form of stereotypes. Multiracial children have been deemed inferior to monoracial individuals and are presumed to be more likely to have major psychological and social problems. Additional assumptions about multiracial children include that their parents are not married, their father is in the military, and the race of each parent being assumed based on stereotypes of common interracial relationships (e.g., Asian mother, white father; black father, white mother).

Informed by Bronfenbrenner (1989), Root's (2000, 2003b) Ecological Framework for Understanding Racial Identity provides a model for understanding the complexity of racial identity development that is both inclusive of multiracial identity and nonlinear. Based on nearly a decade of research, Root's framework illustrates the bidirectional effects of common ecological influences (e.g., family functioning, community attitudes, racial/ethnic identities, racial socialization, and physical appearance) and invisible factors (e.g., regional and generational history of race and ethnic relations, gender, sexual orientation, and class) on multiracial individuals. Root's model is grounded in the understanding that a multiracial person's identity can and will change depending on the ecological context. A multiracial woman named Amina, quoted in Powell (2005), illustrates how her answer to "What are you?" depends on context. If she doesn't want to be bothered, she says "I'm black," but if a coworker asks, she'll share that her mother is Dutch and her father is a black Costa Rican. The idea of racial identity varying based on context represents an important shift in the evolution of racial identity models.

The preceding models suggest that family and community members play a significant role in the development of multiracial persons. They lay out a roadmap that can guide our communities as we strive to better understand the unique identity and developmental issues facing multiracial persons. In order to take an active role in the multiracial movement, we suggest the following actions in which all persons can engage:

1. Create safe spaces for openly communicating with multiracial persons about their unique experiences
2. Talk about race and give multiracial persons an outlet to discuss racial stereotypes and hurtful comments they may have experienced
3. Communicate in relation to the positive aspects and strengths of being multiracial
4. Talk about similarities and differences in multiracial persons' experiences between themselves and others
5. Talk about dating and friendship issues that multiracial individuals may face
6. Introduce multiracial youth to a diverse vocabulary in order to explore and develop their racial identity
7. Introduce children to multiracial-affirmative stories, coloring books, and toys
8. Introduce children and adolescents to projective avenues for expression, including creative writing, painting, and drawing
9. Introduce youth to multiracial role-models and peers, and facilitate interactions and relationships with multiracial persons
10. Include classroom lessons focused on debunking multiracial stereotypes and facilitating awareness of multiracial issues
11. Create and/or participate in a mentoring program with multiracial models
12. Create and/or participate in multiracial groups in school, college, and beyond
13. Sponsor speakers and cultural displays on mixed race topics in relevant organizations
14. Challenge assumptions of monoraciality among family, peers, and so on.

Multiracial-Affirmative Ideology

Society can provide negative and invalidating feedback to mixed-race persons, giving them the message that they are different, a mistake, or undesirable. Even when community members have positive intentions, attitudes about race and ethnicity that are embedded in a larger monoracial paradigm can have harmful consequences for people of racially mixed heritage. However, with exposure and the implementation of multiracial-affirmative ideology, family and community members can send positive messages to foster the healthy identity development of mixed-race persons.

To this end, Root (2004) created a Multiracial Oath of Social Responsibility that affirms dedication to making a positive difference in the world, including improving race relations, fighting all oppression, and recognizing people that have engaged in multiracial-affirmative actions and ideals. The Oath is written from the multiracial perspective, and it is equally important for monoracial persons to embrace a multiracial-affirmative ideology. Douglass stated, "We cannot know true freedom and the celebration of diversity until we can be comfortable and supportive of every individual's right to choose in the matters of race and ethnic identity" (p. 16). Only through the participation of all people can positive change endure for multiracial people. To this end, we propose the following multiracial-affirmative principles.

Be open to racial identity variance. The U.S. Census is not the final word on racial and ethnic identification. Identity is not mandated by genetics or biology, and does not have to match with others' expectations or perceptions. Racial and ethnic identity is not a fact that can be right or wrong. For multiracial persons, racial and ethnic identity is contextual, can change, and therefore does not have to be consistent across situations and environments. It can be psychologically healthy and adaptive for an individual to have multiple racial identities simultaneously. A person's identity development is a subjective process that can ultimately be defined only by the individual.

Avoid assumptions and stereotypes. While it is natural to try to make sense of people through heuristics, assumptions can also lead to making inaccurate conclusions about someone because of the monoracial category ascribed to him or her. Physical attributes, such as complexion, hair, eyes, nose, lips, and height, may influence but do not dictate a person's racial or ethnic identity. Making assumptions impacts all parties involved, usually in negative ways; this is especially the case for the person of mixed race. Mistaking a multiracial person's identity can send an invalidating message about his or her existence. In addition, complimentary stereotypes are still stereotypes. The use of the term *exotic* to describe a mixed-race person can pigeonhole a person's identity. The generalization that "Mixed people are so beautiful or handsome" (Root, 2003a, p. 133) can send an alienating and objectifying message.

Increase self-awareness. The stigma associated with interracial marriage stems from a long history of institutionalized racism in the United States. There is no better example of this than the fact that, as late as 1967, 16 U.S. states had laws banning interracial marriages. This history often biases current perspectives of racially mixed persons as negative and taboo. In order to work toward multicultural competence, psychologists, counselors, and social workers are expected to honestly assess and increase their self-awareness of their biases regarding multiracial people and interracial couples and families. This same expectation can be further applied to all community members and, with increased self-awareness, people can change their faulty attitudes and beliefs about multiracial persons.

Use respectful language; ask appropriate questions. It is important to use the language and terminology that the multiracial person uses for him or herself and avoid imposing the identity labels of others. People should also be open to the mixed race identity options identified by Zack (2006), Renn (2004), and Root (2003b). In the proper settings and circumstances, asking appropriate, open-ended questions can give mixed-race persons the opportunity to share their perspectives on their identity. In order to avoid being offensive, impolite, or wrong, people may tend not to talk with mixed race persons about their heritage. However, such avoidance can contribute to the silencing of people of mixed heritage, and may prevent them from having an equal chance to share about themselves. For example, in a workshop or counseling session, during an exercise about cultural identity, a facilitator could ask "How would you describe your racial or ethnic identity?" Such a question is broad enough to allow multiracial people to project their own thoughts and beliefs about identity into their response. That said, it is also important to be respectful of a multiracial person's right not to explain or self-disclose about their identity. For example, the question "What are you?" can lead multiracial individuals to feel insulted or different.

Drawing from the ideology above, the following are proactive, multiracial-affirmative attitudes to endorse:

1. I will accept the identities that racially mixed people select for themselves and will not pressure them to change their identification according to my own views.
2. I will be open to ethnic and racial identities that I am unfamiliar with and have perhaps never even heard of.
3. I will accept that racial and ethnic identities can change over time.
4. I will not force labels onto others' ethnic and racial identities.
5. I will see multiracial identity as a spectrum, with multiple aspects.
6. I will not assume that someone's physical attributes are equivalent to his or her identity.
7. I will make every effort not to stereotype and make assumptions based on others' ethnic and racial identities.
8. I will tolerate, support, and celebrate the racial and ethnic identity exploration of my family, friends, peers, subordinates, and authority figures.

The multiracial-affirmative ideology and statements given above are a social responsibility that can be empowering and liberating for both mixed-race and monoracial persons.

Racism has a destructive effect on those who engage in racist beliefs and behaviors, as well as recipients of the racist attitudes and acts. In order for United States' racial politics to change, all people must be part of the solution. Society's multiracial language barrier can be overcome through increasing awareness and acceptance of *all/and* and mixed-race identity options, decreasing the perceptual discrepancy between self and society, and embracing the proposed multiracially affirmative actions, ideology, and attitudes. Endorsing a multiracial-affirmative mentality, and avoiding narrow, stereotypical, and categorical conceptualizations of race, will bring about the betterment of the multiracial movement, and a positive transformation in all of society.

NOTE

1. The one-drop rule, otherwise known as racial assignment by hypodescent, is a historical and colloquial term in the United States. According to this rule, to be considered black, one only needs to have one drop of black blood in one's ancestry.

REFERENCES

Bronfenbrenner, U. (1989). Ecological systems theory. In R. Vasta (Ed.), *Six theories of development* (pp. 187–249). Greenwich, CT: JAI press.

Douglass, R. (2003). Evolution of the multiracial movement. In M.P.P. Root & M. Kelley (Eds.), *Multiracial child resource book: Living complex identities* (pp. 13–17). Seattle, WA: Mavin Foundation.

Eckert, S. (2007). Famous multiracial celebrities: New perspectives on race and identity. Retrieved March 1, 2008, from http://racism.suite101.com/article.cfm/famous_multiracial_celebrities.

Erikson, E. (1963). *Childhood and society* (2nd ed.). New York: Norton.

Gaskins, P. (1999). *What are you? Voices of mixed-race young people.* New York: Holt.

Jones, N. A., & Smith, A. S. (2003). A statistical portrait of children of two or more races in Census 2000. In M.P.P. Root & M. Kelley (Eds.), *Multiracial child resource book: Living complex identities* (pp. 3–10). Seattle, WA: Mavin Foundation.

Kelley, M., & Root, M.P.P. (2003). Introduction. In M.P.P. Root & M. Kelley (Eds.), *Multiracial child resource book: Living complex identities* (pp. xiv–xvi). Seattle, WA: Mavin Foundation.

Loving v. State of Virginia. (1967). Retrieved August 7, 2008, from http://en.wikipedia.org/wiki/Loving_v._Virginia.

Lyda, J. (2008). *The relationship between multiracial identity variance, social connectedness, facilitative support, and adjustment in multiracial college students.* Unpublished doctoral dissertation, University of Oregon.

Obama, B. (2008, March 18). *A more perfect union.* Speech presented at the Constitution Center, Philadelphia. Retrieved March 19, 2009, from http://www.huffingtonpost.com/2008/03/18/obama-race-speech-read-th_n_92077.html.

Powell, B. A. (2005). Mixed emotions: The multiracial student experience at UC Berkeley. *NewsCenter.* Retrieved June 3, 2008, from http://berkeley.edu/news/media/releases/2005/03/07_multiracial.shtml.

Renn, K. R. (2000). Patterns of situational identity among biracial and multiracial college students. *The Review of Higher Education, 23,* 399–420.

Renn, K. R. (2004). *Mixed race students in college: The ecology of race, identity, and community.* Albany, NY: SUNY Press.

Root, M.P.P. (Ed.). (1996). *The multiracial experience: Racial borders as the new frontier.* Thousand Oaks, CA: Sage.

Root, M.P.P. (2000). Rethinking racial identity development: An ecological framework. In P. Spickard & J. Burroughs (Eds.), *We are a people: Narrative in the construction and deconstruction of ethnic identity* (pp. 205–220). Philadelphia: Temple University Press.

Root, M.P.P. (2003a). Issues and experiences of racially mixed people. In M.P.P. Root & M. Kelley (Eds.), *Multiracial child resource book: Living complex identities* (p. 134). Seattle, WA: Mavin Foundation.

Root, M.P.P. (2003b). Racial identity development and persons of mixed race heritage. In M.P.P. Root & M. Kelley (Eds.), *Multiracial child resource book: Living complex identities* (pp. 34–41). Seattle, WA: Mavin Foundation.

Root, M.P.P. (2004). Multiracial Oath of Social Responsibility. Retrieved March 19, 2009, from http://www.drmariaroot.com/doc/OathOfSocialResponsibility.pdf.

U.S. Census Bureau. (1992, March). Marital status and living arrangements. *Current population reports, population characteristics, Series P20–468,* December. Washington, DC: U.S. Government Printing Office.

U.S. Census Bureau. (2000). *Racial and ethnic classifications used in Census 2000 and beyond.* Retrieved February 10, 2008, from http://www.census.gov/population/www/socdemo/race/racefactcb.html.

Wardle, F. (1992). *Biracial identity: An ecological and developmental model.* Denver, CO: Center for the Study of Biracial Children.

Wardle, F., & Cruz-Janzen, M. I. (2004). *Meeting the needs of multiracial and multiethnic children in schools.* Boston: Pearson Education.

Zack, N. (2006). *Thinking about race* (2nd ed.). Belmont, CA: Thomson-Wadsworth.

CHAPTER 2

Bicultural Identities in a Diverse World

Angela-MinhTu D. Nguyen, Que-Lam Huynh,
and Verónica Benet-Martínez

In recent years, there has been a surge of interest in the study of biculturalism and bicultural identities. Broadly speaking, bicultural individuals may be immigrants, refugees, sojourners, indigenous people, ethnic minorities, those in inter-ethnic relationships, and mixed-ethnic individuals. More strictly defined, bicultural individuals are those who have been exposed to and have internalized two cultures (Benet-Martínez & Haritatos, 2005; Nguyen & Benet-Martínez, 2007). In this chapter, we reflect on the reasons for the increasing appeal of biculturalism research, present acculturation and identity theories as the foundation for research on bicultural identity, introduce Bicultural Identity Integration (BII; Benet-Martínez & Haritatos, 2005) as a way to understand individual differences in bicultural identity organization, explore the diversity of the bicultural experience through concepts such as segmented assimilation, discuss the implications of biculturalism, and suggest future directions and applications of biculturalism.

WHY BICULTURALISM?

Several factors may have contributed to the rise in interest in studying biculturalism. First, bicultural individuals increasingly comprise a significant proportion of the world's population. In the United States alone, bicultural individuals may include the 13 percent who are foreign-born, the 34 percent who are non-white, and the 20 percent who speak a language other than English at home (U.S. Census Bureau, 2006). In addition, children and grandchildren of foreign-born U.S. Americans are often also bicultural, as are U.S. Americans who have lived or worked in other countries.

Second, biculturalism has garnered attention due to societal-level events such as the civil rights movement, immigration, and globalization. For instance, the civil rights movement resulted in a resistance to assimilation into the dominant Anglo-Protestant American society (Arce, 1981; Atkinson, Morten, & Sue, 1989; Cross, 1978) and the development of pride in the other (i.e., racial, ethnic, cultural) side of one's identity. During this same period, the Immigration and Nationality Act of 1965 permitted immigration into the United States by Asians, Latinos, and Eastern Europeans. Because they are phenotypically different from Anglo Americans, immigrants from these parts of the world have a more difficult time assimilating and blending into the dominant U.S. American society; thus, biculturalism seemed a more feasible identity model for these individuals. More recently, globalization has allowed for greater intercultural contact via work, travel, and the Internet, resulting in increasing numbers of people who are exposed to cultures other than their own and thus may identify as bicultural. Hence, globalization refers to the cultural, economic, political, technological, and environmental connections among people around the world. These and other events in contemporary U.S. society have affected the perceptions of biculturalism, which in turn has promoted research on this topic.

Third, a call for more scientifically rigorous methods in cultural research has highlighted bicultural individuals as an ideal population for conducting experiments in cultural psychology (Hong, Morris, Chiu, & Benet-Martínez, 2000). By virtue of having two cultures that can be independently manipulated, bicultural individuals give researchers a quasi-experimental design ideal for the study of how culture affects behavior (Hong et al., 2000). In addition, previously identified cross-cultural differences can be replicated in experiments with bicultural individuals (Sanchez-Burks et al., 2003). Furthermore, these cross-cultural differences can be examined while controlling for variables that confound national comparisons (e.g., gross national product) by using bicultural individuals in a within-subjects design.

Clearly, recent sociopolitical and historical developments, along with new research interests, have drawn more attention to biculturalism. It is an increasingly common and important social phenomenon that has implications for understanding basic psychological processes, such as identity. Before turning to theory and research on bicultural identity, we first briefly review theories of acculturation and identity from which bicultural identity theories took their roots.

UNDERLYING THEORIES: ACCULTURATION AND IDENTITY

Acculturation at the individual level is defined as the psychological and behavioral changes that occur in people who are exposed to more than one culture (Berry, 2003). In the past, psychologists viewed acculturation as a unilinear process, whereby all acculturating individuals would relinquish their ethnic culture in order to adopt the dominant culture. Currently, acculturation is viewed as a bilinear process, with acculturating individuals facing two key issues: (1) the extent to which they are motivated and/or allowed to maintain their ethnic culture and identity; and (2) the extent to which they are motivated and/or allowed to be involved in the dominant culture. Four acculturation strategies result from the negotiation of these two issues. An individual who does not want to or cannot maintain his/her ethnic culture and identity but seeks to have contact with the dominant culture is using the *assimilation* strategy. Conversely, an individual who seeks to maintain his/her ethnic culture and identity but does not have a desire to or cannot interact with the dominant culture is using the *separation* strategy. One who wishes to or is allowed to maintain his/her ethnic culture while interacting with the dominant culture is using the *integration* or *biculturalism* strategy. Finally, when one has no preference or opportunity for contact with either culture, he/she is using the *marginalization* strategy. There is considerable empirical support for the existence of these different acculturation strategies (e.g., Berry, Kim, Power, Young, & Bujaki, 1989; Tsai, Ying, & Lee, 2000; Ying, 1995), but integration/biculturalism is the most widely endorsed and used strategy by individuals undergoing acculturation (Van Oudenhoven, Ward, & Masgoret, 2006). In summary, acculturation theories offer the conceptual backdrop for theories and research on bicultural identity by highlighting how people change as a result of exposure to two cultures. Next, we turn to basic theories of identity, which have also informed the development of theories about bicultural identities.

Identity has been defined in many different ways by psychologists. It is a striving for continuity of personal character and maintenance of solidarity with the group's ideals and identity (Erikson, 1959); a core sense of self, a coherence of personality, a continuity of self over time, and a self in social context (Grotevant, 1992); the intersection of individual and society (Josselson, 1994); or a life story that has both biographical and social elements and can be used in making identity by emerging adulthood (McAdams, 2001). All of these definitions have a common component: identity is inherently social in nature. In other words, identity can be defined simply as the part of one's self-concept that is related to group membership.

VARIATIONS IN BICULTURAL IDENTITY

According to Phinney and Devich-Navarro (1997), "There is not just one way of being bicultural" (p. 19). Acknowledging that bicultural identity is not uniform across individuals, researchers have attempted to identify types of bicultural individuals. Through a review of the literature, LaFromboise, Coleman, and Gerton (1993) identified two modes of biculturalism: alternation and fusion. Alternating bicultural individuals are highly oriented to both cultures and switch between cultures in accordance with the situation, whereas fused biculturals are highly oriented to an emergent third culture that stems but is also distinct from their two cultures (e.g., Chicano culture). Expanding on La-Fromboise et al.'s (1993) bicultural types, Birman (1994) identified three types of bicultural individuals: blended, instrumental, and integrated. Blended biculturals are the same as LaFromboise et al.'s (1993) fused biculturals. Instrumental biculturals are those who use the integration strategy in terms of their behaviors and the marginalization strategy in terms of their identity. Integrated biculturals are those who use the integration strategy in terms of their behaviors and the separation strategy in terms of their identity. To test these theories, Phinney and Devich-Navarro (1997) interviewed African American and Mexican American adolescents. From their interviews, two types of bicultural individuals emerged: blended and alternating. Both types of bicultural individuals had positive attitudes toward both of their cultures. However, alternating biculturals perceived conflict between their cultures, whereas blended biculturals did not. Furthermore, alternating biculturals were more oriented to their ethnic culture than the dominant culture, whereas blended biculturals were more oriented to the dominant culture than their ethnic culture. One limitation of the terms "blended" and "alternating" is that these labels refer to two distinct but not exclusive domains of the bicultural experience: "blended" refers to bicultural individuals' merging of their two *identities*, whereas "alternating" refers to their change in *behavior* in response to different cultural contexts.

Bicultural Identity Integration (BII)

Building on the research cited above, with further analysis of the literature and new empirical data, Benet-Martínez, Leu, Lee, and Morris (2002) introduced the construct of BII, an individual difference variable that captures the phenomenology of managing dual cultural identities. Theoretically, BII may relate to similar constructs such as nonoppositional versus oppositional identity (Ogbu, 1993) and identity synthesis versus confusion (Schwartz, 2006), but these relationships need to be explored empirically.

More recently, a study showed that BII is not a unitary construct but, instead, encompasses two different and psychometrically independent components (Benet-Martínez & Haritatos, 2005): (1) cultural distance versus blendedness—the degree of dissociation or compartmentalization versus the overlap perceived between the two cultural orientations (e.g., "I see myself as a Chinese in the United States" versus "I am a Chinese-American"); and (2) cultural conflict versus harmony—the degree of tension or clash versus compatibility perceived between the two cultures (e.g., "I feel trapped between the two cultures" versus "I do not see conflict between the Chinese and American ways of doing things"). BII theory emphasizes the *subjective* (i.e., perceptual) elements of distance and conflict between two cultures. This emphasis is a strength of BII theory, as a study of over 7,000 acculturating adolescents in 13 countries found that *objective* cultural differences do not relate to adjustment (Berry, Phinney, Sam, & Vedder, 2006).

Empirical studies suggest that these individual differences in bicultural identity, particularly BII, are psychologically meaningful and have expected relationships with dispositional factors, contextual pressures, traditional acculturation variables, and mental health. Specifically, as indicated by path analyses, cultural distance is related to having a closed-minded disposition, lower levels of cultural competence in and identification with the dominant culture, experiencing strains in the linguistic domain (e.g., being self-conscious about one's accent), living in a community that is not culturally diverse, preferring the separation strategy, and frequently engaging in behaviors associated with only one of the two cultures. On the other hand, cultural conflict is related to having a neurotic disposition, experiencing discrimination, having strained intercultural relations (e.g., being told that one's behaviors are too "American" or too "ethnic"), experiencing linguistic barriers, endorsing values from both cultures, and lower adjustment (Benet-Martínez & Haritatos, 2005; Benet-Martínez, Haritatos, & Santana, 2008; Chen, Benet-Martínez, & Bond, 2008; Nguyen, Huynh, & Benet-Martínez, 2008). In summary, cultural distance is particularly linked to performance-related personal and contextual challenges (e.g., cognitive rigidity, low linguistic fluency, culturally limited surroundings), while cultural conflict stems from strains that are largely intra- and interpersonal in nature (e.g., nervousness, social prejudice, and rejection). See Nguyen and Benet-Martínez (2007) for a further review of empirical findings regarding BII.

OTHER PERSPECTIVES ON BICULTURALISM

Biculturation

Bicultural individuals may learn their two cultures simultaneously, or they may learn one culture before the other (Padilla, 2006). That is, they may learn their ethnic culture first and the dominant culture later, or they may learn the dominant culture first and the ethnic culture later. For example, later-generation Mexican Americans may learn U.S. American culture first and Mexican culture later when they learn Spanish in school, befriend other Mexican Americans, or study in Mexico. Because bicultural individuals are not homogenous in the process of learning their two cultures, the term "acculturation" is too restrictive. Acculturation implies that the ethnic culture is learned before the dominant culture, and thus is more applicable to immigrants and refugees. In response to this, some researchers prefer the term "biculturation," which is the process of adapting to two cultures (Polgar, 1960; Sadao, 2003; Valentine, 1971). This concept is more appropriate than acculturation for many bicultural individuals, such as second-generation children of immigrants or refugees and mixed-ethnic individuals who learn their two cultures simultaneously (Birman, 1994; Padilla, 2006; Szapocznik, Kurtines, & Fernandez, 1980).

Due to later-generation bicultural individuals' biculturation, the ethnic culture is difficult to define. Although an ethnic cultural orientation for first-generation individuals might include participation in cultural activities, ethnic loyalty (or preferences for the ethnic group), and cultural awareness (or cultural knowledge), an ethnic cultural orientation for later-generation individuals may include ethnic pride and ethnic loyalty, without ethnic participation or knowledge (Padilla, 2006; Tsai et al., 2000). Moreover, because first-generation individuals have lived in their ethnic country, their ethnic culture closely approximates the culture of that country. However, the ethnic culture of later-generation individuals might be a crystallized version of the ethnic culture that their ancestors (e.g., parents of second-generation individuals, grandparents of third-generation individuals) brought with them upon migration (Matsumoto, 2000). For example, a recent immigrant from Vietnam brings a Vietnamese culture that is probably reflective of contemporary Vietnam, whereas a second-generation Vietnamese American's Vietnamese culture might be the culture of Vietnam in 1975 (or other year of emigration) when his or her parents left Vietnam for the United States. Besides a crystallized ethnic culture, later-generation individuals' ethnic culture might be an emergent third culture. For example, the ethnic culture of many later-generation Mexican Americans is Chicano culture (a combination of Mexican and U.S. American cultures, but distinct from both) rather than Mexican culture.

Emergent Third Culture

An emergent third culture might be a variation of the ethnic culture to which later-generation individuals are oriented (as mentioned above), or it may be a completely new third cultural orientation (in addition to the original dominant and ethnic cultural orientations). For example, some acculturating individuals using the integration strategy may be oriented to both the dominant (e.g., U.S. American) and ethnic (e.g., Mexican) cultures, whereas others using the integration strategy may be oriented to a third culture created via a combination of dominant and ethnic cultures (e.g., Chicano culture). Because the blending and fusion of cultures is a characteristic of the cultural distance component of BII, these latter individuals may also be described as having low levels of BII distance (or high levels of blendedness). Furthermore, cultural blendedness may be reflective of simultaneously engaging in behaviors associated with two cultures (e.g., speaking "Vietglish," eating fusion food; Nguyen et al., 2008). Note that when applied to adolescents who have lived in more than one country, that is, third-culture kids, "third culture" refers not to an emergent third culture, but to a cosmopolitan, "citizen-of-the-world" culture (Cockburn, 2002).

An emergent third culture is more than just a summation of particular elements from the dominant and ethnic cultures; rather, it often results from a dynamic and instrumental interaction between dominant and ethnic cultures. For example, Chicano culture is composed of Mexican culture, U.S. American culture, Mexican American culture and other cultures (Garza & Lipton, 1982). The notion of a new culture that emerges from a combination of existing cultures has also been referred to as ethnogenesis (Flannery, Reise, & Yu, 2001), transculturation (Comas-Diaz, 1987), and hybridity (Hermans & Kempen, 1998; Hutnyk, 2005; Lowe, 1996; Oyserman, Sakamoto, & Lauffer, 1998). Hybridity is the term most widely used across disciplines, and assumes that cultures are not pure, homogeneous, essentialist, static, or discrete (Anthias, 2001; Hermans & Kempen, 1998; Lowe, 1996; Mahalingam & Leu, 2005). Furthermore, hybridity has been proposed as an acculturating individual's response to pressure by the dominant group to assimilate. In other words, it is a compromise between adopting and resisting the dominant culture, whereby acculturating individuals adopt the dominant culture but modify it to reflect aspects of their ethnic culture (Hutnyk, 2005; Lowe, 1996).

The possibility of being oriented to an emergent third culture has important implications for research on acculturation and biculturalism. The currently accepted bilinear model of acculturation with ethnic and dominant cultural orientations might be replaced by a trilinear model, where the third cultural orientation is the emergent third culture (Flannery et al., 2001). Moreover, this trilinear model might be more applicable to later-generation individuals than either the unilinear or bilinear model of acculturation. As of yet, no study has examined a third cultural orientation or compared a trilinear model to the other models. In addition, future research is needed to delineate the differences between an emergent third culture and the cultural distance versus blendedness component of BII. Emergent third cultures are likely to become more common as the number of later-generation bicultural individuals grows and cultures interacting in the same space continue to fuse and merge.

Pan-Ethnicity

Due to the diversity of societies such as the United States, acculturating individuals, especially those in metropolitan areas and inner cities, might interact with people from other ethnic and racial groups. As a result, they might come to identify with a racial or pan-ethnic group rather than with their specific ethnic group (Rumbaut, 1994). Pan-ethnic labels such as "Asian" or "Latino" were created by U.S. institutions to classify groups of individuals who were seen as racially or phenotypically homogeneous (Espiritu, 1996; Lopez & Espiritu, 1990). Pan-ethnicity is also known as panethnogenesis, or the creation of a culture based on race (Rumbaut, 1994). For acculturating individuals, a pan-ethnic cultural orientation might include behaviors and attitudes that tend to be common across the hyphenated ethnic cultures of that pan-ethnicity. For example, a pan-ethnically oriented young Vietnamese American might identify as "AZN" (shortened form of "Asian"), drive a modified ("tricked-out") imported vehicle, and drink *boba* (a tapioca drink invented in Taiwan). These behaviors are not found in Vietnam and are not unique to Vietnamese Americans; these same behaviors are found among other young Asian Americans, such as Chinese Americans and Korean Americans.

Whether an individual is likely to identify with a pan-ethnic group is better predicted by structural factors (such as race and class) than by cultural factors (such as a common language or religion; Lopez & Espiritu, 1990). Other predictors of pan-ethnicity include being second generation or beyond and having experienced or perceived discrimination (Masuoka, 2006; Rumbaut, 2005). Furthermore, pan-ethnicity is associated with greater pride, social support, political strength, and intergroup interaction (Espiritu, 1996; Okamoto, 2003). Future studies should include a measure of pan-ethnic cultural orientation (e.g., Asian or Asian American) in addition to measures of dominant cultural orientation (e.g., U.S. American) and ethnic cultural orientation (e.g., Vietnamese) when examining acculturation. With increasing diversity in the United States, bicultural individuals might not merely be negotiating how their ethnic culture fits with the dominant culture; rather, they might be negotiating how their ethnic culture fits with other cultures within the United States (e.g., through pan-ethnicity).

Segmented Assimilation

According to Berry's (2003) framework, individuals using the marginalization strategy are neither oriented to the dominant culture nor their ethnic culture; however, it is difficult to consider any individual as being cultureless (del Pilar & Udasco, 2004). Perhaps, these individuals are oriented to a different culture, a culture that has not been given much attention within psychology. Within sociology, the acculturation process most applicable to these individuals is termed "segmented assimilation," and the culture to which these individuals are oriented is the culture of an impoverished, under-privileged, lower-class, inner-city, and reactive racial-minority segment of dominant society (Portes & Zhou, 1993). (Note that sociologists use "assimilation" to mean acculturation or cultural orientation, and not to mean a high dominant cultural orientation in combination with a low ethnic cultural orientation.)

Whereas pan-ethnicity refers to an identity that is determined by race, segmented assimilation refers to an identity that is determined by both race and class (Rumbaut, 1994). That is, acculturating individuals participating in segmented assimilation are those experiencing discrimination based on their race or skin color, those experiencing economic and class inequality, and those living in poverty-stricken inner cities (Portes, Fernandez-Kelly, & Haller, 2005; Portes & Zhou, 1993). Segmented assimilation is some second-generation individuals' response to racial discrimination, the employment barriers that their parents encounter (e.g., limited job access), and rejection from the dominant, mainstream society (Portes & Zhou, 1993). Some correlates of segmented assimilation include dropping out of school and involvement in criminal activities (Portes et al., 2005).

Based on the above descriptions of and findings regarding segmented assimilation, there is reason to believe that at least some, if not all, individuals using the marginalization strategy are also those participating in the segmented assimilation process. For example, like segmented assimilation, marginalization is the acculturation mode for individuals who have been discriminated against due to their race and those who have been unsuccessful at becoming fully assimilated into dominant society (possibly due to rejection; Berry, 2003). Furthermore, as with segmented assimilation, marginalization has been found to be associated with dropping out of school, delinquency, substance abuse, and maladaptation (Berry, 2003; del Pilar & Udasco, 2004; Ward & Kennedy, 1994). Therefore, individuals using the marginalization strategy might not be without a culture; rather, they may be oriented to a culture that is not measured with typical acculturation scales. Future research is needed to determine whether segmented assimilation and marginalization are one and the same, and whether the cultural orientation of marginalized individuals is the culture of disadvantaged, under-class racial minorities in inner cities. Besides pan-ethnicity, segmented assimilation is another way for bicultural individuals to negotiate how their ethnic culture fits with other cultures within a diverse society. In summary, researchers have begun to recognize that biculturalism takes many forms, and the many theories and perspectives on the diversity of the bicultural experience have and will continue to generate new, exciting research on this topic. Particularly as later-generation bicultural individuals increase in numbers, the above concepts of biculturation, emergent third cultures and hybridity, pan-ethnicity, and segmented assimilation will attain greater relevance and importance.

IMPLICATIONS

Researchers have long touted biculturalism as an ideal, calling attention to the many benefits associated with having two cultures (e.g., Berry, 1997; Phinney, Horenczyk, Liebkind, & Vedder, 2001). However, empirically, findings have been mixed as to whether biculturalism is positively or negatively related to adjustment, if at all. Recently, a meta-analysis found that identifying with both cultures may have positive psychological and sociocultural correlates (Nguyen & Benet-Martínez, 2008). The study also suggested that the mixed findings from previous studies were probably due to how biculturalism was measured (i.e., acculturation as unilinear vs. bilinear), with bilinear measures of acculturation yielding moderate effects and unilinear measures yielding null effects. It is perhaps not surprising that bicultural individuals, who tend to have more social and cognitive flexibility (Benet-Martínez, Lee, & Leu, 2006; Tadmor & Tetlock, 2006) and wider behavioral repertoires and competencies, experience greater adjustment and less maladjustment. Conversely, acculturating individuals who do not have dual identities may feel incomplete, fragmented, and culturally homeless (Vivero & Jenkins, 1999), thus becoming the so-called marginal man proposed by early acculturation researchers (Park, 1928; Stonequist, 1935).

Biculturalism research also has implications for public policy. At the institutional level, biculturalism can be promoted via multicultural legislation in some societies. For example, Canada has had policies that encourage the maintenance of all cultures *and* support full participation in the larger society, making biculturalism a national policy since the 1970s (Berry, 2003). In contrast, policies toward immigrants and ethnic minorities in the United States and many other culturally plural societies have been more assimilationistic (i.e., melting pot ideology; Berry, 2003; Van Oudenhoven et al., 2006). Because the majority of acculturating individuals prefer the integration strategy (Van Oudenhoven et al., 2006), it is imperative that researchers study the effect of national policy regarding pluralism on the adjustment of immigrants and other acculturating individuals.

Because most societies are no longer ethnically and culturally homogeneous, biculturalism is an increasingly important worldwide phenomenon that deserves attention. It may be an asset for interpersonal success, corporate success, intercultural relations and communication, and so on. For instance, it is possible that bicultural individuals who are able to resolve intrapersonal cultural differences may also be equipped to resolve interpersonal cultural differences. It seems intuitive that individuals who can accept and appreciate two cultures within themselves would also be able to do so with other cultures and with people from cultures different from their own.

BEYOND BICULTURALISM

Research on the dynamics, components, and variants of biculturalism is relatively new. Beyond implications for understanding dual cultural identities, new biculturalism research and theory can be applied to other types of dual identities including gay, work, and religious identities (Fingerhut, Peplau, & Ghavami, 2005; Luijters, van der Zee, & Otten, 2006; Verkuyten & Yildiz, 2007). In addition, research on biculturalism and other forms of dual identities must take into consideration multiple identities and multiple types of oppression (e.g., gender, race, class, ability, sexual orientation). Identity-relevant factors such as gender, age, sexual orientation, religion, class, and phenotype must be examined in conjunction with acculturation and identity development processes (Reynolds & Pope, 1991).

CONCLUDING THOUGHTS

From this chapter, it should be evident that bicultural individuals are the key to uncovering the dynamics of culture and that the field of acculturation and biculturalism offer many new and exciting opportunities for future inquiries. For the past decade, the field has been transitioning from unilinear to bilinear models of acculturation (e.g., Flannery et al., 2001; Ryder, Alden, & Paulhus, 2000; Tsai et al., 2000), and from a focus on cultural differences and between-individual comparisons to an interest in cultural dynamics and within-individual cultural processes (Benet-Martínez, 2007). In addition, research has focused on outcomes and correlates of acculturation and biculturalism, with little expansion of Berry's (2003) framework. Fortunately, attention to variations in bicultural identity has propelled the field forward. Increasing research on BII has resulted from this theoretical movement. Although topics such as biculturation, emergent third culture and hybridity, pan-ethnicity, and segmented assimilation offer promising new directions to the field of biculturalism, they have remained relatively unexplored within psychology. Moreover, with increasing diversity, other dual identities, such as sexual identity, and the interaction of multiple identities, require more research. Biculturalism is a surprisingly new area of inquiry in psychology; therefore, there is much to be learned and many paths to travel, all with important implications for individuals as well as societies.

REFERENCES

Anthias, F. (2001). New hybridities, old concepts: The limits of "culture." *Ethnic and Racial Studies, 24*, 619–641.

Arce, C. (1981). A reconsideration of Chicano culture and identity. *Daedalus, 110*, 177–192.

Atkinson, D. R., Morten, G., & Sue, D. W. (1989). A minority identity development model. In D. R. Atkinson, G. Morten, & D. W. Sue (Eds.), *Counseling American minorities* (pp. 35–52). Dubuque, IA: W. C. Brown.

Benet-Martínez, V. (2007). Cross-cultural personality research: Conceptual and methodological issues. In R. W. Robins, R. C. Fraley, & R. F. Krueger (Eds.), *Handbook of research methods in personality psychology* (pp. 170–189). New York: Guilford.

Benet-Martínez, V., & Haritatos, J. (2005). Bicultural identity integration (BII): Components and psychosocial antecedents. *Journal of Personality, 73*, 1015–1050.

Benet-Martínez, V., Haritatos, J., & Santana, L. (2008). *Bicultural Identity Integration (BII) and well-being*. Manuscript under review.

Benet-Martínez, V., Lee, F., & Leu, J. (2006). Biculturalism and cognitive complexity: Expertise in cultural representations. *Journal of Cross-Cultural Psychology, 37,* 386–407.

Benet-Martínez, V., Leu, J., Lee, F., & Morris, M. (2002). Negotiating biculturalism: Cultural frame switching in biculturals with oppositional versus compatible cultural identities. *Journal of Cross-Cultural Psychology, 33,* 492–516.

Berry, J. W. (1997). Immigration, acculturation, and adaptation. *Applied Psychology: An International Review, 46,* 5–34.

Berry, J. W. (2003). Conceptual approaches to acculturation. In K. M. Chun, P. B. Organista, & G. Marín (Eds.), *Acculturation: Advances in theory, measurement, and applied research* (pp. 17–37). Washington, DC: American Psychological Association.

Berry, J. W., Kim, U., Power, S., Young, M., & Bujaki, M. (1989). Acculturation attitudes in plural societies. *Applied Psychology: An International Review, 38,* 185–206.

Berry, J. W., Phinney, J. S., Sam, D. L., & Vedder, P. (2006). *Immigration youth in cultural transition: Acculturation, identity, and adaptation across national contexts.* Mahwah, NJ: Lawrence Erlbaum.

Birman, D. (1994). Acculturation and human diversity in a multicultural society. In E. J. Trickett, R. J. Watts, & D. Birman (Eds.), *Human diversity: Perspective on people in context* (pp. 261–284). San Francisco, CA: Jossey-Bass.

Chen, S., Benet-Martínez, V., & Bond, M. H. (2008). *Bicultural identity, language, and psychological adjustment in multicultural societies.* Manuscript under review.

Cockburn, L. (2002). Children and young people living in changing worlds: The process of assessing and understanding the "Third Culture Kid." *School Psychology International, 23,* 475–485.

Comas-Diaz, L. (1987). Feminist therapy with mainland Puerto Rican women. *Psychology of Women Quarterly, 11,* 461–474.

Cross, W. E., Jr. (1978). The Thomas and Cross models of psychological nigrescence: A literature review. *Journal of Black Psychology, 4,* 13–31.

del Pilar, J. A., & Udasco, J. O. (2004). Deculturation: Its lack of validity. *Cultural Diversity and Ethnic Minority Psychology, 10,* 169–176.

Erikson, E. H. (1959). The problem of ego identity. *Psychological issues: Identity and the life cycle: Selected papers* (Vol. 1, pp. 101–171). Oxford: International Universities Press.

Espiritu, Y. L. (1996). Crossroads and possibilities: Asian Americans on the eve of the twenty-first century. *Amerasia Journal, 22*(2), vii–xii.

Fingerhut, A. W., Peplau, L. A., & Ghavami, N. (2005). A dual-identity framework for understanding lesbian experience. *Psychology of Women Quarterly, 29,* 129–139.

Flannery, W. P., Reise, S. P., & Yu, J. (2001). An empirical comparison of acculturation models. *Personality and Social Psychology Bulletin, 27,* 1035–1045.

Garza, R. T., & Lipton, J. P. (1982). Theoretical perspectives on Chicano personality development. *Hispanic Journal of Behavioral Sciences, 4,* 407–432.

Grotevant, H. D. (1992). Assigned and chosen identity components: A process perspective on their integration. In G. R. Adams, T. P. Gullotta, & R. Montemayor

(Eds.), *Adolescent identity formation. Advances in adolescent development* (Vol. 4, pp. 73–90). Thousand Oaks, CA: Sage.

Hermans, H.J.M., & Kempen, H.J.G. (1998). Moving cultures: The perilous problem of cultural dichotomies in a globalizing society. *American Psychologist, 53,* 1111–1120.

Hong, Y. Y., Morris, M. W., Chiu, C. Y., & Benet-Martínez, V. (2000). Multicultural minds: A dynamic constructivist approach to culture and cognition. *American Psychologist, 55,* 709–720.

Hutnyk, J. (2005). Hybridity. *Ethnic and Racial Studies, 28,* 79–102.

Josselson, R. (1994). The theory of identity development and the question of intervention: An introduction. In S. L. Archer (Ed.), *Interventions for adolescent identity development* (pp. 12–25). Thousand Oaks, CA: Sage.

LaFromboise, T., Coleman, H. L., & Gerton, J. (1993). Psychological impact of biculturalism: Evidence and theory. *Psychological Bulletin, 114,* 395–412.

Lopez, D., & Espiritu, Y. L. (1990). Panethnicity in the United States: A theoretical framework. *Ethnic and Racial Studies, 13,* 198–224.

Lowe, L. (1996). *Immigrant acts: On Asian American cultural politics.* Durham, NC: Duke University Press.

Luijters, K., van der Zee, K. I., & Otten, S. (2006). Acculturation strategies among ethnic minority workers and the role of intercultural personality traits. *Group Processes & Intergroup Relations, 9,* 561–575.

Mahalingam, R., & Leu, J. (2005). Culture, essentialism, immigration and representations of gender. *Theory & Psychology, 15,* 839–860.

Masuoka, N. (2006). Together they become one: Examining the predictors of panethnic group consciousness among Asian Americans and Latinos. *Social Science Quarterly, 87,* 993–1011.

Matsumoto, D. (2000). *Culture and Psychology* (2nd ed.). Pacific Grove, CA: Brooks Cole.

McAdams, D. P. (2001). The psychology of life stories. *Review of General Psychology, 5,* 100–122.

Nguyen, A.-M.D., & Benet-Martínez, V. (2007). Biculturalism unpacked: Components, individual differences, measurement, and outcomes. *Social and Personality Psychology Compass, 1,* 101–114.

Nguyen, A.-M.D., & Benet-Martínez, V. (2008). *Biculturalism and adjustment: A meta-analysis.* Manuscript in preparation.

Nguyen, A.-M.D., Huynh, Q.-L, & Benet-Martínez, V. (2008). *The acculturation of values and bicultural identity.* Manuscript submitted for publication.

Ogbu, J. U. (1993). Differences in cultural frame of reference. *International Journal of Behavioral Development, 16,* 483–506.

Okamoto, D. G. (2003). Toward a theory of panethnicity: Explaining Asian American collective action. *American Sociological Review, 68,* 811–842.

Oyserman, D., Sakamoto, I., & Lauffer, A. (1998). Cultural accommodation: Hybridity and the framing of social obligation. *Journal of Personality and Social Psychology, 74,* 1606–1618.

Padilla, A. M. (2006). Bicultural social development. *Hispanic Journal of Behavioral Sciences, 28,* 467–497.

Park, R. E. (1928). Human migration and the marginal man. *American Journal of Sociology, 33,* 881–893.

Phinney, J. S., & Devich-Navarro, M. (1997). Variations in bicultural identification among African American and Mexican American adolescents. *Journal of Research on Adolescence, 7,* 3–32.

Phinney, J. S., Horenczyk, G., Liebkind, K., & Vedder, P. (2001). Ethnic identity, immigration, and well-being: An interactional perspective. *Journal of Social Issues, 57,* 493–510.

Polgar, S. (1960). Biculturation of Mesquakie teenage boys. *American Anthropologist, 62,* 217–235.

Portes, A., Fernandez-Kelly, P., & Haller, W. (2005). Segmented assimilation on the ground: The new second generation in early adulthood. *Ethnic and Racial Studies, 28,* 1000–1040.

Portes, A., & Zhou, M. (1993). The new second generation: Segmented assimilation and its variants. *Annals of the American Academy of Political and Social Science, 530,* 74–96.

Reynolds, A. L., & Pope, R. L. (1991). The complexities of diversity: Exploring multiple oppressions. *Journal of Counseling and Development, 70,* 174–180.

Rumbaut, R. G. (1994). The crucible within: Ethnic identity, self-esteem, and segmented assimilation among children of immigrants. *International Migration Review, 28,* 748–794.

Rumbaut, R. G. (2005). Assimilation, dissimilation, and ethnic identities: The experience of children of immigrants in the United States. In M. Rutter, & M. Tienda (Eds.), *Ethnicity and causal mechanisms* (pp. 301–334). Cambridge, UK: Cambridge University Press.

Ryder, A. G., Alden, L. E., & Paulhus, D. L. (2000). Is acculturation unidimensional or bidimensional? A head-to-head comparison in the prediction of personality, self-identity, and adjustment. *Journal of Personality and Social Psychology, 79,* 49–65.

Sadao, K. C. (2003). Living in two worlds: Success and the bicultural faculty of color. *Review of Higher Education: Journal of the Association for the Study of Higher Education, 26,* 397–418.

Sanchez-Burks, J., Lee, F., Choi, I., Nisbett, R., Zhao, S., & Koo, J. (2003). Conversing across cultures: East-West communication styles in work and nonwork contexts. *Journal of Personality and Social Psychology, 85,* 363–372.

Schwartz, S. J. (2006). Predicting identity consolation from self-construction, eudaimonistic self-discovery, and agentic personality. *Journal of Adolescence, 29,* 777–793.

Stonequist, E. (1935). The problem of a marginal man. *American Journal of Sociology, 41,* 1–12.

Szapocznik, J., Kurtines, W., & Fernandez, T. (1980). Bicultural involvement and adjustment in Hispanic American youths. *International Journal of Intercultural Relations, 3,* 15–47.

Tadmor, C. T., & Tetlock, P. E. (2006). Biculturalism: A model of the effects of second-culture exposure on acculturation and integrative complexity. *Journal of Cross-Cultural Psychology, 37,* 173–190.

Tsai, J. L., Ying, Y.-W., & Lee, P. A. (2000). The meaning of "being Chinese" and "being American": Variation among Chinese American young adults. *Journal of Cross-Cultural Psychology, 31,* 302–332.

U.S. Census Bureau. (2006). American FactFinder. Retrieved March 18, 2008, from http://factfinder.census.gov/home/saff/main.html.

Valentine, C. A. (1971). Deficit, difference, and bicultural models of Afro-American behavior. *Harvard Educational Review, 2,* 137–157.

Van Oudenhoven, J. P., Ward, C., & Masgoret, A.-M. (2006). Patterns of relations between immigrants and host societies. *International Journal of Intercultural Relations, 30,* 637–651.

Verkuyten, M., & Yildiz, A. A. (2007). National (dis)identification and ethnic and religious identity: A study among Turkish-Dutch Muslims. *Personality and Social Psychology Bulletin, 33,* 1448–1462.

Vivero, V. N., & Jenkins, S. R. (1999). Existential hazards of the multicultural individual: Defining and understanding "cultural homelessness." *Cultural Diversity & Ethnic Minority Psychology, 5,* 6–26.

Ward, C., & Kennedy, A. (1994). Acculturation strategies, psychological adjustment, and sociocultural competence during cross-cultural transitions. *International Journal of Intercultural Relations, 18,* 329–343.

Ying, Y.-W. (1995). Cultural orientation and psychological well-being in Chinese Americans. *American Journal of Community Psychology, 23,* 893–911.

CHAPTER 3

Lesbian, Gay, and Bisexual Asian Americans: Coming Out in Context

Nadine Nakamura, Jonathan R. Flojo, and Maria L. Dittrich

Racial and ethnic identity and culture impact the way that sexual orientation is experienced and expressed. However, culture and race are often left out of the sexual orientation discussion. In this chapter, we will focus on how lesbian, gay, and bisexual Asian Pacific Islanders (LGB APIs) experience "coming out" in the context of culture and in various domains. According to the American Psychological Association, *coming out* refers to "the process of acknowledging one's gay, lesbian, or bisexual attractions and identity to oneself and disclosing them to others" (American Psychological Association [APA], 1999, p. 4). A recent report from the National Gay and Lesbian Task Force (Dang & Vianney, 2007) based on a national survey of 860 lesbian, gay, bisexual, and transgender APIs revealed that coming out was among the most important issues.

This chapter will focus on coming out experiences of lesbian, gay, and bisexual APIs. At times, we will use the acronym LGBT, which includes transgender individuals. However, we believe that the transgender experience of gender identity development and disclosure differs from sexual orientation identity development and disclosure. Thus, we cannot assume that the experiences of LGB APIs accurately reflect and represent those of transgender APIs.

We will be discussing API cultures and values with broad strokes in an attempt to be inclusive of the diversity that exists among APIs. This should not imply that APIs are a cultural monolith. A great deal of variation exists between LGBT APIs, including, but not limited to differences in ethnicity, language, religion, socioeconomic status, immigration status, and acculturation level. Language plays an important role in the coming out experience, as the phrase coming out and the concept of sexual orientation do not neatly translate from one language and cultural context to another; this can create unique challenges and obstacles for some LGBT APIs.

Much has been written about the coming out process of Caucasian gays and lesbians; however, there has been much less focus on the coming out process of other ethnic and racial groups. When other racial and ethnic groups are considered, they are often compared to Caucasians, as though the Caucasian experience is the norm. Greene (1997) has suggested that focusing only on the Caucasian experience can obscure issues relevant to ethnic minorities. There are only a few empirical studies on coming out conducted with APIs, and the findings of this research will be highlighted throughout this chapter. Rather than comparing LGB APIs to other ethnic and racial groups, we will instead focus on the role that API culture and identity has on LGB APIs.

The models of the coming out process are based on white, Western, middle-class cultural values, norms, and expectations. The most popular models of the coming out process do not consider other aspects of identity and how these might intersect with sexuality. Several assumptions are made that may not apply to other cultural groups. For example, coming out is described as "an individual process, related to a person's self-concept and identity" (Smith, 1997, p. 287). In addition, not being publicly out is considered evidence of a psychological problem, such as shame, self-hatred, repression, or denial. While self-disclosure is often considered a sign of personal comfort and self-acceptance, within some cultures, sexual and interpersonal relationships are considered private matters that should not be discussed. Thus, coming out may be the expectation for LGBs in Western cultures that place value on individuality and finding oneself, but this may be a quite different process for LGB individuals from more collectivistic cultures that place more value on maintaining harmony than on standing apart from the group. The impact of API cultural values on coming out will be discussed in this chapter.

The coming out experiences of LGB APIs does not occur in a vacuum; thus, these experiences need to be understood in context. The decision to negotiate one's multiple identities (e.g., API, LGB, etc.) is shaped by the specifics of the setting. With this lens, we explore the experiences of LGB APIs in three interrelated areas: within their families, as youth in schools, and in workplace settings.

COMING OUT TO FAMILY

The coming out literature emphasizes that individuals may disclose their sexual orientation to their parents with the expectation that this will have a positive impact on familial relationships. For example, Ben-Ari (1995) reported that gay men and lesbians, along with their parents, felt that increased honesty in their relationship was a major benefit to coming out. The biggest motivation for coming out to their parents, reported by the children, was the desire "not to hide, not to live a lie," followed by wanting to "share happiness with parents" (p. 96). Similarly, Cramer and Roach (1988) found that gay men came out to their parents in an attempt to create a closer relationship; the most common reasons for coming out to them were "a desire to share one's personal life . . . and a desire for more intimacy with one's parents" (p. 87). This reflects the values of openness, honesty, and closeness within Western familial relationships.

In order to understand homosexuality within the API cultural context, it is necessary to identify cultural values with regards to an individual's place in society. While Western cultures place a lot of value on individuality, Asian cultures place value on the collective group. In this way, the situation may be very different for an LGB API who faces losing familial support upon coming out compared to an LGB Caucasian who may value other types of interpersonal relationships equally. The Western value of individual autonomy may allow for an LGB Caucasian person to assert his or her own needs to live an authentic life, whereas an LGB API person who holds more collectivistic values may struggle with putting his or her own needs ahead of the needs of his or her parents and other family members.

Coming out is a difficult issue for many LGB APIs who fear rejection from their families and friends. Many also fear that they will stigmatize their families (Merighi & Grimes, 2000). Family is a very important component in East Asia, for example. Respect, obedience, and loyalty to one's family are cultural expectations. The family is an interdependent collective where gender roles are clearly defined. In addition, homosexuality and sexuality in general are rarely openly discussed in East Asia, which can complicate the coming out process.

Chan (1989) conducted the first study of coming out with an Asian American sample. The participants were 19 women and 16 men who self-identified as lesbian or gay and Asian American (90 percent of the sample was Chinese, Japanese, or Korean American). Most (77 percent) reported that they had come out to at least one family member. Only 26 percent had come out to their parents, which is rather low given that the mean amount of time being out was 6.2 years. More than half of the participants reported that Asian Americans were in denial as to the fact that lesbian and gay Asian Americans even exist (Chan, 1989). Thus, it is not surprising that 77 percent reported that it was harder for them to come out to other Asian Americans.

Bhugra (1997) conducted an exploratory study on coming out by South Asian gay men in the United Kingdom. The sample consisted of 52 gay and bisexual men who ranged in age from 16 to 61, but their length of stay in the United Kingdom and level of acculturation was not assessed. The majority of this sample reported that they attempted to conceal their homosexuality from other people. Friends, followed by cousins, were the first to be informed of the participants' sexual orientation. Parents and work colleagues were the last to be told. Only 35 percent of parents knew of their sons' sexual orientation. Thirty-one percent said that they regretted being homosexual. The most common reason for this regret was "not having children and going against the Asian culture" (p. 554).

Dube and Savin-Williams (1999) studied sexual identity development with 139 gay and bisexual ethnic minority youths between the ages of 16 and 26, including Asian Americans. They looked at racial group differences and found that Asian Americans tended to self-label themselves as gay before having sex with a male, which was not the case for the other racial groups. In fact, Asian Americans reported their first sexual experience with another male to be about three years later than youth from other racial groups. Asian American gay and bisexual male youths were also significantly less likely to have been romantically or intimately involved with women than their counterparts of different racial backgrounds. One possible explanation that the researchers gave was that Asian families are less likely to talk about sex and that there is an expectation that youth will put off intimate relationships until adulthood, when they are ready for marriage. Asian Americans also disclosed their sexual orientation at significantly lower levels. Furthermore, the researchers found a significant inverse relationship between internalized homophobia and disclosure among Asian Americans, where those with more internalized homophobia were less likely to disclose.

More recently, Wong and Tang (2004) examined the coming out experiences of Chinese gay men in Hong Kong. While this sample was Asian, rather than Asian American, this study provides important information on the coming out experience as it occurs in Asia. We include this study, as the experiences of this sample may also reflect those of very recent immigrants from Asia to the West better than studies with more acculturated APIs. The sample was composed of 187 men between the ages of 17 and 35. All participants had disclosed their sexual orientation to someone. Seventy-seven percent of participants had disclosed to their gay friends, 52 percent to their straight friends, 41 percent to siblings, 32 percent to parents, and 20 percent to coworkers. This sequence was found to be similar to studies of Western samples; however, Chinese gay men experienced coming out about five years later than Western men (Wong & Tang, 2004). This difference may be related to cultural differences between Chinese and Western cultures in terms of the importance placed on sexual identity.

Wong and Tang (2004) also examined coming out through the Theory of Reasoned Action (TRA) model. TRA predicts behavior based on behavioral intentions, which are influenced by subjective norms (in this case, measured as attitudes towards homosexuality and being gay) about the target behavior, attitudes and beliefs about outcomes of the behavior (measured as perceived or actual discrimination experiences), and perceived behavioral control (measured as identification and involvement in the gay community). Identification with the gay community and positive attitudes about coming out were significant predictors of coming out (gay identification and greater disclosure).

Gock (2001) proposed an API-specific model of coming out that recognizes that LGB APIs have multiple identities. His Identity Integration and Pride Model includes five states for developing an integrated, positive gay or lesbian API identity. The first, *status quo*, is characterized by an idealist belief that we are all individuals and will be treated as such. This state ignores the homophobia in one's ethnic community and the racism faced in the mainstream LGBT community. The second state is *awareness of identities*, when one realizes their double minority status, which can be emotionally distressing. There can be frustration about not being able to successfully integrate into the LGBT community or the API community, which can lead to compartmentalizing one's life. The third state is *dilemma in allegiance*, when the compartmentalization that occurred in the previous state begins to break down. LGB API individuals in this state feel pulled towards both communities and may experience guilt about choosing one over the other. *Selective allegiance* is the fourth state, during which time the individual finds him or herself identifying primarily with one community. In the fifth state, *integrating identities*, individuals finds themselves moving more fluidly within their identities according to the situation. Gock makes a point to express that one can occupy different states simultaneously, and that the model should be more of a map than a way to label oneself.

Dittrich and Jernewall (2007) examined the order in which individuals came out to family members, as well as reasons for delaying this disclosure, among a sample of 89 LGB APIs between the ages of 18 and 49. These data were part of a larger Internet-based study of the effects of parental trust and solidarity on the process of coming out to parents (Dittrich, 2005). More than half of the participants indicated that they came out to a sibling before they came out to any other family member (28 percent to sisters and 24 percent to brothers), followed by 20 percent who came out to their mother first. In terms of order of disclosure to family members, these results follow a trend similar to that indicated by Wong and Tang (2004).

Dittrich and Jernewall (2007) found that both among participants who had eventually come out to their mothers (72 percent, $n = 64$), and those who came out to their fathers (48 percent, $n = 43$), a variety of reasons for not coming out to them sooner were cited, including fear that they would react in a negative way, feeling that it was not the right time to tell them, not wanting to disappoint or hurt them, and not wanting to put them in an awkward social position. The belief that there would be "strong ethnic and/or religious objections to homosexuality" was also a concern in relation to mothers; this was not as much the case for fathers. Compared to the Caucasian subsample in the original study (Dittrich, 2005), the API group considered not wanting to place their parents in a socially awkward position to be a stronger factor in their decision to delay disclosure. This is consistent with the importance placed on family above self, and the desire to avoid stigmatizing the family that has previously been mentioned.

This study was unique in that comparisons were made between participants born in the United States and participants born abroad, and results indicated that individuals who were born in the United States were significantly more likely to be out to their parents. This may indicate that people born in the United States are more comfortable about being out or place a greater importance on being out, though it is also possible that their families are not in the United States, and so they are less close in proximity to their families and feel less of a need to be out to them. In sum, the Dittrich and Jernewall (2007) study supports previous findings and relevant theories, but also raises questions regarding the possible influence of acculturation and/or immediacy of family contact on the decision to come out to parents.

Participants were invited to write about anything else that they wanted to share about their coming out experience. The variety of responses demonstrates how diverse the LGB API community is and how varied experiences with coming out are.

A 19-year-old gay, Chinese-born man said, "Being a Chinese-born American, it has been hard for me to integrate the two cultures. With parents who try to yank me one way and my identity-forming process tugging me another, I have at times felt that I had to reject one in order to maintain the other. As most aspects of life [sic], I am getting better at balancing the forces. Hopefully, balancing will soon change to integrating" (Dittrich & Jernewall, 2007). This man spoke of the pull he feels between identities, which reflects the dilemma of allegiance that Gock (2001) described in his model. He also expressed a desire for balance and integration. His age may dictate his reliance on his parents not only for an emotional connection, but also for economic support; this may add weight to the conflict he feels between his desire to identify as a gay man and his need to meet the expectations of his parents.

A 23-year-old U.S.-born East Asian woman who self-identified as queer said, "I have never explicitly come out to my parents, but they 'know' anyway, and I'm super close to them and we have a great relationship. And often I have felt pressured by the 'Mom/Dad, I have something to tell you' paradigm to sit down and come out explicitly to them, even though in retrospect it seems not only unnecessary, but also quite wrong for our context" (Dittrich & Jernewall, 2007). This woman referenced the expectation that she conform to a model of coming out that does not culturally fit for her. She mentioned an implicit knowing on the part of her parents that does not require her to tell them that she is queer. Her experience speaks to the need for alternative models of what being out means.

COMING OUT IN SCHOOL

Coming out before reaching adulthood poses its own set of challenges. Family can provide a safe haven for youth or react in an abusive manner. Since youth rely on their families not only for emotional support, but also for shelter and financial support, rejection from family can lead to homelessness in some cases. In addition, youth must contend with what is often a hostile school environment. Unfortunately, youth usually lack the resources and options to improve their home and school environments, meaning that until they reach adulthood, many youth face hostility on a daily basis.

According to the Gay, Lesbian and Straight Education Network's (GLSEN) National School Climate Survey, anti-LGBT harassment and bullying is an everyday occurrence in schools, where youth spend most of their time outside of the home. Three out of four students heard derogatory remarks such as "faggot" or "dyke" frequently or often at school, and nearly 9 out of 10 reported hearing "that's so gay" or "you're so gay"—meaning stupid or worthless—frequently or often. Over a third of students experienced physical harassment at school on the basis of sexual orientation and more than a quarter on the basis of their gender expression. Nearly one-fifth of students had been physically assaulted because of their sexual orientation and over a tenth because of their gender expression. In addition to feeling threatened at school because of their sexual orientation, students of color were more likely to feel unsafe because of their race or ethnicity than Caucasian students (Rankin, 2005).

One consequence of this unsafe academic environment is that it can negatively impact students' scholastic achievement. For example, LGBT students were five times more likely to report having skipped school in the last month because of safety concerns than the general population of students. The average GPA for LGBT students who were frequently physically harassed was half a grade lower than that of LGBT students experiencing less harassment (2.6 versus 3.1). LGBT students who experienced more frequent physical harassment were more likely to report they did not plan to go to college. Overall, LGBT students were twice as likely as the general population of students to report they were not planning to pursue any postsecondary education (Rankin, 2005).

Homma and Saewyc (2007) examined the role of family and school on emotional distress with a sample of mostly Hmong, LGB API students in the Midwest. The results indicated that those who perceived that their families were less caring and who perceived their school climate as negative had more emotional distress.

Varney (2001) discusses another consequence of anti-gay harassment and bullying among API youth. She presents the experience of a high school student who joined a Chinese gang that offered him protection against harassment at school based on his sexual orientation. In addition to physical protection, the gang may also act as a surrogate family to youth who do not feel accepted by their biological families.

According to a report that looked at the experiences of LGBT college students, 20 percent feared for their physical safety, 36 percent had experienced harassment in the past year, and 51 percent concealed their sexual orientation or gender identity to avoid harassment (Rankin, 2003). College students of color also reported experiencing harassment based on race and ethnicity.

Asian Pacific Islander youth often have difficulty finding spaces that support both their API and queer identities. As a result, queer APIs have taken it upon themselves to fill the gap by addressing their needs in already existing organizations or creating new ones. For example, Asian Queers Under 25 Altogether (AQU[25]A) is a group in San Francisco for and run by API queer youth. They have gatherings, workshops, parties, retreats, a peer leadership program, and a drop-in space for youth to hang out. Parents, Family, and Friends of Lesbians and Gays (PFLAG) is an organization that many parents of gay children turn to in order to get support in dealing with their child's sexual orientation and is a resource for many queer people, especially when they are considering coming out. Two chapters have developed to meet the needs of API families: the API PFLAG in Southern California and the San Francisco Bay Chinese PFLAG in Northern California. The API PFLAG website (www.pflag.gapsn.org) discusses options for coming out, giving an example of an older Chinese American man who has a "don't ask, don't tell" relationship with his parents. This man never openly discussed his sexual orientation with his parents and they never asked him about it, but when he would visit them overnight with his partner, the two of them would share the guest bedroom. This is just one way that API PFLAG provides queer APIs with a perspective beyond that of the mainstream, which may feel more culturally congruent.

COMING OUT IN THE WORKPLACE

As members of at least two marginalized communities, LGB API workers are affected by discrimination. Racism, heterosexism, and homophobia are elements that limit occupational success. Not only is success negatively affected, but racism and heterosexism influence workplace disclosure of one's sexual orientation. Cultural expectations, the workplace environment, and interpersonal factors significantly impact the career experiences and the workplace coming out process for Asian American LGBT individuals.

Few studies in the vocational psychology and career development literature examine the intersection of sexual orientation and other aspects of identity such as race/ethnicity. Little empirical evidence directly addresses the workplace experiences of LGB API individuals and LGB API workplace sexual identity disclosure. The lack of empirical work describing the experience is not indicative of the importance of the workplace for LGB API individuals. In fact, LGB API individuals are concerned about the workplace. In the 2007 National Gay Lesbian Task Force survey of LGBT APIs, 28 percent of respondents indicated that job discrimination/ harassment was the most important factor facing all API in the United States (Dang & Vianney, 2007). On the list of concerns, job discrimination and harassment was the fourth most endorsed issue. Twenty-nine percent of respondents indicated that job discrimination/harassment, the fifth most endorsed issue, was the most important issue for LGBT APIs. Although there is a lack of empirical evidence describing the LGB API workplace experience, through an examination of the LGB literature and the API literature, one can begin to identify the salient issues impacting the coming out process for LGB API individuals.

API Workplace Experiences

While LGB identity can be considered an invisible stigma, API identity can be considered a visible stigma. In contrast to other occupational and academic stereotypes for other ethnicities, APIs are perceived as having high educational and occupational attainment. In addition, Asian Americans' occupational interests tend to be concentrated in technical and scientific fields.

Much has been written and discussed relating to the relatively high educational attainment of APIs. Unfortunately, these generalities and the general acceptance of the Model Minority Myth mask discrimination and differential success rates between Asian ethnic groups and hide difficulties in career advancement. For Asian Americans, higher educational attainment may not be translating into occupational success. Barringer, Takeuchi, and Xenos (1995) analyzed 1980 Census five percent Public Use Sample data and examined educational attainment and income for multiple races and ethnicities. Barringer and colleagues assert that when compared to white counterparts, Asian Americans do not have income parity. In addition, APIs have experienced difficulty in attaining management positions. Even in industries with a high concentration of APIs, Woo (2000) asserts that Asian Americans are underrepresented in management.

Acculturation can be considered a powerful moderator variable in the career experiences of Asian Americans. Not only did Tang, Fouad, and Smith (1999) find that families influenced career decision-making; they also found that acculturation had an impact. Asian Americans with higher levels of acculturation were less likely to choose stereotypical science and technology-related occupations. With a sample of 39 Asian Americans working in two corporations who attended a career development workshop, Leong (1991) found acculturation to be positively related with job satisfaction and negatively related with job stress. In a second study consisting of a sample of 27 Asian Americans, Leong (2001) found positive supervisor appraisals to be related to acculturation. In an examination of the career adjustment of 56 Asian American corporate workers, Leong (2001) discovered higher acculturation to be associated with higher levels of work satisfaction and lower levels of job stress.

LGB Workplace Discrimination and Workplace Disclosure

Workplace settings have a profound effect on the workplace experience of LGB workers, especially regarding personal and professional safety. Perceptions of workplace discrimination influence the coming out decisions of LGB workers. Twenty-five to eighty percent of LGB workers report having been discriminated against at least once (Bradford, Ryan, & Rothblum, 1994; Croteau & Lark, 1995; Croteau & von Destinon, 1994). Forty-four to 60 percent of LGB workers anticipate future discrimination (Croteau, 1996; Croteau & Lark, 1995). LGB workers employ a range of strategies to disclose or hide their sexual identity. In their private lives, LGB workers have the opportunity to be open about their sexual orientation, but in their public lives at work, LGB workers may be forced to change pronouns in discussing their partners (e.g., for a gay man, changing "he" to "she"), may be unable to place pictures of their partner in their work areas, and may have to censor their sharing about their weekend plans.

Ragins and Cornwell (2001) suggest that workplace disclosure is more than a function of discrimination. The workplace climate shapes the disclosure of LGB workers. They suggest that other factors such as workplace policies and the presence of supportive coworkers and supervisors are just as important. Button (2001) found that gay and lesbian employees who worked in settings that were more equitable and treated them fairly had higher degrees of workplace disclosure. Rotosky and Riggle (2002), surveying 118 gay male and lesbian couples, learned that employee disclosure was best predicted by the presence of supportive workplace policies and relatively low levels of internalized homophobia among employees. Griffith and Hebl (2002) found that workplace disclosure was predicted by (in order of relative strength) a gay-supportive workplace environment, disclosure to heterosexual friends, and self-acceptance. These robust findings were replicated by Ragins, Singh, and Cornwell (2007), who discovered that the degree of disclosure/outness in the workplace was predicted by the presence of LGB coworkers and supportive supervisors and coworkers.

While the vocational literature does not address the LGB API experience specifically, the separate literatures on LGBs and APIs gives us an understanding of some of the challenges that LGB APIs face in the workplace. Most adults spend a considerable amount of time in the workplace. Coming out in this environment can have drastic implications, including being fired from one's job. The API vocational literature suggests that APIs are often not at income parity in comparison to other racial/ethnic groups. In addition, APIs are underrepresented in management. Taking these features together, we can infer that the workplace can be a challenging environment for LGB APIs and that this topic warrants further research.

CONCLUSION

In the context of heterosexism and racism, LGB API individuals navigate the disclosure of their sexual orientation on a daily basis in multiple domains. This chapter has explored the cultural and societal influences that uniquely impact the coming out narratives of API LGBs in families, schools, and workplaces. Given the dearth of research focusing on the intersection of race and sexual orientation, we often try to understand the experiences of LGB API individuals by relying on literature that addresses sexual orientation in other racial groups or that speaks to heterosexual API experiences in various settings. More research is needed to fully understand sexual orientation disclosure as it pertains to APIs and, since there is tremendous diversity within the API population, we speculate that there will be differences based on ethnicity, acculturation, language, religion, and many other cultural and demographic factors. Increased understanding of the coming out experiences of APIs will help therapists to provide more culturally appropriate recommendations for LGB API clients. In addition, LGB API individuals will benefit from having more resources that speak to their specific experiences as ethnic and sexual minorities as they attempt to navigate environments that can be racist and homophobic.

Coming out is not a finite event, but is instead a lifelong process. Heterosexism supports the assumption that all people are heterosexual unless otherwise stated. Therefore, LGB APIs will face the issue of coming out in every arena that they enter. We explored some of these domains such as family, school, and workplace settings, but there are many more spaces that LGB APIs occupy. Future research should consider unique issues that LGB APIs face in other settings, such as religious institutions. APIs are very religiously diverse and, therefore, being out will be easier in some churches and religions than in others. Some LGB APIs will find themselves in conflict between their sexual orientation and their religious beliefs, which can be spiritually and emotionally painful. More research is needed to help clinicians who want to provide psychological support to these clients.

We acknowledge that this chapter does not include the transgender experience. While gender identity and sexual orientation are often discussed in one breath, we believe that transgender APIs have unique and important experiences and challenges that go beyond sexual orientation. Future research should examine the transgender API experience, while recognizing the diversity of experiences that will be informed by ethnicity, acculturation, language, socioeconomic status, education, religion, and a myriad of other demographic factors.

REFERENCES

American Psychological Association. (1999). *Just the facts about sexual orientation and youth: A primer for principals, educators, and school personnel.* Retrieved January 5, 2007, from http://www.apa.org/pi/lgbc/publications/justthe facts.html.

Barringer, H. R., Takeuchi, D. T., & Xenos, P. (1995). Education, occupational prestige, and income of Asian Americans. In D. T. Nakanishi & T. Y. Nishida (Eds.), *The Asian American educational experience* (pp. 146–164). New York: Routledge.

Ben-Ari, A. (1995). The discovery that an offspring is gay: Parents', gay men's, and lesbians' perspectives. *Journal of Homosexuality, 30,* 89–112.

Bhugra, D. (1997). Coming out by South Asian gay men in the United Kingdom. *Archives of Sexual Behavior, 26,* 547–557.

Bradford, J., Ryan, C., & Rothblum, E. D. (1994). National lesbian health care survey: Implications for mental health care. *Journal of Consulting and Clinical Psychology, 62,* 228–242.

Button, S. B. (2001). Organizational efforts to affirm sexual diversity: A cross-level examination. *Journal of Applied Psychology, 86,* 17–28.

Chan, C. S. (1989). Asian lesbians: Psychological issues in the "coming out" process. *Asian American Psychological Association Journal, 12,* 16–18.

Cramer, D. W., & Roach, A. J. (1988). Coming out to mom and dad: A study of gay males and their relationships with their parents. *Journal of Homosexuality, 15,* 79–91.

Croteau, J. M. (1996). Research on the work experiences of lesbian, gay, and bisexual people: An integrative review of methodology and findings. *Journal of Vocational Behavior, 48,* 195–209.

Croteau, J. M., &. Lark, J. S. (1995). On being lesbian, gay or bisexual in student affairs: A national survey of experiences on the job. *NASPA Journal, 32,* 189–197.

Croteau, J. M., & von Destinon, M. (1994). A national survey of job search experiences of lesbian, gay, and bisexual student affairs professionals. *Journal of College Student Development, 35,* 40–45.

Dang, A., & Vianney, C. (2007). *Living in the margins: A national survey of lesbian, gay, bisexual and transgender Asian and Pacific Islander Americans.* New York: National Gay and Lesbian Task Force Policy Institute.

Dittrich, M. L. (2005). Coming out to parents: Parental trust and solidarity among only children and non-only children. *Dissertation Abstract International, 66*(7), 3945. (UMI No. ATT 3183135.)

Dittrich, M., & Jernewall, N. (2007, January). *Coming out to parents: Trends and observations among Asian Americans.* Paper presented at the National Multicultural Conference and Summit, Seattle, WA.

Dube, E. M., & Savin-Williams, R. C. (1999). Sexual identity development among ethnic sexual-minority male youths. *Developmental Psychology, 35,* 1389–1399.

Gock, T. S. (2001). Asian-Pacific Islander issues: Identity integration and pride. In B. Berzon (Ed.), *Positively gay: New approaches to gay and lesbian life* (pp. 247–252). Berkeley, CA: Celestial Arts.

Greene, B. (1997). Ethnic minority lesbian and gay men: Mental health and treatment issues. In B. Greene (Ed.), *Ethnic and cultural diversity among lesbians and gay men* (pp. 216–239). Thousand Oaks, CA: Sage Publications.

Griffith, K. H., & Hebl, M. R. (2002). The disclosure dilemma for gay men and lesbians: "Coming out" at work. *Journal of Applied Psychology, 87,* 1191–1199.

Homma, Y., & Saewyc, E. M. (2007). The emotional well-being of Asian-American sexual minority youth in school. *Journal of LGBT Health Research, 3,* 67–78.

Leong, F.T.L. (1991). Career development attributes and occupational values of Asian American and White American college students. *The Career Development Quarterly, 39,* 221–230.

Leong, F.T.L. (2001). The role of acculturation in the career adjustment of Asian American workers: A test of Leong and Chou's (1994) formulation. *Cultural Diversity and Ethnic Minority Psychology, 7,* 262–273.

Merighi, J. R., & Grimes, M. D. (2000). Coming out to families in a multicultural context. Families in Society: *The Journal of Contemporary Human Services, 81,* 32–41.

Ragins, B. R., & Cornwell, J. M. (2001). Pink triangles: Antecedents and consequences of perceived workplace discrimination against gay and lesbian employees. *Journal of Applied Psychology, 86,* 1244–1261.

Ragins, B. R., Singh, R., & Cornwell, J. M. (2007). Making the invisible visible: Fear and disclosure of sexual orientation at work. *Journal of Applied Psychology, 92,* 1103–1118.

Rankin, S. R. (2003). *Campus climate for gay, lesbian, bisexual, and transgender people: A national perspective.* New York: The National Gay and Lesbian Task Force Policy Institute.

Rankin, S. R. (2005). Campus climate for sexual minorities. *New Directions for Student Services, 111,* 17–23.

Rotosky, S. S., & Riggle, E.D.B. (2002). "Out" at work: The relation of actor and partner workplace policy and internalized homophobia to disclosure status. *Journal of Counseling Psychology, 49,* 411–419.

Smith, A. (1997). Cultural diversity and the coming out process: Implications for clinical practice. In B. Greene (Ed.), *Ethnic and cultural diversity among lesbians and gay men* (pp. 279–300). Thousand Oaks, CA: Sage Publications.

Tang, M., Fouad, N. A., & Smith, P. L. (1999). Asian Americans' career choices: A path model to examine factors influencing their career choices. *Journal of Vocational Behavior, 54,* 142–156.

Varney, J. A. (2001). Undressing the normal: Community efforts for queer Asian and Asian American youth. In K. K. Kumashiro (Ed.), *Troubling intersections of race and sexuality: Queer students of color and anti-oppressive education* (pp. 87–103). Lanham, MD: Rowman & Littlefield.

Wong, C. Y., & Tang, C. S. (2004). Coming out experiences and psychological distress of Chinese homosexual men in Hong Kong. *Archives of Sexual Behavior, 33,* 149–157.

Woo, D. (2000). *The glass ceiling and Asian Americans: The new face of workplace barriers.* Walnut Creek, CA: AltaMira.

CHAPTER 4

Interracial Marriage: Current Perspectives and Unanswered Challenges

Janice M. Steil, Allison M. Rothman, Lisa E. Harris,
Gideon S. Kim, and Justin P. Steil

When we announced our engagement to my parents, my mother leaned in close and, looking straight into his eyes, told my fiancée, "You know, Lisa's not white. Have you thought about that? Do your parents know? Because they may not like that and you need to be ready for what people will say when they find out." (Lisa E. Harris, personal communication, May 14, 2008.)

Over the last decade, a number of biracial persons have achieved positions of prominence in the United States. Tiger Woods, son of an African American father and an Asian mother, is one of the world's best and most celebrated golfers. Halle Berry, Academy Award–winning actress, is the daughter of an African American father and a white mother. Norah Jones, celebrated musician, is the daughter of a white mother and an Indian father, while Barack Obama, the current president of the United States, is the son of a white mother from Kansas and a black father from Kenya. While much attention has been paid to these accomplished individuals, much less attention has been paid to the interracial marriages that produced them. Yet, their very presence is a reflection of the extent to which interracial marriage is a rapidly growing phenomenon in the United States. What are the implications of this increasing rate of intermarriage as a reflection of and, simultaneously, a catalyst for social change? Given our society's historic reliance on rigid classifications, especially in regard to race, do these marriages result in identity conflicts for the partners, both as individuals and as a couple? To what extent do interracial couples find family and societal support for their choice of partner? To what extent do they struggle with negative responses to the breaking of what some have labeled "the last taboo" (Qian, 2005, p. 35)? And what are the implications for partner and couple well-being? In this chapter, we explore these questions in the context of what is known and what is not known about the factors associated with the growing phenomenon of interracial marriage.

Interracial marriage has been defined as the marrying of two people of differing races. The concept of interracial marriage is made more problematic by agreement among most contemporary researchers that race is a socially constructed category unsupported by biology. Nevertheless, the concept of race continues to be a highly salient feature of the U.S. social structure, affecting individual identity, access to resources and social interaction. Because race is a socially constructed category, it is also socially contingent and its boundaries and significance change with changing social conditions and identities. Thus, a marriage between someone of Japanese descent and someone of Korean descent could be seen by some as an interracial marriage and by others as an intraracial marriage, depending on time, place, and the identifications of those involved. The existing research, however, mostly focuses on marriages across the racial and ethnic categories identified in the U.S. Census: non-Hispanic whites, blacks, Hispanics or Latinos, Asians and Native Americans.

Interracial marriage is seen as a form of exogamy (marrying outside of one's social group). For most of U.S. history, such marriages have not only been stigmatized, but also prohibited. As recently as 50 years ago, in the case of *Loving v. Virginia*, an African American woman and a white man were prosecuted for being married and living in the state, thereby violating the law against "mixing or blending races in marriage or breeding" (Miscegenation, 2009). In 1967, when the case reached the Supreme Court, the Court ruled that antimiscegenation laws were illegal, striking down Virginia's statute as well as similar laws in 15 other states. Yet, as recently as 1998, 38 percent of voting South Carolinians voted to retain the legally enforceable clause in the state constitution forbidding interracial marriages (Yancey, 2001), and it was only in the year 2000 that the state of Alabama repealed its own ban on these relationships.

CHANGING DEMOGRAPHICS

The Supreme Court ruling of 1967 coincided with a number of social changes, including increased attention to civil rights and expanding educational and employment opportunities for people of color. While not fully explanatory, it is more than coincidental that the rate of interracial marriage has almost doubled every decade since that ruling. In 1970, there were approximately 321,000 interracial marriages in the United States. In 1980, that number had risen to about 1 million; it then increased to 1.5 million in 1990 and 2.9 million in 2000 (King & Bratter, 2007). Yet, despite the rapid increase in absolute numbers, the relative percentage of interracial marriages remains rather low, having grown from less than one percent of all marriages in 1970 to approximately seven percent today (Qian & Lichter, 2007; Simmons & O'Connell, 2003).

In contrast to antimisegenation laws aimed at preserving so-called racial purity and racial hierarchy, interracial marriage is viewed by many as a measure of inclusion and as a "barometer of the extent to which racial boundaries are atrophying" (Golebiowska, 2007, p. 268). In the social sciences, measures of social prejudice, including the Bogardus Social Distance Scale, use the extent to which respondents are willing to accept the marriage of their daughters to a member of another race as the most significant measure of social acceptance. Others see interracial marriage as an engine of social change (George & Yancey, 2004; Root, 2001), promoting interaction among the families, friends, and colleagues of those who have married, potentially leading to a greater appreciation of the other's culture (Romano, 2003; Yancey & Yancey, 1997). In addition, the increase in multiracial children leads to a blurring of racial boundaries and identifications, thereby achieving what antimisegenation laws were designed to prevent.

DEMOGRAPHICS OF INTERRACIAL MARRIAGE

Racial Demographics

Sociologists have been instrumental in using national data, particularly those of the U.S. Census, to analyze patterns of interracial marriage. Working from the perspective of interracial marriage as a measure of social acceptance, most focus on rates of intermarriage between the various racial and ethnic groups with the majority group, non-Hispanic whites. It is also the case, however, that these comparisons are the ones for which there is the most data; though only four percent of whites are involved in interracial marriages, 92 percent of all interracial marriages include a white partner (Bentley, Mattingly, Hough, & Bennett, 2003; Qian, 2005). Hispanics, Native Americans, and Asians are most likely, while African Americans are least likely, to marry into white families (Blackwell & Lichter, 2000; Harris & Ono, 2004; Qian, 1997).

Rates of intermarriage for immigrant groups are often associated with the length of their residency in the United States. Comparing native- and foreign-born blacks, native-born African Americans are more likely to marry others who label themselves as black, such as West Indians, Africans, and Puerto Rican nonwhites, than they are to marry whites, but are more likely to intermarry with whites than are nonnative black immigrants (Qian & Lichter, 2007). Among Asian Americans, Japanese Americans have intermarriage rates of 20 percent for men and 41 percent for women, while Vietnamese Americans and Asian Indians, both more recent immigrant groups, have intermarriage rates of 3 percent for men, 10 percent for women and 8 percent for men, 5 percent for women, respectively (Xie & Goyette, 2004).

Overall, mixed-race individuals are more likely to marry whites than single-race minority individuals, and this is true for Asian Americans as well. Multiracial Asian Americans have even higher rates of intermarriage than the nonmultiracial, with 44 percent of men and 54 percent of women married to whites (Batson, Qian, & Lichter, 2006).

Sex Demographics

Rates of intermarriage often vary significantly by sex. These differences are modest among whites, Latinos and Native Americans, but substantial among African Americans and Asian Americans. African American men are more likely to marry white women than African American women are to marry white men. Indeed, black men are almost three times as likely to marry white women than the reverse, such that in 73 percent of black-white couples, the husband is black and the wife is white (Batson et al., 2006; Porterfield, 1982). The opposite is true for most Asian ethnicities. According to the 2000 U.S. Census, an Asian American woman is twice as likely to have a non-Asian husband (23%) than an Asian man is to have a non-Asian wife (12%). For Filipinos, the difference is almost threefold (33% of women versus 13% of men) and the contrast is even greater for Korean Americans (27% of women versus 4% of men) (Xie & Goyette, 2004).

According to Xie and Goyette (2004), some of this difference is attributable to military men who have met and married their wives during their service in Asia. Yet sex differences in the rate of interracial marriage are so large and so consistent across all Asian groups that this theory does not fully explain the differences. Further, data restricted to U.S.-born Asian Americans show a similar pattern (49% of U.S.-born Asian American women have interracially married, versus 38% of men). Asian Indian Americans are the only major Asian group in which women do not interracially marry more often than men (5% for women and 8% for men) (Xie & Goyette, 2004).

WHY THE CHANGING DEMOGRAPHICS?

The rising rate of interracial marriages has been attributed to a number of factors, ranging from changing immigration patterns resulting in greater racial diversity in the United States to greater acceptance of diversity among the population at large, especially among the young, who have studied and worked with more diverse peer groups, and the rising age of marriage, which both expands exposure to diverse communities and limits parental control (Rosenfeld & Kim, 2005).

Level of education, in particular, is considered a strong predictor of minority intermarriage with whites, as it provides increased opportunities for contact in both school and work settings. Consistent with this perspective, intermarriage with whites increases for Asians and Hispanics as their level of educational attainment increases. Thus, high intermarriage rates, particularly between Asians and whites, may be explained, in part, by the fact that Asian Americans are four times more likely to complete a college education than are African Americans and Hispanics (Qian & Lichter, 2007; Xie & Goyette, 2004). Educational attainment, however, does not fully explain racial differences in the rates of intermarriage. Latinos, whose levels of education do not match those of Asians, have similar levels of intermarriage with whites. Furthermore, the discrepancy between education and rates of intermarriage is especially notable among African American women who, at approximately four percent, have one of the lowest rates of intermarriage and for whom, according to some, "race apparently trumps educational attainment" (Qian & Lichter, 2007, p. 90).

WHO ACCEPTS INTERRACIAL MARRIAGE?

Sociologists have also looked at the factors associated with the acceptance or rejection of interracial marriage. African Americans are generally more accepting of interracial marriage than whites (Jacobson & Johnson, 2006). In 1972, 76 percent of African Americans approved of interracial marriage, as compared to less than 30 percent of whites. In 1997, the percentages had changed to 83 percent for African Americans and 67 percent for whites, while a 2000 survey showed that 37.3 percent of non-Hispanic whites opposed a close relative of theirs marrying a black person and less than a quarter (23%) embraced the idea (Golebiowska, 2007). In general, the factors associated with level of endorsement or rejection of interracial marriage parallel those associated with endorsement or rejection of racial prejudice generally. Income, education, and urbanization are all positively associated with approval. The younger, better educated, wealthier, less religiously devout, and ideologically liberal whites are more approving of interracial marriage than their older, less well educated, and more religiously devout counterparts (Golebiowska, 2007; Johnson & Jacobson, 2005). There are also differences by geographic region, such that rates of intermarriage are highest in the most racially diversified region of the country, the West (George & Yancey, 2004). In contrast, rates of interracial marriage have been lowest in the South, where resistance has been particularly strong, but findings suggest that these differences are diminishing (Gullickson, 2006).

PSYCHOLOGICAL PERSPECTIVES

There are few systematic psychological studies of interracial couples. Because of the recent nature of the growing rates of interracial marriage, the few studies that have been reported tend to be based on in-depth interviews with small clinical or convenience samples. Almost all of these have been studies of marriages between African Americans and whites, with little attention to other ethnic or racial groups. Most have focused on the motives for partner involvement in an interracial marriage, while others have focused on societal and family pressures and the partners' methods of coping.

Motivational Explanations

Almost all studies, it seems, include a motivational component. As an anomaly, out-of-race marriages, it seems, must be explained. Who marries exogamously and why? The findings frequently pathologize both the partners and their motives. Whites who intermarry are often portrayed as "misfits" and "loners"; or as individuals with low self-esteem who are, either consciously or unconsciously, rebelling against their families and society (Gullickson, 2006; Lewis, Yancey, & Bletzer, 1997). Other theories center on issues of sexuality, including sexual curiosity and notions of exoticism. As Perry and Sutton (2006) point out, given the long history of black-white relations in the United States, sexuality becomes a particularly important site for the construction of difference. Black men have often been narrowly defined in terms of a dangerous, powerful sexuality; women of color have often been portrayed as racialized exotic others (Perry & Sutton, 2006). Still others have looked at interracial marriage as a means of social advancement in which high status blacks (or other minorities) seek to exchange their economic achievement status for the higher racial status of a white spouse.

Lewis et al. (1997) conducted one of the few systematic studies of racial as compared to nonracial motives in interracial marriages. Little support was found for factors such as the sexual novelty and excitement of someone from another race. Most respondents focused on issues of common interests and goals and personal (as compared to racial) attractiveness. Other studies found that partners emphasized the importance of love, companionship, compatibility and the desire to be seen as normal and ordinary people who choose to marry for the same reasons as any other couple (Killian, 2001; Leslie & Letiecq, 2004; Rosenblatt, Karis, & Powell, 1995). As one of the respondents in Rosenblatt et al.'s (1995) study noted, "You look for a person to be with, not a race or color" (p. 25).

Evidence in support of the social exchange perspective is mixed. In a study of personal advertisements from those seeking biracial relationships, Yancey and Yancey (1997) hypothesized that whites would be more likely to express a desire for assets (e.g., indicators of professional status or achievement), whereas blacks would be more likely to offer assets to offset their lower racial status. Contrary to the hypothesis, they found that sex, not race, was the most significant predictor of who seeks or offers relationship assets (with women as the seekers).

Others have noted that, overall, individuals who marry interracially tend to come from the same social class. Yet, not only African American men, but also Latino and, to a lesser extent, Asian men are more likely to be married to a white woman with less education than themselves than to a white woman at the same educational level. But this is not a pattern unique to interracial marriages. Marriage researchers have long written of the marriage gradient, in which women seek to "marry up," that is, to marry men with higher income and status potential than themselves. While, historically, this was a practice originating in women's lesser access to education and high-status professions, and may be in the process of change, it at least lends some broader context. In same-race marriages, it is seen as women marrying up to achieve social advantages; in cross-race marriages, it seems to be seen as men marrying down for the same reasons.

RELATIONAL CHALLENGES

While the dominant response of those in interracial marriages seems to reflect a yearning for so-called normalcy, the response of others most often reflects our highly race-conscious society. African Americans are more supportive of interracial unions and more likely to have another interracial marriage in the family than are whites (Leslie & Letiecq, 2004). Yet, blacks also suffer disapproving reactions. African American men who marry white women may be seen as racial defectors who are reducing the already limited marriage pool for black women, while black women who marry white men may be seen, by some, as "sleeping with the oppressor." White families fear a loss of status and societal disapproval, and worry about their daughters' and sons' safety, as well as their economic future (Rosenblatt et al., 1995).

Societal hostility varies, ranging from stares, derogatory jokes, and catcalls that "put a shadow over interracial intimacy" (Kennedy, 1999, p. 17) to discrimination in levels of service in stores, seating in restaurants, employment, housing, and medical care, to police harassment (Leslie & Letiecq, 2004; Rosenblatt et al., 1995).

RESPONDING TO THE STRESSES

How, then, do interacial partners respond to these stressors? Among the most frequent responses noted in interview studies is the tendency on the part of partners to downplay the significance of race in their relationship. Killian (2002), on the basis of in depth interviews with 10 black-white couples, noted a general policy of minimizing the relevance of race. In half of Killian's couple respondents, there was a policy of "no race talk." Though black members of the couples were more likely to notice and be emotionally affected by negative public reactions, it was expected that black partners would not discuss racial issues from their families of origin or their experiences of discrimination in their current lives in racially mixed company. Others describe themselves as constantly on guard, avoiding places where they think they will not be welcome or will be at risk, going out of their way when making reservations, for example, to let people know in advance that they are an interracial couple, and selecting a supportive community of friends. A significant amount of energy, it seems, is directed at "avoiding, deflecting, minimizing or sliding away from" confrontation (Rosenblatt et al., 1995, p. 175). To what extent, then, is the felt need for these coping patterns associated with measures of partner well-being?

WELL-BEING

Using a five-year pool of data from the National Health Interview Survey, Bratter and Eschbach (2005) conducted one of the few systematic studies to date of the association between the racial composition of couples and levels of partner distress. In each of their analyses, Bratter and Eschbach compared rates of dysphoric distress by race and gender for those in same race as compared to other race marriages. Rates of intermarriage paralleled those from other surveys. For married men, 97 percent of whites were married to same race women, followed by 88 percent of Asians, 87 percent of Blacks, 83 percent of Hispanics and 41 percent of Native Americans. For women, 97 percent of whites were married to same race men, followed by 96 percent of blacks, 82 percent of Hispanics, 74 percent of Asians and 45 percent of Native Americans. Also consistent with other studies, the majority of African Americans, Asians, Hispanics and Native Americans who were not in same-race marriages were married to whites. Of the intermarried who were not married to whites, most African Americans were married to Hispanics, as were the majority of intermarried whites.

Well-being was assessed using the K-6 scale, a screening measure for nonspecific psychological distress. Consistent with the hypothesis, rates of distress varied by gender and race. Intermarried white women were significantly more likely to report higher distress rates (12.5%) than white women with white husbands (8%). Increased rates of severe distress were found for intermarried white women in every pairing, including those married to African Americans, Hispanics, and Native Americans; although the difference did not reach statistical significance for white women married to Asians. Subsequent analysis, using measures of socioeconomic status, suggested that perhaps 50 percent of this increase in psychological symptomatology could be explained by socioeconomic disadvantages accruing to white women in intermarriages compared to those with same-race partners. The remaining half, however, remains unexplained.

By contrast, distress rates for white men did not differ significantly for the interracially as compared to endogamously married (6.7% as compared to 5.7%), with the exception of white men who were married to Native American women (13.5%). Indeed, for all groups, that is, men and women of all races for whom there was a large enough sample to analyze, the highest distress rates were found for those married to Native Americans. By contrast, rates of distress did not increase for men or women of any racial group intermarried with whites.

Fu, Tora, and Kendall (2001) examined marital happiness among a sample of the intermarried living in a multi-ethnic community in Hawaii. Overall, they found that the interracially married were more likely to have considered divorce. Furthermore, wives in interracial marriages were less happy than wives in intraracial unions. Paralleling the findings of Bratter and Eschbach, however, husbands were less affected, showing no significant differences in happiness by type of marriage.

How are we to understand these differential patterns of well-being? What do we know of the factors associated with marital quality among the interracially married? What is the role of discrimination? What is the role of social support or the loss thereof? What are the strategies of successful coping? In a preliminary attempt to address these questions, Leslie and Letiecq (2004) examined the role of social support, experience of discrimination, and racial identity as predictors of marital quality in a sample of 76 black-white interracially married couples. Findings showed that, particularly for African American partners, racial identity was the strongest predictor of marital quality. For African Americans, the stronger their black identity and the higher their tolerance for other races, the greater the level of love they reported, the more positively they evaluated their marriage, and the more they worked to maintain it. What mattered most was pride in one's own race that did not devalue or diminish other races and cultures.

SUMMARY OF THE RESEARCH
AND UNANSWERED QUESTIONS

While there have always been interracial marriages in the United States, a number of factors converged in the 1960s and 1970s leading to their rapid proliferation. These include changing immigration patterns, greater racial tolerance, greater interracial contact through increased educational and employment opportunities for people of color, and a loosening of parental and community control through greater geographic mobility and a later age of marriage. Due to the recency of the phenomenon, research is at a nascent stage. To date, sociologists, using data from the U.S. Census, have documented the rising rates as well as the differential frequency of interracial marriage across different groups. Seeking to identify the factors associated with differences in the rates of marriage to whites across racial groups and for both women and men of different racial groups, they have examined the role of group size (smaller groups have fewer potential same-race partners from which to choose), recency of immigration (more recent immigrants often have less opportunity for interracial contact), and educational level (higher education is often associated with a loosening of racial ties and affords more opportunity for equal status interracial contact). Yet, none of these factors is fully explanatory. Hispanics, for example, are a large and fairly recent immigrant group, whose level of education does not parallel that of Asians, a smaller immigrant group, and yet they have similar rates of intermarriage with whites as Asians do. Other researchers show differential rates of well-being. Women in interracial marriages may be less happy than men; white women seem to evidence the highest levels of stress. Why?

Much of the research to date is based on small samples and few draw on the rich psychological literature on a number of topics, including stigma, stereotypes, entitlement, and power. Yet, each of these theoretical perspectives has the potential to enrich our understanding of the challenges and benefits of interracial marriage. It seems impossible to understand the differences in the rates of interracial marriage across groups without considering the impact of racial stereotypes. As Qian (2005) points out, the lighter the skin color, the higher the rate of intermarriage with white Americans. Hispanics who label themselves as racially white are most likely to marry non-Hispanic whites. Asian Americans and Native Americans are next. Hispanics who do not consider themselves racially white have low rates of intermarriage with whites. African Americans are least likely of all racial minorities to marry whites. According to Qian (2005), "Darker skin in America is associated with discrimination, lower educational attainment, lower income and segregation" (p. 35). What role, then, do racial stereotypes play in the distinctly low rates of white intermarriage with African American women?

Most researchers today see stereotypes as functional. Cognitively, they facilitate the processing of information by grouping discrete bits of information into coherent categories. Socially, however, they often serve to maintain status hierarchies (Sidanius & Pratto, 1999). For the powerful, they can be integral to belief systems that justify the advantages of their position as appropriate and deserved. Similarly, when internalized by the less powerful, stereotypes can justify their position of disadvantage as equally deserved, thereby serving to maintain the status quo. Lisa's mother, in the quotation that opened this chapter, was well aware of the hierarchies of color. To some extent, at least, she had internalized her disadvantaged position. She greeted her daughter's engagement with anxiety provoked by the anticipated disapproval of her in-laws, among others, when they learned that their son was engaged to a woman who was "not white."

Yet, we must go beyond stereotypes associated with skin color alone. For how do we explain the low rates of intermarriage with Asian men as compared to high rates with Asian women? Pyke (2004), in an analysis of 100 interviews with daughters of Korean and Vietnamese immigrants, found that they frequently juxtaposed derogatory images of Asian masculinity with positive images of white masculinity. Stereotypes of Asian men portrayed them as "effeminate, non athletic, submissive, wimpy, small in stature, nerdy and asexual and, on the other hand, as hyper masculine martial arts masters or gang members who are threatening and domineering particularly in their personal relationships with women" (p. 3). Thus, Asian men are portrayed as either too masculine or not masculine enough, making them less desirable partners to Asian American women (as well as non–Asian American women). In contrast, stereotypes of white men portrayed them as "embodying the ideal masculinity" (p. 3). Compared to Asian American men, they are regarded as tall, attractive, athletic, romantic, caring, and egalitarian heterosexual partners. According to Pyke, the imagery of these stereotypes penetrates the consciousness of society, bolstering the power of white men by making Asian American women available to them as sexual partners and contributing to the high rates of outmarriage among Asian American women as compared to men. Clearly, here as elsewhere, race and gender do not act in isolation, but interact in complex ways with the hierarchies of power and the power of social stereotypes.

And how are we to understand the differential rates of well-being between interracially married white women and white men if we do not consider issues of gender and power? Traditionally, women's status as compared to men's has been more dependent on whom they marry. Bratter and Eschbach's (2005) study suggested that white women who marry out-of-race fare less well than their same-race married peers in terms of socioeconomic status (SES). According to the authors, this loss of SES may explain up to 50 percent of white women's increased symptomotology levels. But how then are we to explain the remaining 50 percent? And why are white women affected more than white men? Are white women more vulnerable than their white male counterparts to diminished social status? White males have traditionally been associated with the highest levels of status, power, and privilege in U.S. society. Are white men also more able than white women to retain their privileged state in the context of interracial marriage?

We see that sense of identity can be the most significant predictor of couple well-being, particularly for African Americans, who suffer the greatest social stigma and are most likely to experience discrimination. A secure sense of identity can contribute to effective coping with external pressures and disapproving reactions from family, friends, and strangers. Yet, what about issues of couple identity? While interracial couples may be seeking normalcy—"we're no different than anybody else" (Rosenblatt et al., 1995, p. 24)—there are inevitable challenges. For all newly married couples, there is the challenge of learning about each other and partner family of origin, of integrating different family customs, practices, and expectations, and developing a couple identity. How, then, is this different for those who marry interracially? Are the cultural differences in terms of the issues of food, money management, etiquette, and child rearing, among others, more challenging? Do partners knowingly or unknowingly bring culturally based differences in their sense of entitlement and privilege to these negotiations? How are these managed? Do some practice their cultures separately? How does this compare with couples in which one "gives up" his or her culture to practice in the other? Who gives up, and with what effects?

Negotiations take place in an external context that conceptualizes race as dichotomous and ascribes different values to these dichotomies. Furthermore, as a culture, we often marginalize that which we perceive as different. White partners may be experiencing these issues for the first time. How do these external factors influence the process of identity development? How do they affect the ability to appreciate and maintain both cultures? How do they affect the ability to honor and maintain the multiple identities of the partners and the relationship? One of the most frequent findings from previous studies was the silencing of race talk. Is this the result of couples seeking to deny difference? If so, how effective is it and what is its cost? Or is this due to the differences in sensitivities and perceptions of those who are advantaged rather than disadvantaged by racial and color hierarchies? Those with higher status are often less affected by and sensitive to racial slights. How do these factors differentially affect those in minority-majority as compared to minority-minority marriages?

As a nation, the United States has had a long and troubled history with race. While most social scientists today view race as a socially constructed category with no biological bases, longstanding biases persist, affecting both our opportunity horizons and the course and patterns of our social interactions. The growing rate of interracial marriage is seen as a reflection of increased interracial interaction and tolerance. Yet, interracial marriage can also be seen as a site of cultural conflict with important implications for the culture, families, and individuals involved. Globalization and immigration will continue to diversify our society. The rate of interracial marriage will continue to grow. Yet, in this review, we have found that interracial marriage is primarily an arena of unanswered questions. Much is required to better understand the experience of interracial marriage and to achieve a fuller grasp of the challenges, benefits, and factors associated with the well-being of this growing constituency in our increasingly diverse society.

REFERENCES

Batson, C. D., Qian, Z., & Lichter, D. T. (2006). Interracial and intraracial patterns of mate selection among America's diverse Black populations. *Journal of Marriage and Family, 68,* 658–672.

Bentley, M., Mattingly, T., Hough, C., & Bennett, C. (2003, April 3). Census quality survey to evaluate responses to the census 2000 question on race: An introduction to the data. *Census 2000 Evaluation B3*. Washington, DC: U.S. Census Bureau.

Blackwell, D. L., & Lichter, D. T. (2000). Mate selection among married and cohabitating couples. *Journal of Family Issues, 21*, 275–302.

Bratter, J. L., & Eschbach, K. (2005). "What about the couple?" Interracial marriage and psychological distress. *Social Science Research, 35*, 1025–1047.

Fu, X., Tora, J., & Kendall, H. (2001). Marital happiness and inter-racial marriage: A study in a multi-ethnic community in Hawaii. *Journal of Comparative Family Studies, 32*(1), 47–60.

George, D., & Yancey, G. (2004). Taking stock of America's attitudes on cultural diversity: An analysis of public deliberation on multiculturalism, assimilation and marriage. *Journal of Comparative Family Studies, 35*(1), 1–19.

Golebiowska, E. A. (2007). The contours and etiology of whites' attitudes toward black-white interracial marriage. *Journal of Black Studies, 38*(2), 268–287.

Gullickson, A. (2006). Black/white interracial marriage trends, 1850–2000. *Journal of Family History, 31*(3), 289–312.

Harris, D. R., & Ono, H. (2004). How many interracial marriages would there be if all groups were of equal size in all places? A new look at national estimates of interracial marriage. *Social Science Research, 34*, 236–251.

Jacobson, C., & Johnson, B. (2006). Interracial friendship and African American attitudes about interracial marriage. *Journal of Black Studies, 36*(4), 570–584.

Johnson, B., & Jacobson, C. (2005). Contact in context: An examination of social settings on whites' attitudes toward interracial marriage. *Social Psychology Quarterly, 68*(4), 387–399.

Kennedy, R. (1999). How are we doing with loving? Race, law and intermarriage. *Interrace, 45*, 14.

Killian, K. (2001). Crossing borders: Race, gender and their intersections in interracial couples. *Journal of Feminist Family Therapy, 13*(1), 1–31.

Killian, K. (2002). Dominant and marginalized discourses in interracial couples' narratives: Implications for family therapists. *Family Process, 41*(4), 603–618.

King, R. B., & Bratter, J. L. (2007). A path toward interracial marriage: Women's first partners and husbands across racial lines. *The Sociological Quarterly, 48*, 343–369.

Leslie, L. A., & Letiecq, B. L. (2004). Marital quality of African American and White partners in interracial couples. *Personal Relationships, 11*, 559–574.

Lewis, R., Jr., Yancey, G., & Bletzer, S. (1997). Racial and nonracial factors that influence spouse choice in Black/White marriages. *Journal of Black Studies, 28*(1), 60–78.

Miscegenation. (2009). Wikipedia. Retrieved September 24, 2008, from http://en.wiktionary.org/wiki/miscegenation.

Perry, B., & Sutton, M. (2006). Seeing red over black and white: Popular and media representations of interracial relationships as precursors to racial violence. *Canadian Journal of Criminology and Criminal Justice, 48*(6), 887–904.

Porterfield, E. (1982). Black-American intermarriage in the United States. *Marriage and Family Review, 5*, 17–34.

Pyke, K. (2004, August). *Internalized gendered racism in Asian American women's accounts of Asian and white masculinities.* Paper presented at the annual meeting of the American Sociological Association, San Francisco, CA. Retrieved

September 16, 2008, from http://www.allacademic.com/meta/p109437_index.html.

Qian, Z. (1997). Breaking the racial barriers: Variations in interracial marriage, 1980 and 1990. *Journal of Comparative Family Studies, 30*(4), 579–597.

Qian, Z. (2005). Breaking the last taboo: Interracial marriage in America. *Contexts 4*(4), 33–37.

Qian, Z., & Lichter, D. T. (2007). Social boundaries and marital assimilation: Interpreting trends in racial and ethnic intermarriage. *American Sociological Review, 72*, 68–94.

Romano, R. (2003). *Racemixing: Black-white marriage in postwar America.* Cambridge, MA: Harvard University Press.

Root, M. (2001). *Love's revolution.* Philadelphia: Temple University Press.

Rosenblatt, P. C., Karis, T. A., & Powell, R. C. (1995). *Multiracial couples: Black and white voices.* Thousand Oaks, CA: Sage Publications.

Rosenfeld, M. J., & Kim, B. S. (2005). The independence of young adults and the rise of interracial and same-sex unions. *American Sociological Review, 70*(4), 541–562.

Sidanius, J., & Pratto, F. (1999). *Social dominance: An intergroup theory of social hierarchy and oppression.* New York: Cambridge University Press.

Simmons, T., & O'Connell, M. (2003). Trends in educational assortative marriage from 1940 to 2003. *Demography, 42*, 621–646.

Xie, Y., & Goyette, K. A. (2004). *The American people census 2000: A demographic portrait of Asian Americans.* New York: Russell Sage Foundation.

Yancey, G. (2001). An analysis of resistance to racial exogamy: The 1998 South Carolina referendum. *Journal of Black Studies, 31*(5), 635–650.

Yancey, G., & Yancey, S. (1997). Black-white differences in the use of personal advertisements for individuals seeking interracial relationships. *Journal of Black Studies, 27*(5), 650–667.

CHAPTER 5

Women of Color and the Glass Ceiling in Higher Education

Debra M. Kawahara and Anabel Bejarano

Although changes in work participation for women, particularly white middle-class women, have been documented, there are participation patterns such as pervasive occupational segregation, underrepresentation in leadership positions, and inequities in compensation that continue to exist. In academia, for instance, women faculty tend to earn less than their male counterparts and are less successful in obtaining competitive grant funding. Furthermore, women only make up 15 percent of full professors in the social/behavioral and life science fields (Committee on Maximizing the Potential of Women in Academic Science and Engineering et al., 2006). For women of color, their experiences are further compounded by the double jeopardy of the social oppressions of being minorities in race and gender, as well as other possible statuses such as sexual orientation or disability. It has been argued that people of color's employment patterns must be seen through the lens of longstanding racism in American society, demonstrated by the large number found in the lower socioeconomic class. To add to these oppressions is the larger number of women of color who are of immigrant status; immigrants have the lowest employment rates and are overrepresented in the lowest socioeconomic levels in the United States. Thus, the difficulties faced by women and people of color are exponentially exacerbated for women of color.

In this chapter, we highlight experiences common to women of color who are academics, namely non-Caucasian females in higher education or female academics of color, across racial and ethnic groups and academic fields, in order to name, categorize, and reify what may otherwise be mistakenly considered a uniquely subjective phenomenon. The fact that many female academics of color, regardless of racial/ethnic membership or academic discipline, describe similar struggles and experiences is, in and of itself, noteworthy. Despite the numerous external and internal challenges described by women of color in academia, we will address their resiliency and protective factors that have facilitated their journey.

THE GLASS CEILING AND THE CONCRETE WALL DEFINED

After newspaper articles were published in the 1980s, three major findings were cited as an impetus for Congress to pass the Glass Ceiling Act as part of the Civil Rights Acts of 1991. They included the under representation of women and minorities in management and decision-making positions; the existence of artificial barriers in the advancement of minorities and women; and the awareness that U.S. corporations were aware of the benefits derived from a diverse workforce and were increasingly relying on women and minorities to meet work requirements.

The Glass Ceiling Act charged the U.S. Secretary of Labor with studying the glass ceiling problem and providing recommendations. The glass ceiling was defined by the U.S. Department of Labor (1991) as preventing qualified individuals from advancement in organizational and managerial positions due to artificial barriers based on attitudinal or organizational bias. The Federal Glass Ceiling Commission was created to study not only the systemic barriers and biases for women, but also for minorities, that prevented movement into management.

The commission concluded that gender and race segregation was evident in the present-day American labor force, with white men occupying most of the top corporate management positions. Furthermore, the glass ceiling has been acknowledged in academia as well. According to Chait and Trower (2001), women comprised 56 percent of all undergraduates in 2001 compared to 42 percent in 1971. However, in comparison to the changes in the student demographics, the U.S. faculty profile remains largely white and male. Women currently represent only 37 percent of full-time faculty, while faculty of color continue to represent a very small percentage of the professoriate, at 17 percent in 1997 (U.S. Department of Education, 2002). Specifically, for faculty of color, Asian Americans have increased the most from 2.2 percent in 1975 to 4.5 percent in 1997, whereas African Americans have remained at the same level, at approximately 5 percent, and Latinos have shown a slow increase from 1.4 percent in 1975 to 2.8 percent in 1997 (U.S. Department of Education, 1998, 2002).

The barriers that are the result of attitudinal or organizational bias for women of color are further compounded based on the combined effects of the intersection of race and gender. In addition to the glass ceiling that all women face in the workplace, women of color also face a so-called concrete wall or sticky floor first. Sanchez, Hucles, Sanchez-Hucles, and

Mehta (2007) suggested that this concrete wall is built and maintained by the continuation of racism, stereotypes, outsider status, invisibility and hypervisibility, lack of opportunity to engage in networks, challenges regarding authority and credibility, conflicts of work and family responsibilities, and lack of commitment to the advancement of diverse persons.

BARRIERS AND CHALLENGES

Stereotypes

One of the most frequently reported barriers to professional advancement is stereotypes, particularly when a woman of color is the only visible minority, specifically racial/ethnic and/or female, in the organization. The stereotypes imposed on them are often negative and are even more complex due to the interaction of race, gender, and possibly other diverse statuses that they must overcome. For women of color, others' expectations are for the women to meet these stereotypes, even if the stereotypical perceptions are inaccurate and fail to acknowledge their true strengths and contributions. However, if the woman of color counters the stereotypes, she may also find that there are consequences of not meeting the expectations of others, such as attributions of being difficult or not fitting into the department.

Steele (1997) discussed the stereotype threat effect that is evident when people of color find themselves in a hostile and unwelcoming environment. When the person of color has a heightened awareness and evaluation of an unsafe environment, this environment lowers or impedes the person's performance and achievement. Research found that performance was reduced when stereotypes were activated in both people of color and women prior to engaging in the associated task. Thus, an environment that allows stereotyping to occur may actually maintain a situation where women of color are not able to perform at their best.

A further consequence of the stereotyping effect is the internalization of the stereotypes of others. The insidious effect of stereotypes has been shown, whereby the individual may begin to question his or her ability or believe that the perceptions are correct. The self-doubt and possible decrease in self-confidence and self-esteem may prevent and hinder a woman of color's pursuit of her career and development.

Inequitable and Exclusionary Practices

Another cited barrier is the exclusion from important information or opportunities that would advance an individual's career. In educational settings, the following barriers have been found: institutional practices and opportunities that favor men and restrict the options for women (e.g., job tracking, majors); inequitable distribution of resources (e.g., salary, scholarships); and inequitable educational experiences or opportunities.

Two of the ways by which the inequitable and exclusionary practices are implemented are the so-called old boy's network and tokenism. The old boy's network is utilized to determine who will be allowed into the circle amongst more senior or influential and powerful persons within the institutions and, eventually, who will occupy leadership and administrative roles. Unfortunately, because women of color are often seen as different, they are considered a threat to those who currently have the power, as well as a future threat to changing the power structure. As a result, the woman of color may be excluded or blocked, either intentionally or unintentionally, from assignments, projects, committees, or information that may assist her future career plans.

Through tokenism, a woman of color is caught in a paradoxical situation of invisibility and hypervisibility. On the one hand, being the only one or one of the few minorities amongst the majority makes the woman of color stand out; she is typically noticed for anything that may be considered different, deficient, erroneous, or problematic on her part, including appearance, speech, or behavior. Yet, the woman of color also feels that she is isolated, ignored, and/or excluded from formal and informal networks and activities. This is further exacerbated if the woman of color is perceived to be a token based on affirmative action, which brings with it a set of assumptions and stereotypes associated with not being qualified.

The cumulative effect of this dynamic barrier can set the woman of color further and further behind her peers, ultimately making her a less viable candidate for future opportunities and positions relative to others. Unless she is given opportunities and/or experiences to develop and grow within the institution, she will then have to work even harder to seek them out and participate in them while maintaining her academic workload.

Insufficient Mentoring and Networking

Research has consistently shown the beneficial outcomes of mentoring: enhanced promotion rates, higher salaries, accelerated career mobility, improved professional identity, greater professional competence, increased career satisfaction, greater acceptance within the organization, and decreased job stress and conflict. Yet, Catalyst (2003) found that 23 percent, or only one in four, senior-level corporate women were satisfied with the availability of mentors in organizations. Furthermore, women of color faculty members may be excluded from informal and formal mentoring and networking for various reasons such as stereotyping, as well as being seen as different or threatening, or not fitting the profile of a supposed leader or superstar. As with other barriers, this can certainly impact the woman academic of color's opportunity to gain knowledge and experiences that would assist in her current and future advancement. The barriers to sufficient mentoring and networking appear to be a critical component in blocking one's professional development and progression, as mentors assist in learning to navigate the institution's landscape and offer support and links to opportunities and influential persons.

Personal and Familial Responsibilities

For many women of color, balancing the demands of their career as well as personal and familial responsibilities can be challenging and taxing. On the one hand, academia often sets high expectations and standards of productivity and effectiveness in teaching, research and scholarship, and service/governance, especially during the years before tenure is secured. The Western values of independence, self-sufficiency, a strong work ethic, and achievement underlie the rigorous workload, schedule, and activities expected from a faculty member. These characteristics, along with being able to fit socially within the academic department and university, are often considered when hiring and evaluating the performance of a potential and actual faculty member. The pressure on younger or newer faculty, in which women of color are more highly represented, is even more important because there is a set time frame to gain tenure or lose their position.

However, the importance of family, immediate as well as extended, may be at odds with career demands for female faculty of color. Women, in general, bear much of the responsibility for children, parents, and/or other family members, and universities tend to lack family-friendly policies. Furthermore, many women of color come from cultures that emphasize an individual's role or duty to aid in family matters or assistance with other family members whenever possible. Given the success and intelligence of these women, they may often be sought for their knowledge and ability to deal with problems or crises. However, if the female faculty member of color chooses personal or family matters over her academic responsibilities, she may be looked down upon. To compound this further, she may be evaluated poorly without consideration for the academic structure and responsibilities that may have caused unreasonable and unrealistic expectations of her. In this case, the female faculty member of color is caught in a dilemma of how to adhere to her familial obligations while still meeting the demands of the academic position.

The Intersection of Gender, Ethnicity, and Class

Women of color who attain a postsecondary degree are often, though not always, trailblazers within their extended family and family of origin. They are typically the first in their family to have achieved within the traditional and hierarchical structure of the academy. Unlike white faculty members, they disproportionately come from working class families, given the demographic profile of communities of color in the United States. Because the behaviors, beliefs, and attitudinal predispositions are shaped by the socioeconomic class in which we are raised, faculty of color often lack the cultural capital and Western, white, individualistic, middle-class-based value system that exists in academic departments. White female faculty members are also challenged to perform in an androcentric environment, yet faculty of color are burdened by the triple jeopardy of gender, race, and often class. As stated by Dr. Sonia Nieto (2006), a self-proclaimed Nuyorican, "I had not been socialized with the dispositions, behaviors, or tastes that would have made the academy a 'natural' place for me to be" (p. 249).

Bettie (2003) captured the essence of class-influenced behaviors and attitudes in her use of the term *class as performance* in her work with adolescents from diverse groups. This conceptualization lends itself to the academy and expectations of an individual's behavior. Specific, ill-fitting behavioral and attitudinal characteristics that female faculty of color are faced with include: self-focused individual competition; an inflexible separation between the world of work and family life; continuity between class status and family of origin; styles of speech and expression (e.g., limited nonverbal mannerisms, volume, grammar); and styles of dress. Not having inherited white privilege and middle-class grooming and socialization experiences during their formative years creates an uneven playing field for these women, given the foundations of academia. Therefore, due to the class disparity, these women may not always be aware of the tools, unspoken rules, or strategies for success. This dynamic may also lend itself to the unfortunate and oft-expressed feeling that an individual is an interloper and does not fit in or belong in academia; that she is an outsider.

Similar interpersonal dilemmas as an outcome of the intersection of gender, race or ethnicity, and class origins for female faculty of color in the academy can be seen through their numerous personal accounts of their experiences. These accounts are often scholarly, first-person narratives that utilize a qualitative self-study approach to dissect and analyze individual experiences in the academy against a backdrop of racism, sexism, and marginalization. Across the narratives, it is common to begin with a somewhat confessional statement regarding the initial lack of awareness that other female faculty of color underwent similar experiences of racism, sexism, and forms of marginalization. Yet, the authors believed in the benefits of making their experiences known for their own healing, to give voice to the struggle, and in the hope that others like them would find comfort in knowing they were not alone.

Recurring concerns expressed by these women with regard to majority students included feeling disrespected, having their expertise and credentials questioned, being the first teacher of color and authority figure these students had encountered, and receiving negative and hurtful teaching evaluations that affected the promotion and tenure process. Several authors described observations of their mere presence and unavoidable visibility serving as the stimulus for student's stereotypical beliefs and associations about people of color.

Additionally, these women were usually assigned to teach the only course on multiculturalism in their department. Within this course, the constructs and systemic deconstruction of privilege and power typically aroused resistance from majority students. Therefore, these faculty members were tasked and taxed by being the first scholars to invite white and privileged students to critique their place in the world, while representing the other against whom their privilege is made possible. Because these classes are often emotionally charged and experiential in nature, student complaints about the instructor and her teaching methods and rigor could then bring into question her abilities and credentials. Graduate study does not prepare one for the psychological, interpersonal, and group dynamics inherent in such an undertaking.

The paradox of being assigned to teach courses on multiculturalism is that the female faculty member of color may intentionally focus her research agenda on issues of race and culture within her discipline. When the scholar of color maintains a dual role of faculty member and advocate for social justice via research and community involvement, her work is often not considered by the academy to be legitimate *scholarly* material. Furthermore, qualitative and action-research models are not unilaterally embraced as empirical or evidence-based research in the social sciences. Loder et al. (2007) speculated that their work would be more respected if they were crunching numbers. Culture- and race-based research is often considered so-called watered-down scholarship by the academy, and journals that have such scholarly work as its main focus are similarly discredited.

These negative experiences contrast with the role of faculty members of color as mentors and role models for ethnic minority students. Their presence is critical to the recruitment, retention, and success of students of color. For example, research found that the percentage of women faculty was a significant predictor of subsequent success for female undergraduates. Furthermore, the psychological impact of seeing someone who looks like a minority student and is succeeding provides a concrete example that it is possible for the student to achieve as well. Yet, given the tokenism that results from having only one or very few faculty members of color, faculty described a workload in which they are not credited for being the so-called go-to person for minority students in their department, university, and discipline, in addition to being the go-to person for majority students or colleagues considering issues of diversity in their work.

RESILIENCY AND PROTECTIVE FACTORS

The role of spirituality and religion in the lives of female faculty of color cannot be overemphasized. Regardless of their ethnic origins, authors consistently credit their survival and success in the academy to their spiritual anchors. These spiritual anchors may take the form of traditional organized religion, strength derived by lessons and memories of their ancestors, and/or meditation and spiritual practice. Garner (2006) describes and refers to spirituality and its role in her psychological survival as a form of empowering resistance. It is important to make time for quiet reflection and spiritual practice as one navigates the unpredictable waters of the academy.

Maintaining a connection and identity within individuals' community of origin is an additional source of strength. In light of our shifting identity as we accommodate to the academy, faculty of color recommend that we not lose sight of our family, community, and those we represent. Nieto (2006) recommends that we develop all of our identities, valuing each one equally despite the pressures to assimilate to the academy. Female faculty members of color who approach scholarly activity from a social justice perspective and believe in the value of activist intellectual work derive much fulfillment in their endeavors. Embracing the role of a scholarly advocate for neglected communities or populations may strengthen the individual's resolve during challenging periods.

STRATEGIES FOR BREAKING AND SURPASSING THE GLASS CEILING

External: Organizational

Organizational Commitment to the Advancement of Women of Color. Before placing responsibility on the individual, organizations must make a commitment to providing an optimal working environment for these women to thrive and succeed. This must be demonstrated by policies and procedures that are inclusive of women of color and provide career opportunities that allow them to build their skills and showcase their abilities to others within the academic institution. In addition, the onus must be on the university administration to create a climate that clearly communicates the value of these women to the university and the need for developing their talents to their fullest. Assessment and evaluation of the university's administration and faculty in meeting these goals would make the university accountable to progress.

Cultural Awareness and Sensitivity of University Administration and Personnel. Institutional change needs to be promoted and implemented by those at the upper echelons of the university who set policies and procedures. Moreover, the administration and university personnel must be willing to examine the cultural values and structures that are inherent within the system and how these may create and place artificial barriers that maintain the status quo. Furthermore, administrators and university personnel need to engage in their own reflection on the intentional and unintentional ways that bias and prejudice may be influencing them and their decisions, as well as their interactions.

Hiring, Retaining, and Promoting Women of Color

Proof of the educational institution's commitment to the advancement of women of color is through the hiring, retention, and promotion of women of color. This provides clear evidence of an organizational climate that is conducive to the advancement of women of color. This can be achieved through promoting the importance of diversity in the university administration and faculty's racial and gender composition by senior academic leaders' identification of a clear, concrete goal.

In addition to demonstrating the university's commitment, the increase in women of color in academic and/or administrative positions can also reduce the stereotyping of women of color. As the increase in the number of women of color occurs, the variations among the women of color will make it more difficult for the generalizations to be reinforced and used. Furthermore, the lifestyles and experiences of the women of color can become part of the norms, as opposed to being unique or different to others who comprise the university.

Communication Networks

Related to the above, the administration and department heads must include these women of color in communications across the university, share information, and make an effort to choose them for difficult and highly visible assignments and projects. As noted above, women of color may not be included in formal and informal networks, so efforts must be made to improve the transparency of the inner workings of the university. Further, mentoring programs that include persons from similar racial and gender backgrounds, as well as from the upper administration and senior management positions, must be instituted.

Student Evaluations

Student evaluations need to be considered within the sociocultural context in which the female faculty member of color is situated. Research at Arizona State University by the Faculty Women's Association has consistently found that women of color receive lower teaching evaluations. Given the premium placed on student evaluations in the promotion and tenure process, these evaluations should be weighed in the context of resistance and racism encountered by faculty, particularly for evaluations of courses on diversity and multiculturalism. There needs to be increased awareness on the part of institutions of this phenomenon and dynamic.

Additional Research

Given the similarities in the experiences of female faculty of color, it will be necessary to develop qualitative, quantitative, and mixed methods research to add to the current base of autobiographical literature in order to understand and make changes toward a more equitable work environment in the academy. Perhaps institutions of higher learning will be more compelled by findings that are in their language and therefore difficult to refute. Marbley (2007) suggests that research on the experiences of female faculty of color is not widely known, given both its marginalization within disciplines and its fragmentation across disciplines.

Internal: Individual Strategies

Self-Awareness and How the Individual Is Seen by Others. One important step is to gain knowledge of an individual's own cultural worldview, values, and beliefs, as well as being able to identify others' cultural worldviews, values, and beliefs. This will allow an evaluation of what values and beliefs may be in line with the university's culture and mores, and what may contradict or be in conflict with them. Further, an assessment of how others view the individual may be important in understanding how they are interacting with and evaluating him or her. Both assessments will hopefully illuminate the individual's cultural profile, skills, and strengths, as well as areas that could be improved and developed.

Exceptional Achievements. Women who were successful and resilient despite the glass ceiling barriers described above exceeded performance expectations and established a recognizable area of expertise. This allowed these women to be sought out and to take on difficult and/or highly visible projects, making them stand out from others. Further, Mainiero (1994) interviewed successful career women and found that they described themselves as being success-driven workaholics and taking smart and savvy risks.

Excellent Communication. In addition to their exceptional achievements, these women had excellent communication skills and were able to have a communication network that helped them stay informed and use the information to assist in their career. Oral and written communication abilities are critical competencies to succeed in an academic setting. These include being able to communicate effectively during meetings, conference calls, and large group presentations, as well as to write scholarly articles, memorandums, and position papers well.

Learning to Say "No." As women of color, faculty are often spread thin and debilitated in their energies to conduct research and publish by the myriad of projects and committees within and outside the university. During Bejarano's first year as an assistant professor, a male colleague recommended at a meeting that she say "yes" to everything in which she was asked to participate. He went on to explain that it is important to contribute, be perceived as a team player, and learn how things work by being very involved in the department. While there is no doubt that he meant well by his advice, he did not have an understanding of the differences in their respective "places" within the university. She politely responded that she didn't think the strategy would be helpful for her; instead, she would be mindful of what she became involved in as a junior member of the faculty and would thereby conserve her time and energy. Clearly, agreeing to all requests had worked for him as a white male, but the same approach would be quite detrimental for a woman of color.

Related to being mindful of commitments made, it is also important to devote energy to committees and projects that one is genuinely interested in and that may contribute to one's research interests. Bejarano had the experience of receiving unsolicited advice from a white male colleague against joining a committee focused on Latino students and related issues in place of a standard committee to which she had been assigned. Despite the condescending tone and words used in his electronic communication, she listened to her internal voice and interest in devoting her available committee time to a cause that held personal and professional meaning for her.

Mentoring. Cultivating and maintaining mentoring relationships will take time and effort. For those seeking mentoring, a proactive approach will need to be taken to engage with numerous mentors throughout an academic's life, as one mentor will not be able to fulfill all of her career needs. Furthermore, Hyun (2005) recommends a good mentee/protégé does his/her homework by following up on any work or development that the mentor has suggested, and shows respect to the mentor by being prepared for meetings and demonstrating consistent progress in the areas of assistance. Hyun reported having two to three significant mentors in her own career during different developmental periods.

Building and Maintaining a Professional Support Network. The establishment of a professional development and support group by and for faculty of color is strongly recommended. Given the advantages of the electronic age, these groups may function effectively across states and countries. Loder et al. (2007) suggested that the potential of such a group is enhanced by the following group characteristics: adopting a womanist worldview or identity; the shared need for a culturally affirming and validating professional experience; and striving for excellence while comentoring colleagues of color.

In terms of more concrete and practical strategies to obtain tenure, Ferreira (2006) recommends that, early on, one should inquire not only about the requirements for tenure, but also what counts as scholarship at the university; organize three folders in which to gather documentation of one's research, teaching, and service contributions; and organize one's time in order that two to three days each week are reserved for writing. She also reminds early career female faculty of color that it is never too early to begin organizing and orienting oneself toward promotion and tenure.

REFERENCES

Bettie, J. (2003). *Women without class: Girls, race and ethnicity.* Berkeley: University of California Press.

Catalyst. (2003). *What keeps women from reaching the top?* Retrieved July, 2008, from http://www.womensmedia.com/new/Catalyst-Women-Executives.shtml

Chait, R., & Trower, C. (2001). Professors at the color line. *New York Times,* Op-Ed, p. A27.

Committee on Maximizing the Potential of Women in Academic Science and Engineering, National Academy of Sciences, National Academy of Engineering, and Institute of Medicine (2006). *Beyond bias and barriers: Fulfilling the potential of women in academic science and engineering.* Retrieved July, 2008, from http://www.nap.edu/atalog/11741.html

Ferreira, M. M. (2006). Succeeding in academia: Practical strategies for achieving tenure and promotion at research universities. *Advancing Women in Leadership, 221.* Retrieved June, 2008, from http://0-proquest.umi.com.library.alliant.edu

Garner, R. (2006). Standing on the frontline: Having the courage to teach. *Advancing Women in Leadership, 22.* Retrieved June 2008, from http://0proquest.umi.com.library.alliant.edu

Hyun, J. (2005). *Breaking the bamboo ceiling: Career strategies for Asians.* New York: Harper Collins.

Loder, T. L., Sims, M. J., Collins, L., Brooks, M., Voltz, D., Calhoun, C., et al. (2007). On becoming and being faculty leaders in urban education and also being African-American . . . Seems promising. *Advancing Women in Leadership, 231.* Retrieved June 2008, from http://0proquest.umi.com.library.alliant.edu

Mainiero, L. A. (1994). On breaking the glass ceiling: The political seasoning of powerful women executives. *Organizational Dynamics, 22,* 5–20.

Marbley, A. F. (2007). Finding my voice: An African-American female professor at a predominantly white university. *Advancing Women in Leadership, 231.* Retrieved June 2008, from http://0proquest.umi.com.library.alliant.edu

Nieto, S. (2006). A Nuyorican in the academy. In T. R. Berry & N. D. Mizelle (Eds.), *From oppression to grace: Women of color and their dilemmas within the academy* (pp. 244–256). Sterling, VA: Stylus Publishing.

Sanchez, P., Hucles, P., Sanchez-Hucles, J., & Mehta, S. C. (2007). Increasing diverse women leadership in corporate America: Climbing concrete walls and shattering glass ceilings. In J. L. Chin, B. Lott, J. Rice, & J. Sanchez-Hucles (Eds.), *Diverse voices in leadership* (pp. 228–244). New York: Wiley.

Steele, C. M. (1997). A threat in the air: How stereotypes shape the intellectual identities and performance of women and African Americans. *American Psychologist, 52,* 613–629.

U.S. Department of Education. (1998). *Fall staff in postsecondary institutions, 1995* (National Center for Education Publication No. NCES98–228). Washington, DC: U.S. Government Printing Office.

U.S. Department of Education. (2002). *Digest of education statistics, 2001* (National Center for Education Statistics Publication No. NCES 2002–130). Washington, DC: U.S. Government Printing Office.

U.S. Department of Labor. (1991). *A report on the glass ceiling initiative.* Washington, DC: U.S. Government Printing Office.

CHAPTER 6

Narratives to Heal: A Look at Contrasting Mythologies

Jean Lau Chin

The use of narratives has been popular through the ages to capture the meaning and essence of the human condition through literature and storytelling. It is an emotional bridge and a journey for both the storyteller and listener. It can provide a therapeutic atmosphere and a healing environment through which individuals, families, and communities can bond and nurture one another. The experience of immigration is a journey; it is traumatic, but necessary for those who seek opportunity and asylum from economic, religious, political, and social oppression. Narratives can be used to capture the journey of immigration and the identities of immigrants, both unique and shared; they can be used to heal from the crises and trauma encountered along the way. Differences of culture, worldview, and experience will make for different narratives, and bridges are needed to capture those differences for communication, tolerance, and adjustment. The psychological themes of immigration include: abandonment, loss, guilt, and trauma. They involve conflict and regeneration, intergenerational and bicultural identity, acculturation and assimilation.

In this era of diversity and globalization, we sometimes forget the immigrant origins of almost all of those who live in the United States. It is easy to close the doors of opportunity to newcomers who do not "look or act like us" and blame the ills of society on their presence. It is easy to forget the struggles and hardships of our immigrant ancestors if we cannot empathize with their experiences. To embrace diversity in our minds and actions, we need to reach into our psyches through our narratives to bring about common bonds amidst differences. We often remind ourselves to learn from our history, lest we repeat our mistakes of the past. Narratives document these histories; they provide a process to transcend our biases, conflicts, and insecurities, which prevent us from treating others as we want to be treated—narratives can be used to nurture and to heal. The narratives that follow illustrate this.

CREATING FAMILY LEGEND

In *Learning from My Mother's Voice: Family Legend and the Chinese American Immigration Experience* (Chin, 2005), I honor my mother in documenting her oral history while celebrating the legacy of Chinese Americans in the United States. And celebrate we must, since immigration itself is a journey and a traumatic experience. To celebrate is to empower, and to transform that journey into a bonding and healing experience. Though the context of my mother's story is situated in New York City and in the lives of Toisanese immigrant families, the themes are shared by all immigrants and generations. *Learning from My Mother's Voice* is a bridge between the contrasting American and Chinese cultures and the intergenerational gaps of parent and child. There are lessons to be learned—lessons that urge all of us to use life's journey to record our family narratives, to nurture and to heal. This is both a process and a product.

The process is one of self-reflection and creating the intergenerational bonds to provide hope for the future and restore faith in the present for those who have faced the trauma of immigration. The product is the creation of family legend, a product that preserves what could be forgotten by future generations. It is the saga of surviving and striving among immigrants. The psychological themes of immigration remain constant across diverse groups—they include loss, abandonment, guilt, and trauma. The content may differ; the solutions may change. In connecting with the past, immigrants and their offspring can build the bridge toward achieving a bicultural identity. The journey of immigration includes the dreams, disappointments, and frustrations that become the legends that not only bond us, but also put us in bondage. Cultural and personal mythology and storytelling bonds families as the stories are shared and passed on through the generations. These same narratives can put us in bondage when immigrant families are unable to step outside their stories of survival, suffering, trauma, and hardship. While all immigrants share the dream of a better life, not all are successful. Sometimes that dream is only achieved for their children; often, the dream is better than the reality in which they live—resulting in the need to embellish, distort, and use these narratives to cope with a bitter reality. It is out of these dreams that legends are created.

In creating family legend, the narratives or stories both change and remain the same. One may hear the same story repeated by one's immigrant parent over and over. With careful listening, there may be slight changes to the experience; there may be embellishments to the facts. As a result, some will question whether we are representing reality or creating art and fiction; however, the question is irrelevant if we understand its purpose.

The changing content captures the psychological state of mind of the storyteller; the embellishment or distortion of facts identifies the need. What psychological phenomenon does the storyteller need to communicate or preserve? In creating family legend, what stories capture the pain, struggle, loss, or guilt of the immigration experience, and why is there a need to preserve it? As these narratives change with the situational context and evolve over time, so does the psychological ethos of the storyteller and the families who receive them.

"The New Colossus," the famous sonnet written by Emma Lazarus in 1883, has been affixed to the inner walls on the pedestal the Statue of Liberty since the early 1900s. It has come to symbolize the statue's universal message of hope and freedom for immigrants coming to America and people seeking freedom around the world. The Statue of Liberty is more than a monument; it is a legend. Called the *Copper Lady* by Chinese immigrants, it is one of the most universal symbols of political freedom and democracy. It is the gateway to New York City, where many Chinese immigrants landed; it is a place visited by many tourists; it is the place from which the immigration legend begins.

USE OF NARRATIVES

In the psychological sciences, the use of narratives, stories, oral history, interviews, and so on, has been viewed as pseudoscience, lacking in empirical rigor, or merely preliminary to randomized controlled studies. These qualitative methods are often less valued as contributions to knowledge, while attempts to quantify them often result in meager or insignificant findings. I would submit that narratives are more able to capture the richness of human struggles, the intensity of emotion, and chronicle the human journey through stages of life than is possible in randomized controlled experiments. It is a different way to validate what we find in seeking truth and knowledge.

The use of narratives as a method for diagnosis and psychotherapy can facilitate psychological healing. As a therapeutic tool, to invite the client to tell his/her story is to invite the emotion and impact of life experience. Its purpose is to address identity—to find it, to develop a positive sense of identity and self-esteem, and to use it for bonding families, communities, and cultures. To listen to this story and enable the client to modify its outcome may the most important therapeutic effect. Clients can be stuck in their stories as if frozen in time; therapists can help their clients to complete their stories, to move on from the tragic ending, to revisit their relationships with parents and family, and to forgive.

Lastly, the use of narrative is personal—for individuals and families to share the common bond of their life experience. For Jews to share the Holocaust, for Japanese Americans to share the internment experience, for Chinese Americans to share the effects of the discriminatory anti-Asian legislation, for African Americans to share the effects of slavery—these are all stories to be remembered and shared by cultural groups, and stories to connect us all. These stories reflect the journey.

THE HERO'S JOURNEY

Campbell (1949/1972) wrote *The Hero with a Thousand Faces,* first published in 1949, to describe the archetypal hero found throughout world mythologies. The themes and stages that he describes characterize the journey taken by many as they travel through life. A summary of the mono-myth is given below.

A hero is called to adventure. He may initially refuse the call. He ventures forth from his common day world into a region of supernatural wonder. He may encounter fabulous forces there, and faces numerous challenges. He may be aided by some divine being or tempted by a strong adversary. A decisive victory is won. The hero may refuse to return, but comes back from this mysterious adventure with the power to bestow boons on his fellow man.

Campbell describes the stages of this journey as including: (1) a call to adventure, (2) a road of trials, (3) achievement of the ultimate boon, (4) a return to the ordinary world, and (5) application of his boon. These stages include separation, initiation, and return. We see this theme in myths across cultures. Some have found the hero's journey to be masculine in nature, as described by Campbell, and contrast it with fairy tales, which are female in nature. Campbell inspired the *Star Wars* movies by George Lucas (1977) about Luke Skywalker, an adolescent, in his call to adventure to save us from the Evil Empire. His adventure brings him face to face with Darth Vader, a powerful archenemy, later revealed to be his father who turned to the dark side. Innocence and good survives and becomes supreme once again.

Bettelheim (1976), in *The Uses of Enchantment,* speaks to the meaning and importance of fairy tales for all children (male and female), in terms of educating, as well as supporting and liberating the emotions of children, and mastering the psychological problems of growing up—overcoming disappointment, coping with rivalry, gaining self-worth, and acquiring moral obligation. Bettelheim speaks to the juxtaposition of good and evil in many fairy tales and myths; the fairy tale hero is often isolated initially, and grows to be capable of achieving meaningful and rewarding relations with those around him.

JOURNEY OF IMMIGRATION

We should characterize immigration as a journey, and as a journey that does not end upon arrival in the host country. The theme of a hero's journey is one that can be well applied to immigration; but unlike the hero's journey, it does not end with the return home. This is useful to avoid pathologizing the issues faced by immigrant families in their quest—as failures at assimilation or marginalized identities. The use of narratives provides a strength-based approach by looking at the journey of immigration as part of normal developmental process in coping with crisis and trauma. Many cultures or faiths have narratives of a journey that unites them and leads them to the promised land; the *Story of Moses*, embraced by many of the Jewish faith, describes how Moses led the Jews in their escape from Egypt to freedom. *Journey to the West* and its hero, the Monkey King, is a classic Chinese epic that captures this journey.

CONTRASTING MYTHOLOGIES

As we journey through life, we seek to reach a state of enlightenment. Immigrant families similarly make their journey in a quest for freedom and enlightenment. Despite many similarities in the hero's journey across cultures, there are significant differences; these are best seen in the contrasting mythologies between Eastern and Western cultures. While the Garden of Eden lies in the East for Westerners, the Jade Mountain of the Queen Mother, Hsi Wang Mu, lies in the West for Asians. According to Western and Asian mythology, those who seek enlightenment need only travel there to eat its fruit. In both traditions, there is but one forbidden fruit: the apple from the Garden of Eden or the peach from the Jade Mountain—the former for those seeking knowledge, the latter for those seeking immortality. The eating of either fruit has wrought havoc for those who disobey. However, the images of women differ in Eastern and Western mythology. The balance of power shifts. It is Eve who tempts Adam to eat the forbidden apple (i.e., the woman tempts the man), while it is Monkey King who steals the immortal peach from the Queen Mother (i.e., the son steals from the mother).

Early American pioneers were westward bound, while Chinese immigrants went eastward in search of the Golden Mountains of the West; they met in California during the Gold Rush and built the transcontinental railroad. These contrasting metaphors between Eastern and Western cultures reflect important similarities and differences. *Journey to the West* and *Star Wars* are two sagas that illustrate some of these differences between Asian and Western cultures. Both are stories of adventure with underlying themes of character transformation and the achievement of enlightenment.

Monkey King and *Journey to the West*

Journey to the West, a renowned sixteenth-century epic written by Wu Ch'eng, is an allegorical rendition of a journey in search of the scriptures; it is mingled with Chinese fables, fairy tales, legends, and demon adventures with origins in the Taoist and Buddhist religions (Wu Ch'eng, n.d.). It is based on the true story of a famous Chinese monk, Xuan Zang (602–664 C.E.), who lived in the seventh century. Over years of traveling on foot to what is now India, the birthplace of Buddhism, to seek the Sutra, the Buddhist holy book, he goes through trials and tribulations. After returning to China—or to Tang Mountain (Tang San), as China was called at that time—his translation of the sutras into Chinese contributed greatly to the development of Buddhism in China.

In the main part of the story, the three disciples who join Hsuan-Tsang on his quest—the clever and impudent Monkey, the gluttonous Pig, and the river spirit, Sha Monk, in other words, mind, body, and spirit, travel for 16 years, encounter 81 adventures with supernatural and mythic beings, and fight fearsome battles with demons and spirits, all the while guided by a compassionate Kuan Yin goddess. The external adventures are colorful, action-oriented, and full of fantasy; the four travelers need to differentiate truth from fiction and demons from spirits, and avoid being fooled by appearances. These external adventures are paralleled by inward explorations of the human psyche within each of the characters, who become enlightened and are transformed in the process of this journey.

The narrative of Toisanese Chinese immigration to the United States is captured in *Journey to the West.* Its hero, Monkey King, is a smart but rebellious character who needed to face 81 dangers before he achieved enlightenment. While many agree that Monkey King, who is full of cunning, prowess, and wisdom, is also an allegory for a rebellious spirit against the then untouchable feudal rulers in China, it is also an allegory for the journey of immigration today. The transformation of Monkey King captures the psyche and transformation of Chinese American immigrants (http://www.china-on-site.com/pages/comic/comiccatalog1.php).

Monkey King was a rebellious and extraordinary being, born out of a rock and fertilized by the grace of Heaven. Being extremely smart and cunning, he learned all the magic tricks and kung fu from a master Taoist; he is able to transform himself into 72 different forms, such as a tree, bird, beast of prey, or bug as small as a mosquito to sneak into an enemy's belly and fight him from the inside. Using clouds as a vehicle, he can travel 180,000 *li* (miles) in a single somersault; he carries a huge iron bar that can expand or shrink at his command as his favorite weapon in his feats.

He claims to be king in defiance of the authority and Supreme Being—the Great Jade Emperor (i.e., fights against social injustice and racism). This act of treason, coupled with complaints from the masters of the four seas and hell, invites the relentless scourge of the heavenly army. After many showdowns, the emperor, unable to defeat him, has to offer the monkey an official title to appease him. He becomes enraged when he learns that the position is nothing more than a stable keeper; he revolts and fights his way back to earth to reclaim his title as king. Eventually, the heavenly army subdues him with the help of all God's warriors. Because he has a bronze head and iron shoulders, all methods of execution fail and

Monkey King dulls many a sword inflicted upon him. As a last resort, the emperor commands that he be burned in the furnace where his Taoist minister, Tai Shang Lao Jun, refines his pills of immortality. Instead of killing him, the fire and smoke adds to Monkey King a pair of fiery golden crystal eyes that can see through what people normally cannot. He fights his way down again. Finally, with Buddha's help, Monkey King is suppressed under a great mountain known as the Mount of Five Fingers and he cannot move. Five hundred years later, he is rescued by the Tang priest, Hsuan Tsang, and becomes his disciple on the journey to the West in search of the scriptures.

Monkey King remains rebellious and formidable against the parental authority figures; his transformation is not unlike that of Chinese American immigrants in evolving a bicultural identity. His journey is also symbolic of the quest for social justice; the challenges posed by the 81 trials he faced are not unlike the fight against the -*isms* of race, gender, age, and class. As Monkey King so aptly puts it, he can leap a thousand *li* to get to where he wants to in a second, but he must accompany the Tang priest on foot to reach his destiny in 16 years. The developmental process of transformation cannot be rushed.

The character of Monkey King is not unlike the unbreakable spirit of Chinese American immigrants. Early Toisanese immigrants were described as cunning and rebellious for their tendency to be inscrutable—similar to the portrayals of Monkey King, negative to Westerners, but loved by the Chinese as a smart and spirited character. Initially welcomed and recruited as sources of cheap labor from the mid-1800s, the sentiment toward Chinese turned to fear and suspicion during the first half of 20th century. We now see this sentiment toward the undocumented Latino farm laborers coming to the United States, and at the time it resulted in anti-Asian legislation: immigration quota systems were instituted to keep Chinese immigrants out; ordinances of unfair taxation targeted the Chinese; the civil rights of a fair trial were denied; Chinese immigrants were assaulted and killed in raids on Chinatowns. Many Chinese immigrants defied rules that they considered senseless and unjust, resulting in years of illegal immigration as they sought to survive and reunite with families in the United States.

Star Wars

Journey to the West is not unlike the popular Western epic *Star Wars*, termed a "modern developmental fairy tale" by McDermott and Lum (1980), and a hero's journey as defined by Campbell (1949/1972). *Star Wars* takes place in another galaxy at a future time. In the story, Luke Skywalker is called to adventure by R2D2's holograph of Princess Leia—a leader of the Alliance to restore the Republic—who has been captured and taken aboard the evil Galactic Empire's mobile command station, the impregnable Death Star. Prior to her capture, she entrusts the plans to destroy the Death Star to R2D2, the little robot, hoping he and his care-taker, C3PO, also a robot, can reach a former general of the Old Republic, Obi-wan Kenobi. Luke initially refuses the call because his uncle Owen re-minds him of his family responsibilities. When he returns to find his uncle killed and the family farm burned by imperial stormtroopers, however, he has no reason to stay on his home planet, Tantooine. Divine interven-tion arrives in the form of Obi Wan Kenobi, who provides him with his father's light saber. They engage Han Solo, a mercenary pilot, to rescue Princess Leia.

The adventure centers around three characters—Luke Skywalker, Han Solo, and Princess Leia—who are forced to band together by circumstance rather than friendship. Luke experiences a series of trials—trying to save Princess Leia, falling into the trash compactor, battle with Darth Vader and the stormtroopers. Obi Wan dies at the hands of Darth Vader, but returns as the inner voice for Luke. Despite great odds and many adven-tures, the trio, with the help of The Force is able to destroy the Death Star, escape from the exploding ship, and restore the Republic. They are also transformed in the process with the support of The Force, and recognized for their valor.

CONTRASTS

This saga has the elements of fantasy, supernatural powers, good versus evil, and action also found in *Journey to the West*. There are also significant contrasts between the two stories that distinguish their cultural origins. In *Journey to the West*, the parents are symbolically represented by female authority figures—the spiritual and supreme beings of Kuan Yin and Hsi Wang Mu, who watch over the travelers. In *Star Wars*, the parent is rep-resented by a male authority figure, Obi Wan Kenobi, who watches over the trio while Darth Vader, another male authority figure, thwarts, threat-ens, and almost destroys them; these men represent two sides of a power-ful force. The need to destroy the parental authority figures in Western mythology, as the hero goes through his transformation and maturation, contrasts with Asian mythology where the benevolent parental authority figure remains intact.

Both Monkey King and Luke Skywalker long for adventure and are impatient; their transformation is analogous to adolescent maturation. In *Journey to the West*, components of self are embodied in the characters of Monkey, Pig, and River Spirit, that is, impulse, bodily desire, and spirit; the developmental task is in their moderation and containment. In *Star Wars*, Luke's idealism is pitted against Han Solo's cynicism, selfishness, and sense of omnipotence; the developmental task is in his self-expression.

Repressed images of childhood are depicted in both sagas. The barroom in *Star Wars* resembles a frontier saloon and embodies visual evidence of evil and ugliness, representing the present corrupt world. In *Journey to the*

West, the seduction by the material world is represented in the substory of the Seven Spider Spirits. The Tang Priest is lured into Gossamer Cave by seven spider spirits disguised as beautiful women; his rescue by Monkey and Pig emphasizes the importance of interdependence and teamwork.

The fight between good and evil is a spiritual one in Monkey King, that is, against demon spirits; for Luke Skywalker, it is a concrete fight against the evil Empire. In *Star Wars,* the ultimate fight is between father and son as Luke discovers that Darth Vader is his father. In Western literature, the son (Luke) must often be victorious over the powerful father figure; in Asian literature, the son (Monkey King) is transformed with forgiveness and the granting of immortality by the powerful mother figure (Hsi Wang Mu).

The journey for each is also different. Han Solo and Luke Skywalker set out to destroy the evil forces; they succeed because the vulnerability of Death Star was in its designer's inability to conceive of the fact that one small space ship could be a threat to it—symbolizing the failing of the father to see the threat of the son. Monkey King makes a journey to seek the scriptures—for enlightenment as opposed to conquering. Luke must conquer and overcome Darth Vader to achieve his maturity and manhood. Monkey King must subdue his impulsive and temperamental tendencies to achieve enlightenment; the crown he wears (given to him by His Wang Mu) tightens to give him headaches whenever he has bad thoughts. The rebelliousness and cunning of Monkey King is internal, and must be contained in order to succeed over the demons and spirits outside.

These differences reflect different worldviews of man against nature. In the Asian culture, man must establish harmony with nature; in Western culture, man must overcome it. Both epics are appealing because they tap into the meaning of life; self-identity and value systems; separation and individuation; achievement of maturity; and overcoming of problems of dependency, abandonment, and death. They reflect a journey not unlike that of immigration.

WARRIOR WOMEN

The hero's journey is often considered a male journey, symbolizing the rite of passage for boys. For women, whose history and contributions were often subordinated to men in both the West and the East, the story of the *Woman Warrior,* both in its classic (*Ode to Mulan,* 2009) and contemporary (Kingston, 1989) versions, captures the strength and resiliency of women in male dominated cultures.

One of the most celebrated characters in the Chinese culture, Hua Mulan is the heroine of the Five Dynasties (420–588 C.E.) whose power is her ability to surpass the military skills of men. She is a young woman who loves and reveres her aging father so much that, when he is called to battle, she goes in his place disguised as a man, since he does not have a son.

For 12 years, she distinguishes herself in military battle as a warrior and leads the army to victory. She develops a friendship with a fellow military general, whom she later marries after revealing her true self to him. She refuses further promotions, and instead returns home to her parents and family to fulfill her obligations to them.

While the hero's journey is generally viewed as masculine, this is one of few stories of a woman's valor. Chinese American immigrant women are the women warriors of today; they have faced great odds and challenges in supporting families and culture as they coped with poverty and survival in male-dominated Confucian societies and a racist America. The need for disguise is not unlike the double bind dilemmas faced by women today—social demands of females and leaders are often contradictory.

LEARNING FROM MY MOTHER'S VOICE

While the narratives discussed above are classics, this narrative is personal and directly addresses the journey of immigration. *Learning from My Mother's Voice* is an oral history about my mother (Chin, 2005). My mother lived in Nanking, China, and escaped three days before the Japanese invaded during World War II leaving behind the *rape of Nanking*. In leaving China to join my father in America, she had to leave her 5-year-old son, my brother; they would not be reunited for 50 years. Her promise to him was that she would bring him to America. She kept that promise. He arrived in America at the age of 55, now himself a grandfather. My mother frequently relived and retold this story throughout her life. Through the years, we heard stories of the poverty in China, of our uncles and their families who starved to death, contrasted with China's beauty as my mother both yearned to return and was glad she escaped. We experienced her nurturing as my mother created tonics to heal and restore our health; her teachings always reminded us of who we were and what our obligations were, and she insisted that we remain a family through the family meals and celebrations. Invariably, her stories would return to the trauma of separation from her son, and the loss of her own mother when she was five. My mother journeyed to the West, leaving behind that which she knew and loved, in search of a better life.

This brief narrative of my mother's story mirrors the stories that many are likely to hear from immigrant parents in the process of growing up. The stories are often heard with impatience in youth, but with rapture in adulthood. At times, they may lose their potency, only to resurge when threats to identity, survival, or bonding occur. It is these stories that I urge readers to document—as ways to bond families through crises and trauma, and as ways to come to terms with the pain of separation and guilt of leaving others behind.

NARRATIVES OF JOURNEY AND STRENGTH ACROSS CULTURES

The hero's journey is found in many cultures. Those from different cultures will provide different worldviews; all will capture the journey of life experience toward truth and justice. *Journey to the West* from the Chinese culture has common elements with Western classics such as Homer's *Odyssey* (1997) in Greece and Swift's *Gulliver's Travels* (1726/2001) in England, as well as the modern day *Star Wars* from the Americans.

All are narratives of a journey that includes the fight to seek truth and justice and to achieve transformation. They are all different from one another as well. The journey and themes of strength will play out differently in diverse cultures. In Western narratives, the return is often one of a conqueror coming to claim the prize, often the beautiful maiden or woman (e.g., Odysseus reclaiming his wife Penelope from the suitors). In Eastern narratives, the return is often one of inner transformation with the ability to enter a higher order of enlightenment (e.g., Monkey King entering Buddhahood). This distinction demonstrates the importance of differences across cultures.

The narratives are used in this volume on Diversity in Mind and in Action to capture the journey of immigration, and to inspire all to create their own family and immigration legends. Too often, immigration is viewed as the replacement of traditional, old country, outdated beliefs with the ways of modern, independent thinking and freedom, without recognizing the importance of capturing the themes of strength and resilience needed by immigrant families, of identity and bonds embraced by immigrants, and of transformation resulting from the experience.

LESSONS TO BE LEARNED

These narratives carry with them messages and lessons to be learned in our personal journeys and professional charges. We carry these narratives in our minds; and while there are commonalities, the differences make a difference. Each holds his or her story to be unique, but the narrative is experienced as common across cultures. Holocaust survivors, freed slaves, and internment camp survivors all share in their psyches and identities the common crisis and trauma of losing one freedom. Here are some lessons to be learned.

Lesson 1: Warrior Lessons—Celebrate Strength

Women typically grow up with *bondage messages*. They are taught that women are weak, subservient, or victims. Women are taught early on that they need to be rescued or, alternatively, that they are cunning and manipulative, and their power must be feared. We must replace these messages with *bonding images*. Women need to embrace having the fertilizing power of the Moon Goddess. They can draw on their connectedness and their nurturing, strengths among women, to form family and intergenerational bonds. A Woman Warrior can celebrate strength and pride. The barricades of racism and stereotypes block and silence women and men alike.

Lesson 2: Bicultural Identity

How often are we given the bondage message to Be American? Or told that Being Westernized is modern, so give up traditional ways? Or that there is only one way? A more bonding image would support the idea that one can achieve a Yin-Yang Balance in one's identity. All can avoid the stereotypic comparisons about race and cultures that constrain our identities. Instead, we can engage in a bi-directional process to achieve a bicultural identity.

Lesson 3: Contradictions of Culture

Too often, we are given the bondage message that "We are all the same; we are simply human." This obliteration of difference leaves us all with the false sense of commonality when, in fact, true contrasts can be enriching and bonding. We should be able to live with the contrasting images of the Jade Mountain in the West versus the Garden of Eden in the East existing in the Chinese and American cultures, respectively. It is important to embrace diversity and difference. As contrasting cultural views are placed side by side, we may find that denial and splitting is necessary to maintain integrity, since some things cannot be integrated.

Lesson 4: Immigration Is Traumatic—Loss and Abandonment

So many immigrants stay within the confines of ethnic ghettos that limit and restrict their opportunities—a bondage experience. To cope with the trauma and loss, they often cling to the familiar, even when its time has passed. To free themselves, they need to acknowledge the trauma of immigration, mourn the losses of that which is left behind, and resolve abandonment guilt. They can bond with the shared experience of a new life. Too often, we focus on the new without adequately grieving the old.

Lesson 5: Journey of Immigration

Immigration is a journey. When the United States was defined as a melting pot, this became a bondage message because it denied access to those who could not become like the majority by virtue of the color of their skin or shape of their eyes. The unbreakable spirit of Monkey King is a more bonding image, suggesting that all immigrants can make that journey to reach enlightenment.

Immigrants must survive and create for themselves a new identity in a strange new world. It is a journey that takes them through many transformations of suffering and pain, confusion and anger, before they achieve enlightenment at the end of that journey. These transformations, both pathological and adaptive, speak to the many adventures that immigrants have on their way. It is a journey that must be made, one that should not be forgotten; it is a developmental process.

Lesson 6: Creating Immigration Legends

Lastly, the image of Chinese women in bound feet symbolized a bondage in which custom defined beauty with a practice that deformed feet and prevented women from traveling far. This is no different from the covering of women in the Muslim faith or clitorectomies for fear of women's sexuality. The bonding images of *Crouching Tiger, Hidden Dragon* reverberates with how women must uncover their inner strength, and families need to create their own immigration legends to preserve the memories and build the bonds of family and culture to pass on to the next generation.

The oral histories, the letter writing, the travels, and ultimately, the stories, create cultural myths, family bonds, and immigration legends. Immigrant families work to survive; they live to see the day that their children will fulfill their promise in the new world. Many fear that their children will forget their saga of struggle and suffering.

The journey of immigration, the task of survival, and the memories left behind are all part of creating a new identity and bonding. The stories that speak of suffering and strength, of poverty and riches, must be told. It is the bitter that makes us know the sweet. It is the cold that makes us know what is hot. It is the spicy that lets us know what is mild. It is the bondage messages that make us know the bonding images of empowerment and allow us to find our voices.

REFERENCES

Bettelheim, B. (1976). *The uses of enchantment: The meaning and importance of fairy tales.* New York: Alfred A. Knopf.

Campbell, J. (1949/1972). *The hero with a thousand faces.* Princeton, NJ: Princeton University Press.

Chin, J. L. (2005). *Learning from my mother's voice: Family legend and the Chinese American experience.* New York: Teachers College Press.

Homer. (1997). *The odyssey.* New York: Penguin Books.

Kingston, M. H. (1989). *The woman warrior: Memoirs of a girlhood among ghosts.* New York: Random House.

Lucas, G. (1977). *Star wars*. Retrieved July 21, 2008, from http://us.imdb.com/title/tt0076759/.

McDermott, J. F., & Lum, K. Y. (1980). *Star Wars*: The modern developmental fairy tale. *Bulletin of the Menninger Clinic, 44*(4), 381–390.

Ode to Mulan. (2009). YellowBridge. Retrieved on March 31, 2009, from http://www.yellowbridge.com/onlinelit/mulan.php.

Swift, J. (1726/2001). *Gulliver's travels*. New York: Penguin Books.

Wu Ch'eng. (n.d.). *Journey to the West: Monkey king*. Retrieved May 2002, from http://www.china-on-site.com/pages/comic/comiccatalog1.php.

CHAPTER 7

Asian American Immigrant Mental Health: Current Status and Future Directions

Stephen Cheung

The United States has become a more and more diverse society in the past two decades. Asian Americans comprise one of its fastest-growing ethnic groups. This rapid increase is fueled mainly by immigration. According to Census 2000, about 61.4 percent of Asian/Pacific Islander Americans are foreign-born, as compared to approximately 10.4 percent of the overall U.S. population who are foreign born (Cheung, Yan, Huang, & Hong, 2006). These numbers indicate that a vast majority of Asian Americans are immigrants or come from families in which one or both parents are immigrants. This rapidly growing Asian American immigrant (AAI) population is not homogeneous, but is rather heterogeneous. Let us take a closer look at the breadth of these diverse communities.

First and foremost, Asian Americans make up more than 30 distinct groups that represent more than 32 primary languages plus many dialects (Hong & Ham, 2001; Lee, 1997). Asian Americans who came to the United States in recent decades can be grouped into two categories: immigrants and refugees. Immigrants are individuals who voluntarily move from their home countries to settle in the United States for a variety of reasons, such as family reunion, economic advancement, political freedom, and so on. On the other hand, refugees are those who flee from their home countries due to political unrest, war, and threats of persecution and death. Regardless of the reasons for migration, Asian American immigrant and refugee families are typically faced with a number of challenges in adjusting to life in the United States. These challenges often include multiple losses during and after migration, acculturative stress in its manifold forms, prejudices and discrimination, language and cultural barriers, and so forth (Cheung, 2001; Cheung et al., 2006; Hong & Ham, 2001; Lee, 1997; Sue & Sue, 2008).

Apart from the immigrants and refugees from Asia, there is a third subgroup of AAIs, namely, the undocumented immigrants from Asia. These undocumented Asian American immigrants (UAAIs) have attracted occasional media coverage in recent years, but have received hardly any attention from mental health professionals. There appear to be at least two groups of UAAIs: those who came to this country out of their own volition, and those who came here against their will (e.g., those exploited by unscrupulous individuals via people trafficking, etc.). Both subgroups of UAAIs are confronted with graver and more stressful problems than documented Asian American immigrants and refugees (i.e., constant fear of being discovered and deported by the United States Citizenship and Immigration Services (USCIS), financial hardship due to unemployment or underemployment, lack of access to health and mental health services, and a host of other issues related to their lack of legal status in this country). In addition to the aforementioned problems, the subgroup of the UAAIs that came to this country against their will would more likely suffer from different forms of abuse and the aftermath of abuse, even if the abuse was finally terminated.

Other than these three major subgroups of AAIs, there are an increasing number of children born to these AAI subgroups. Being exposed to the mainstream European American cultures through the mass media and education, these American-born Asian Americans (ABAAs) are usually more acculturated to the mainstream cultures, and have their own unique worldviews, needs, strengths, and challenges that are quite different from those of their parents or grandparents. Sometimes these divergent perspectives, values, needs, and levels of acculturation among the two or three generations can create tension, engender conflict in the family, and result in mental health problems.

As indicated above, there is heterogeneity among AAIs, including diverse subgroups and a myriad of mental health needs. Due to space constraints, this chapter will best serve as a concise overview of Asian American immigrant mental health (AAIMH). It will first briefly review the existing theoretical, clinical, and research literature on AAI mental health. Then, it will highlight some of the current clinical principles and treatment strategies, as well as innovative trends, in providing mental health services to Asian American immigrants. It will illustrate the applications of these treatment principles and strategies with case examples throughout the chapter. The chapter will conclude with recommendations for future research, theory building, clinical applications, and advocacy for services for Asian American immigrant mental health.

REVIEW OF THEORETICAL, CLINICAL, AND RESEARCH LITERATURE ON ASIAN AMERICAN IMMIGRANT MENTAL HEALTH

Although Asians have been immigrating to the United States for decades, there is a dearth of theoretical, clinical, and research literature on AAI mental health.

From a multicultural therapy perspective, the majority of the theoretical and clinical literature on AAI mental health has entailed various adaptations of the existing psychotherapeutic models, based on European American individualistic worldviews, to the needs of AAIs. These different adaptations have, in their own way, stressed how to assess and intervene in the mental health issues of AAIs and reported successes in doing so (Cheung, 2001, 2005, in press; Cheung et al., 2006; Cheung & Hong, 2004, 2005; Ho, 1997; Hong & Ham, 2001; Kim, 1985, 1997; Lee, 1997; Lee & Mok, 2005; Sue & Sue, 2008). In the past decade, such postmodern theories as constructivism and social constructionism have further refined and polished some of our multicultural thinking in working with AAIs. In the following, I will discuss these current well-regarded principles and strategies, followed by some innovative and transformative ideas.

According to Cheung (2001, 2005, in press), in order to provide culturally competent and clinically sound mental health services for AAIs, one needs to know oneself, one's clients, and learn how to use oneself and apply one's knowledge and skills most culturally sensitively to one's clients.

Knowing Oneself

It has been poignantly articulated that

[P]reparation involves self examination—and, where needed, modification—of racial attitudes and values. Racial prejudice is extensive, and not even well intentioned helping professionals escape its impact on thoughts, attitudes, and values. In many respects, and especially with regard to racial prejudice, professional development requires modification of personal perspectives and values. Even professional values may conflict with the values of ethnic and minority groups. For example, many practice theories and assumptions reflect western, middle-class values (e.g., individualism and self-determination) that conflict with familialism and group responsibility valued by many minority groups. Professionals should strive to be aware of their own racial stereotypes and cultural values which are at odds with those of their minority clients. (Davis & Proctor, 1989, p. 119)

As emphasized above, even the most conscientious and compassionate helping professionals can have their own biases, stereotypes, and prejudices and will require self-reflection, self-awareness, and self-management. Added to the aforementioned warning, caveat, and prescription is an established body of literature on cultural identity development for ethnic minorities, including AAIs, and for European American mental health professionals (Helms, 1985, 1995; Ivey, D'Andrea, Ivey, & Simek-Morgan, 2007; McGoldrick, Giordano, & Gracia-Preto, 2005; Pontereotto & Pedersen, 1993; Pontereotto, Utsey, & Pedersen, 2006; Sue & Sue, 2008). These cultural identity development theories posit that individuals have varying levels of consciousness about their ethnic/racial backgrounds. These levels of consciousness affect how they perceive themselves, as well as others with similar cultural backgrounds and worldviews, and others with different cultural worldviews. These perceptions, in turn, influence how they interact with others. To be effective with AAIs, it is important that the therapist recognizes his or her own cultural identity level of awareness vis-à-vis that of his clients. The stages that describe the maturation process of the AAI's cultural identity development include: naiveté, encounter, naming, reflection on self as a cultural being, and multiperspective internalization (Ivey et al., 2007; Sue & Sue, 2008). Similar cultural identity theory was developed for white counselor trainees with the following stages: pre-exposure, exposure, zealotry or defensiveness, and integration (Pontereotto & Pedersen, 1993; Pontereotto et al., 2006).

In view of the perils of racial prejudices and the impacts of one's cultural identity development on one's self-perception and others-perception, it is definitely incumbent upon the mental health professional not only to examine him or herself, but also seek trusted feedback from colleagues, supervisors, consultants, or even personal therapists, to minimize his or her blind spots. Just as we help our clients to be more self-aware, flexible, and capable of problem-solving and adapting to life circumstances, so should we continue with this kind of ongoing life journey ourselves as mental health professionals.

Knowing One's Clients

In addition to knowing oneself, one definitely needs to acquire knowledge and skills in working with one's clients. This means that one understands the dilemmas of AAIs from their cultural perspectives. In other words, one appreciates the physical and psychosocial environment of AAIs; their unique cultural viewpoint on mental health; their expectations of the role of their therapist, themselves as clients, and the therapy format, process, and outcomes; and some of the culturally competent treatment principles and strategies for these clients.

Understanding the Physical and Psychosocial Environment of One's Clients

To understand one's clients and their dilemmas and problems from their cultural perspective involves knowing their environmental constraints and socio-emotional reality. There are some differences in the physical and social environments of the four subgroups of AAIs due to their unique backgrounds and contexts. Although there is intragroup variance in each of the subgroups, I will briefly discuss each subgroup based on its most common and salient characteristics in the following.

Asian American Immigrants (AAIs)

The therapist needs to recognize that immigrants from Asia may have experienced material, emotional, and relational losses before, during, and after their migration. Moreover, upon arrival in the United States, they may encounter acculturative stress in its multifarious forms. For instance, the adults or parents of a family have to find not only new employment for themselves, but also new schools for their children; and on top of that, both adults and children have to adjust to their respective new jobs and new schools. In adapting to their new environment, they also need to make new friends and rebuild their social support network so as to replace the one that they left in their country of origin. As they adjust to the sociocultural environment of the United States, different family members will have to adapt to their new roles within the family. For example, because the children can usually learn English and acculturate faster than their parents or adult family members, they tend to interpret English documents for their adult family members, and sometimes become the spokespersons for their families when their families interact with the outside world. In so doing, the children reverse their roles with their parents; that is, they take care of their parents and the family needs, although their parents or other adults in the family are supposed to take care of them and their needs. The cumulative stress and strain related to the adaptation to all these changes may exacerbate any preexisting health or mental health problems, or precipitate new ones.

Asian American Refugees (AARs)

Depending on the pre-migration situation of his home country, AARs may have been impacted by political unrest, persecution, and torture, and by their accompanied traumas, including war traumas, in their home country. In addition to adapting to the United States like immigrants from Asia, AARs may experience the effect of their premigration experience; this can debilitate, or complicate, their post-migration adjustment (Hong & Ham, 2001; Rumbaut, 1995; Uba, 1994).

Undocumented Asian American Immigrants (UAAIs)

As for the UAAIs who came to the United States willingly, they not only had to deal with the adjustment issues of the immigrants and refugees, but also the fear of deportation. In contrast, the UAAIs who came to the United States against their will suffered even more than any of the afore-mentioned subgroups because they may have additionally been subject to various forms of severe exploitation and abuse, including threats to their safety, as well as imprisonment, deportation, and persecution upon return to their home country. If these individuals were fortunate enough to escape from their abuse and gained their freedom in this country, they would not only have to contend with the myriad challenges of the other subgroup of UAAIs, but also the aftermath of their own traumatic experience of being smuggled, threatened, abused, and tortured while in the United States. In fact, owing to their lack of social support and acute psychosocial disadvan-tages, this subgroup is more vulnerable to mental disorders than the other subgroups (Law, Hutton, & Chan, 2003). Despite their egregious suffering and vulnerability, UAAIs have received the least public and professional attention, as if they were an invisible minority without a voice.

American-Born Asian Americans (ABAAs)

ABAAs are the offspring that are born to the previous subgroups of AAIs. Most of them are exposed not just to the mainstream European American individualistic cultures, or the particular Asian culture of their parents, but to both. Being influenced by two cultures can be confusing and frustrat-ing for some. The reason for this is that children are usually not taught to function well in both cultural worlds because, a lot of times, neither their parents, nor their schools, nor their friends can fully understand their experi-ences, let alone help these individuals to process them. More often than not, ABAAs choose one culture over another, ultimately identifying with either the mainstream dominant cultures or the culture of their parents. In con-trast, others can acculturate, assimilate, and function well in both cultures. Based on some preliminary data, this subgroup of ABAAs has more of a tendency to intermarry (i.e., marry someone who is not from their parents' cultural group) (Hong & Ham, 2001). Unfortunately, some others choose to acculturate or assimilate to neither culture and become marginalized.

As underscored earlier, AAIs are diverse populations with subgroups, and some of the subgroups even have subgroups within them. In order to provide culturally consonant mental health services to AAIs, one needs to be cognizant of the diversified characteristics and needs of the different subgroups as well as the mental health treatment implications of their historical background and current psychosocial and sociocultural realities.

For instance, the first three subgroups of the AAIs (i.e., the AAIs, AARs, and the UAAIs) are foreign-born and likely to have a strong cultural identity with their country of origin; that is, they may espouse collectivistic cultural worldviews that are different from the European American individualistic worldviews of the prominent psychotherapeutic approaches. They may therefore have a collective sense of self and view problems not so much from the standpoint of their own welfare as from that of the well being of their family or community. Furthermore, they may have indirect communication and problem-solving styles with the purpose of preserving interpersonal harmony and promoting the welfare of their kinsmen and communities. Because of these differences, strict adherence to the dominant psychotherapeutic approaches based on European American individualistic worldviews will result in premature termination and/or ineffective and even deleterious treatment outcomes. Therefore, to provide effective mental health services to AAIs, one should intentionally adapt one's treatment approach culturally sensitively to the individual needs and contexts of one's AAI clients (Cheung, 2001, 2005, in press; Hong & Ham, 2001; Ivey et al., 2007; Sue & Sue, 2008).

For ABAAs, especially for those who either identify with the mainstream European American cultures or function well in both the mainstream cultures and Asian American cultures of their families, one may apply the mainstream psychotherapeutic approaches with little modification. The question remains: When does one adapt and when does one apply the dominant psychotherapeutic approaches directly to the AAIs? The answer is to distinguish between AAIs who identify more with Asian American cultural worldviews and those who identify less with these worldviews. For those who espouse more of an Asian American cultural worldview, adaptation of the mainstream European American psychotherapy is needed; for those who identify less with the Asian American worldviews, but more with the mainstream worldview, direct application of the dominant psychotherapeutic approaches would be appropriate.

A brief discussion of cultural identification and how to assess it is in order. Cultural identification, simply put, refers to the complex processes in which the AAI consciously or unconsciously acculturates to, or appropriates, the values, social norms, and behavioral and attitudinal characteristics of the United States on the one hand, and maintains his or her cultural identity and characteristics on the other (Berry & Sam, 1997; Hong & Ham, 2001). There are psychological instruments to measure an AAI's acculturation to the United States, such as the Suinn-Lew Asian Self-identity Acculturation Scale (Suinn, Richard-Figueroa, Lew, & Vigil, 1987). Besides using a psychological measurement to evaluate a client's acculturation, one can assess the cultural identification of one's client by paying attention to the following in the assessment interviews:

1. Preferred food
2. Preferred language(s) used at home
3. Preferred TV programs watched at home

4. Festivals and holidays observed
5. Childrearing practices
6. Ethnic and cultural pride
7. Cultural identification
8. Pre-immigration history as well as during and post-immigration experiences
9. Other factors

Items 1–5 on the list indicate one's preferences for food, language(s), entertainments, cultural celebration, and childrearing practices; they reflect how much one identifies with the social customs, cultural values, and worldviews of one's home country. Cultural and ethnic pride can sometimes be expressed indirectly through references to the accomplishments of one's country of origin, or openly and directly as in the following: "We Koreans do things this way," or "We are so proud that our team entered the semi-final of the World Cup soccer game!" One's cultural identification can easily be inferred from these comments.

Lastly, it is understandable that one's positive or negative experiences before, during, and after migration to the United States affect one's identity and affiliation with one's home country, as well as one's receptivity and affinity toward the social norms and cultural practice of one's host country.

If a client closely identifies with the cultural worldviews of his or her country of origin, a therapist would have to adapt his or her approach culturally congruently to the client based on the therapist's self-awareness, as well as knowledge and skills in working with AAIs. Ardent adherence to the prominent psychotherapeutic orientations without modifications will likely alienate the therapist from the client and result in a rupture in the therapeutic relationship and, therefore, ineffective treatment.

Cultural Worldview of Mental Health and Expectations of Therapy

As has been well documented, AAIs' perception of health and mental health is quite different from that of mainstream European Americans (Lee, 1997; Lee & Mok, 2005). As opposed to the dichotomy of health and mental health espoused in the Western individualistic cultural worldviews, health and mental health are not two separate issues, but one, to most AAIs who identify with Asian American cultural worldviews and values. In addition, most Asian American cultural worldviews value self-control as a sign of virtue and maturity, and view full expressions of one's emotions as immaturity and a lack of self-discipline. With their cultural worldviews on mental health and the cultural value of self-control and maturity, some AAIs prefer to express their somatic problems (which are more socially acceptable than their open talk about how they feel emotionally) when asked about their emotional well-being; others may be at a loss when it comes to answering any questions about their emotional or mental health.

Apart from their different view on health and mental health, AAIs tend to underutilize mental health resources because of several internal barriers. Internal barriers refer to the barriers that stem from one's cultural upbringing and conditioning. These internal barriers include lack of knowledge of mental health and its service delivery system, familism, stigma in seeking mental health help, language and cultural barriers, and, for some AAIs, lack of resources (e.g., transportation) to access services.

1. *Lack of knowledge of mental health and its delivery system.* As said before, for Asians who identify with Asian American cultures, mental health is a foreign concept. Because they do not fully understand and embrace mental health from a Western European American perspective, it is logical that they do not know much about its nature and its service delivery system. This is why they do not make full use of it (Cheung, 2001).

2. *Familism.* This refers to the cultural practice of keeping one's problems to oneself and one's family instead of sharing them with individuals outside of the family. The reason for this is that by sharing one's problems with people outside of the family, one brings shame and disgrace to the family and oneself. For many Asian Americans, there is a cultural taboo against "washing one's dirty laundry in public" due to the fear of losing face for oneself and one's family (Hong & Ham, 2001).

3. *Stigma in seeking mental health help.* Along with AAIs' concept of health and mental health, having mental health problems manifested in unproductive and sometimes aberrant behavior causes discomfort, shame, and stigma not only to oneself, but also to one's family. This is because most AAIs who identify with Asian American cultural worldviews construe mental disorders as a hereditary problem that is passed on from one generation to the next, or, worse still, as the reaping of the negative consequences of some immoral behavior committed by a previous generation (Lee, 1997).

4. *Language and cultural barriers.* A lot of foreign born AAIs immigrated to the United States in their adulthood and find it more challenging to acquire the proficiency in English and learn the cultural nuances necessary to fully benefit from mainstream mental health services. They usually come for mental health services as their last resort. For example, Q., a 22-year-old female from South Vietnam, became psychotic and threatened to kill her parents with a kitchen knife. Inevitably, she was hospitalized and held involuntarily. Once stabilized, she was sent to a community mental health center for follow-up services. Raised in rural Vietnam, both Q. and her parents had difficulty communicating with the psychiatrist and the treatment team in English. Although an interpreter was used, the treatment team made some sociocultural errors by prematurely asking very personal and pointed questions in their intake session. After the first session, Q. and her family felt misunderstood and shamed; they decided not to return for treatment. Despite a phone call from the treating therapist, Q. did not come back.

This brief example illustrates several common phenomena. First, there were language and cultural barriers on both sides of the therapeutic transaction. Neither the treatment team nor the client could communicate clearly in a common language. Although an interpreter was used, many nuances in language were probably lost in the translation. In addition, culturally acceptable etiquette, including verbal and nonverbal communication, was not employed out of a lack of knowledge, which led to mutual misunderstanding. There also seems to have been a clash between the Western European American worldviews and Eastern Vietnamese American worldviews on mental health and help-seeking behavior, including expectations of each other's roles in treatment. For instance, the European American mental health treatment team expected that the client and her family would respond to questions asked with candor so that they could accurately diagnose the disorder and plan appropriate treatment; the Vietnamese American immigrant family expected the treatment experts to respect their privacy and provide relief for their pain without prying into their personal life. There was a mismatch between the worldview and approach of the treatment team and the needs of the clients.

5. *Lack of resources (e.g., transportation) to access services.* Because of the language and cultural barriers discussed earlier, some AAIs cannot obtain a driver's license, and also have difficulty using public transportation on their own. Consequently, they have to rely on their family members, relatives, or friends for keeping their mental health appointments. Sometimes, their lack of transportation and other resources to access mental health services becomes an additional barrier (Cheung, 2001).

External Barriers for Asian American Immigrant Mental Health

Aside from these internal barriers, AAIs face several major external barriers that make mental health services less accessible or successful. These barriers include the scarcity of culturally competent mental health programs and professionals for AAIs, as well as a lack of ongoing quality training and supervision for mental health professionals that serve AAIs. In the past two decades, although there has been more discussion on culturally competent mental health services, there are still a disproportionately small number of culturally consonant mental health services for Asian Americans in the United States. Currently, there are two models of service delivery system for AAIs: the *integrative model* and the *parallel model.* The integrative model is usually situated in a mainstream community mental health center in which a few professionals who specialize in AAI mental health provide services to AAIs. In contrast, the parallel model is a community mental health center in which the services of the program are designed specifically for AAIs. Within this model, the mental health services are comparable to those offered at the mainstream centers, but are fully staffed by teams of culturally competent professionals and are mainly for AAI populations (Hong & Ham, 2001).

Within the U.S. mental health system, there are far more integrative models than parallel models that are in place to serve AAIs. Several specific barriers or problems are found in an integrative model. First, the very few culturally competent professionals in a community mental health center of the integrative model are very often overwhelmed by the needs of their AAI clients. Compared to their counterparts that serve the mainstream European American clients, they have much less professional backup support because they are the only professionals that speak their clients' language and know the cultural worldviews and clinical needs of their clients. When their caseload is full, other mental health professionals will have to fill in. Depending on their awareness, knowledge, and skills, the other mental health professionals might adhere rigidly to their training based on European American cultural worldviews. They might consequently misinterpret the problems of the AAIs; either over-pathologize or under-pathologize them; and misdiagnose and provide the inappropriate treatment for them. As a result, a lot of AAIs do not return for treatment after the first session. This rather common phenomenon indicates a mismatch between the worldview and treatment approaches of the mental health professionals and the needs of the clients.

The current methods of overcoming these internal and external barriers include the following interventions on both a macro- and a micro-level. On the macro-level, most community mental health centers (CMHCs) that specialize in working with AAIs have spent as much time and effort as possible to reach out and educate the AAI communities about mental health and mental health services despite their heavy caseload. They have done so creatively through ethnic-specific mass media like newspapers, radio, or TV stations, and also via educational and training programs such as English, Tai Chi, and parenting classes, computer literacy clubs, and so on. They also advocate for more funding for culturally competent mental health services, and more culturally sensitive continuing education training for therapists who are educated in mainstream mental health training programs, as well as for those that specialize in AAI mental health.

On a micro-level, professionals in the AAI community mental health community centers (AAICMHCs) have been highly innovative, resourceful, and flexible so as to engage AAI clients in mental health services in view of the limited funding and the enormous internal and external barriers they face. They have tried different new and culturally competent ways to lower these barriers. For instance, in contrast to their European American counterparts, they have paid attention to decorating their lobby and offices in such a way that they reflect the cultural worldviews of their AAI clients and their families. Some examples are the display of Asian American pictures, plants, and decorations as well as magazines, newspapers, and publications in Asian languages. The purpose of this is to make the AAICMHC a welcoming and culturally relevant place for AAIs. Along with their outreach and education efforts, most AAICMHCs have tried to make their services easily accessible by locating themselves in the neighborhoods of AAIs as much as possible. In response to the common transportation problems of AAIs, some of the centers offer one-stop services; that is, they provide health, social, and mental health services in their center. For clients who need psychotropic medications as well as non-medical mental health services, they accommodate their clients by offering both services in one client visit. In further removing the internal barriers to receiving mental health services, they provide timely, culturally competent, and clinically effective services to the client and his or her family during their client's crisis (e.g., in case of an involuntary hospitalization because he or she is a danger to him or herself or others, or is gravely disabled). By so doing, they not only help resolve the crisis, but also promote the client's trust in mental health services as well as in the therapeutic relationship. Moreover, they make use of cultural festivals and events to promote mental health treatment compliance and mental health. For example, some AAICMHCs have spent time and effort in celebrating Lunar (Chinese) New Year with their AAI clients and their families each year. With much deliberation and creativity among team members, they have decided on a different mental health theme each year. Take the theme of "the Year of the Boar" for example. Using lessons that can be learned from the positive characteristics and functions of a pig at the New Year celebration and throughout the year, the treatment team has helped clients to focus on the different possible facets of their mental health recovery in next twelve months. They have also used national events (e.g., welfare reform) to promote their clients' mental health. In training the next generation of mental health professionals for the AAIs, these CMHCs have long done so by examples, on-the-job training, and so forth.

Expectations of the Therapist, Oneself, Treatment Content, the Process, and Outcomes

AAIs whose cultural identification is Asian American usually espouse a collectivistic worldview and value hierarchical family and societal arrangements. As said before, within their collectivistic worldviews, they would prefer the welfare of their family to that of themselves individually when solving their problems, and expect that their therapist would understand that. As for their cultural value of hierarchical family and societal arrangements, they often see the therapist as an expert and defer to him or her. They expect the expert to help them to solve their presenting mental health problems like a medical doctor would help them to solve their physical ones. They would take the position of a learner willing to learn and follow practical instructions to solve their problems. They would therefore expect mental health treatment to be more of a learning process between a teacher/mentor and a student. Being quite pragmatic, they would also expect good advice or directives from the therapist, as well as quick results (i.e., having their problems resolved in a short span of time as the outcome of their therapy).

In response to this set of expectations from the AAI client, it is expedient for the therapist to employ two sets of treatment principles: namely, *pacing and leading*, and *credibility and gift-giving*. Pacing refers to the active implementation of the adage of "begin where your client is at." What I mean by *active* is that, instead of passively responding to one's client out of empathy, one "takes the initiative to pace" with one's client. In other words, one actively engages the client by intentionally following the client's lead and matching with the client's cultural worldviews. This includes the client's expectations of one's therapeutic role, activities, and style. For some clients, pacing may mean that one will share a little about oneself so as to establish rapport, for this is culturally congruent. Also, one may give appropriate and useful advice and recommendations, as one is intentionally flexible in one's roles. Being flexible in one's roles means that, aside from being a therapist who just listens, reflects or interprets what one hears, one is willing to take on the role of a counselor, adviser, coach, teacher, consultant, case manager, community worker, advocate, culture-broker, service-broker, and so on, when needed. The purpose of being flexible in one's roles is again to meet the cultural expectations of one's client in order to gain his or her respect, trust, and confidence. By doing so, one will gain trust, cooperation and collaboration from one's client. Once trust is established, one can *lead* one's client in a collaborative manner to change and grow in such a way that the client's self-esteem, self-efficacy, and problem-solving and adaptation capability are enhanced.

Besides pacing and leading, one is wise to cultivate credibility and gift-giving. Credibility refers to one's trustworthiness and ability to understand the client's predicaments from his or her perspective. One way to establish credibility is to show the client one's knowledge and skills in understanding and helping him or her. Because AAIs with Asian American cultural identity tend to value education and defer to expert authority, one would appropriately share one's educational credentials and past experiences in mental health and/or in working with clients with similar backgrounds as the client. *Gift-giving* doesn't mean that one offers gifts at Christmas or at Lunar New Year, but refers to giving the client some tangible or heartfelt emotional gifts in the early sessions so that the client feels helped and stays in treatment. Take the following clinical vignette as an example.

A., a successful 40-year-old businessman from Taiwan, was referred by a colleague of mine to call me about his 17-year-old daughter's bulimia of four years' duration. He sounded sad, ashamed, and self-reproaching over the phone, as I explored with him the nature, duration, severity, and frequency of his daughter's bulimia. I quickly established my credibility by doing at least two things: on the one hand, by referring to my years of experience in treating eating disorders; and on the other hand, by demonstrating my knowledge and skills in asking germane questions regarding his daughter's bulimia, as well as in understanding, empathizing with, and validating him about his plight, feelings, wisdom, and initiative to seek help for his daughter. As I offered him gifts in the form of empathic understanding and support, I also paced with him in meeting his cultural expectations of an expert by providing additional gifts in the form of psycho-education about the nature and impact of bulimia and its general treatment approach. Lastly, in giving him gifts, and meeting his cultural expectation of an expert, I further paced with him by creating realistic hope that his daughter's condition could improve very much with appropriate treatment.

In the phone conversation of about twenty to thirty minutes, I utilized the aforementioned principles of pacing and leading as well as credibility and gift-giving to meet his cultural expectations of an expert and to offer him gifts in therapy in such way that he felt that talking with and seeing me would be worthwhile, for it helped him to feel better and more hopeful to solve his problems.

Awareness of More Culturally Congruent Treatment Approaches

As discussed earlier, AAIs respect and value collective welfare, education, and pragmatic action-oriented problem solving. There are several approaches that are more intrinsically congruent or syntonic to AAI cultural worldviews. They are different systemic approaches that involve the welfare of the family, such as structural and strategic family therapy (Cheung, 2001; Kim, 1985), and therapy that encompasses psycho-education and skills teaching like cognitive-behavior therapy. These approaches can easily be adapted to help AAIs because they relate to the wellbeing of the family and they provide action-oriented interventions and skills acquisition. I would like to further clarify that psychodynamic, humanistic/existential, communication, interpersonal, and group approaches can also be adapted to the AAI populations if one applies the treatment principles and strategies discussed in this chapter.

Postmodernism and Multiculturalism: Refinement of Our Thinking and Interventions

As said before, multicultural therapy requires that the therapist possess self-awareness and other-awareness, as well as knowledge and skills in working with AAIs. In short, it requires "some knowing" of the AAI populations that one is going to work with. This helps one to connect with one's AAI clients by meeting their cultural expectations of a therapist; furthermore, it helps one to empathize with and validate one's clients, and normalize their dilemmas. However, if this is employed to the extreme, one can err by stereotyping one's client, either positively or negatively.

In the past decade of postmodernism, constructivism and social constructionism have contributed to the respectful understanding of our clients' suffering in their phenomenal world by taking on a therapeutic stance of "not knowing." Constructivism posits that one cannot perceive true objective reality and that what one perceives is influenced by the assumptions one makes about one's world including other people, objects, events, and one's relationship with them. In other words, the assumptions one brings to one's situations affect how one perceives and interprets one's situations. Social constructionism further asserts that the reality one constructs "is mediated through language, and is socially determined through our relationships with others and the culture's shared sets of assumptions" (Goldenberg & Goldenberg, 2008, p. 21). In other words, one's constructed reality is influenced by one's social interactions with others as well as by one's ethnic, racial, cultural, national, family, socioeconomic, and religious contexts. There are several implications of social constructionism. First, the therapist and his client all bring their assumptive framework to analyze and interpret a situation; the therapist should not confuse this with the real situation. Second, he should not regard what he sees in a family as existing in the family, but understand that it is the product of his own assumptions about people, problems, and families, as well as his interactions with them. Third, the client knows his or her life best, and is therefore the expert on his or her life; his or her therapy should therefore not be directed by the therapist, but should be driven by the client.

Constructivism and social constructionism have added to and refined our current thinking about multicultural therapy in that one of the most respectful therapeutic stances with one's client is "not knowing." Not knowing means that one does not impose one's preconceived notions, stereotypes, biases, and prejudices on one's clients; instead, one humbly and openly engages in a therapeutic conversation with one's clients in order to co-construct the most appropriate reality for one's clients. Certainly, employing merely "not knowing" would go against some of the AAIs' cultural worldviews and values; notwithstanding, employing only "some knowing" would also do our clients injustice because one could misunderstand one's clients by stereotyping them. The most ideal stance appears to be an integration of "some knowing" with "not knowing" in accordance with the needs, problems, interpersonal styles, and cultural expectations of mental health services of our clients. Certainly, the optimum mixture of these two therapeutic stances depends on the myriad of client variables, therapist variables, and relationship variables between the client and the therapist.

CONCLUSION

As discussed above, Asian American immigrants (AAIs) are a very diverse population with numerous mental health needs. In order to provide culturally competent mental health services to AAIs, one needs to acquire self-awareness, as well as cultural knowledge and skills, in working with them. This involves realizing one's own cultural identity development vis-à-vis that of one's client. In progressing in the developmental stages of one's cultural identity through self-reflection and intentional immersion, training, consultation, supervision, and so on, one will recognize more of one's self-perception and others-perception as well as one's possible biases, stereotypes, and prejudices. As one manages one's thoughts, feelings, and behaviors more effectively, one can acquire more pertinent cultural knowledge and skills in working with AAI communities. Incorporating the contributions of such post-modern theories as constructivism and social constructionism, one would not impose on one's clients the therapeutic orientations that are based on European American individualistic worldviews; instead, one would judiciously employ such a therapeutic stance of "not knowing and some knowing." When working with AAIs who identify with the more traditional Asian American collectivistic cultural worldviews, one would employ a not knowing therapeutic stance so as to fully understand the dilemmas of one's clients from their vantage point on the one hand, and would also employ a some knowing stance in meeting the AAIs' cultural expectations of their therapist as the expert/ teacher, themselves as patients/learners, and the therapeutic content and process, on the other. One should adapt some of the more culturally congruent therapeutic orientations for AAIs in the context of treatment, or adapt one's favorite therapeutic approaches culturally competently to one's AAI clients.

In response to the internal and external barriers that keep AAIs from receiving quality mental health services, mental health professionals, who specialize in working with AAIs, have to be very resourceful, overcoming these hurdles by intervening on both the micro- and macro-level. Due to limited funding for mental health services for AAIs, these mental health professionals have been creative in engaging AAIs in treatment, educating AAI communities on mental health needs and issues, and advocating for more funding for mental health programs and professionals, as well as training and supervision for these professionals.

Despite some progress in the aforementioned areas, much work still needs to be done to move AAI mental health to a more desirable level. For example, on a macro-level, more advocacy efforts are needed to obtain more funding for programs, research, and training for AAIs. Among these efforts, one would advocate for a policy that requires mandatory Continuing Education Unit (CEU) training on cultural competency in working with diverse populations within each two-year license renewal cycle for mental health professionals. Although certain service delivery guidelines have been established for working with diverse populations (American Counseling Association, 2003; American Psychological Association, 2003), there needs to be more buy-in among educators and supervisors of the mental health professions to inculcate these guidelines in mental health professionals in training (i.e., graduate students, interns, residents, etc.) and to ensure that these guidelines are followed in practice.

On a micro-level, in addition to the existing efforts and progress in outreaching and educating the AAI communities and clients, as well as the training of the second generation of mental health professionals to serve AAIs, more seasoned mental health professionals would continue to support and encourage professional publications in which the diverse mental health needs of the AAIs are explicated and exemplary practices are reported. What is more, rigorous research will be conducted and published in the field of AAIMH. Mental health professionals from the second or the third generation of ABAAs, who desire to serve their cohort, should be supported to share their experiences and insights with the larger professional community through publications. Because of the many gaps in the professional literature on AAIMH, a more focused effort to fill these gaps would be needed. To accomplish this, increased periodical review of the field and the literature is highly recommended. Moreover, handbooks that include researchers, theoreticians, and practitioners' contributions of their expertise would facilitate more conversations and even collaboration among groups of professionals who have devoted their time and effort to improving the mental health of Asian American immigrants.

REFERENCES

American Counseling Association. (2003). *Multicultural counseling competencies.* Alexandra, VA: Author.

American Psychological Association. (2003). *Guidelines on multicultural education, training, research, practice, and organizational change for psychologists.* Washington, DC: Author.

Berry, J. W., & Sam, D. L. (1997). Acculturation and adaptation. In J. W. Berry, M. H. Segall, & C. Kagitcibasi (Eds.), *Handbook of cross-cultural psychology* (2nd ed., Vol. 3, pp. 291–326). Needleham Heights, MA: Allyn & Bacon.

Cheung, S. (2001). Problem-solving and solution-focused therapy for Chinese: Recent developments. *Asian Journal of Counselling, 8*(2), 111–128.

Cheung, S. (2005). Strategic and solution-focused couples therapy. In M. Harway (Ed.), *Handbook of couples therapy* (pp. 194–210). New York: John Wiley & Sons.

Cheung, S. (in press). Solution-focused brief therapy. In J. Bray & M. Stanton (Eds.), *Handbook of family psychology.* New York: Wiley-Blackwell Publishers.

Cheung, S., & Hong, G. (2004). Family therapy with children: Sociocultural considerations. *The Family Psychologist, 20*(3), 14–15.

Cheung, S., & Hong, G. (2005). Clinical Application of Attachment Theory: Cultural implications. *The Family Psychologist, 21*(2), 15–16.

Cheung, S., Yan, S., Huang, J., & Hong, G. (2006, February). Psychological services for immigrant Asian American families: Community perspectives. Paper presented at American Psychological Association Expert Summit on Immigration, San Antonio, TX.

Davis, L., & Proctor, E. (1989). *Race, gender, and class: Guidelines for practice with individuals, families, and groups.* Englewood Cliffs, NJ: Prentice Hall.

Goldenberg, H., & Goldenberg, I. (2008). *Family therapy: An overview.* Belmont, CA: Thomson Higher Education.

Helms, J. E. (1985). Toward a theoretical explanation of the effects of race on counseling: A Black a White model. *Counseling Psychologist, 12,* 153–165.

Helms, J. E. (1995). An update of Helm's white and people of color identity models. In J. Ponterotto, M. Casaa, L. Suzuki, & C. Alexander (Eds.), *Handbook of multicultural counseling* (pp. 98–110). Thousand Oaks, CA: Sage.

Ho, M. K. (1997). *Family therapy with ethnic minorities* (2nd ed.). Thousand Oaks, CA: Sage.

Hong, G. K., & Ham, M. D. (2001). *Psychotherapy and counseling with Asian American clients: A practical guide.* Thousand Oaks, CA: Sage.

Ivey, A. E., D'Andrea, M., Ivey, M. B., & Simek-Morgan, L. (2007). *Theories of counseling and psychotherapy: A multicultural perspective* (6th ed.). Boston: Allyn & Bacon.

Kim, S. (1985). Family therapy for Asian Americans: A strategic-structural framework. *Psychotherapy, 22*(2), 342–348.

Kim, S. (1997). Korean American families. In E. Lee (Ed.), *Working with Asian Americans: A guide for clinicians* (pp. 125–135). New York: Guilford Press.

Law, S., Hutton, M., & Chan, D. (2003). Clinical, social, and service use characteristics of Fuzhounese undocumented immigrant patients. *Psychiatric Services, 54*(7), 76–87.

Lee, E. (Ed.). (1997). *Working with Asian Americans: A guide for clinicians.* New York: Guilford Press.

Lee, E., & Mok, M. (2005). Asian Families: An overview. In M. McGoldrick, J. Giordano, & N. Garcia-Preto (Eds.), *Ethnicity and family therapy* (3rd ed., pp. 269–289). New York: Guilford Press.

McGoldrick, M., Giordano, J., & Garcia-Preto, N. (Eds.). (2005). *Ethnicity and family therapy* (3rd ed.). New York: Guilford Press.

Ponterotto, J. G., & Pedersen, P. B. (1993). *Preventing prejudice: A guide for counselors and educators.* Newbury Park, CA: Sage.

Ponterotto, J. G., Utsey, S. O., & Pedersen, P. B. (2006). *Preventing prejudice: A guide for counselors, educators, and parents* (2nd ed.). Thousand Oaks, CA: Sage.

Rumbaut, R. G. (1995). Vietnamese, Laotian, and Cambodian Americans. In P. G. Min (Ed.), *Asian Americans: Contemporary trends and issues* (pp. 232–270). Thousand Oaks, CA: Sage.

Sue, D. W., & Sue, D. (2008). *Counseling the culturally diverse* (5th ed.). New York: John Wiley & Sons.

Suinn, R., Richard-Figueroa, K., Lew, S., & Vigil, S. (1987). The Suinn-Lew Asian Self-identity Acculturation Scale: An initial report. *Educational and Psychological Measurement, 47,* 401–407.

Uba, L. (1994). *Asian Americans: Personality patterns, identity, and mental health.* New York: Guilford.

CHAPTER 8

The Psychology of Undocumented Latinos: Living an Invisible Existence

Lucila Ramos-Sánchez

What is it like to live undocumented in the United States? This is a question to which most people give little thought, yet there is an emerging population of undocumented Latino immigrants who face the daily reality of living in fear because of their immigration status. In a review of Latino immigration, the Pew Hispanic Center (2006) estimated that upwards of 500,000 undocumented individuals have immigrated each year since 2000, and that approximately 11.1 million undocumented immigrants were residing in the United States as of 2006. Of the total undocumented population, individuals of Mexican descent made up the largest group at 6.2 million, or 56 percent, while 22 percent were from other Latin American countries. California had the largest concentration of undocumented Latino immigrants, reaching approximately 2.5 million (Pew Hispanic Center, 2006). This may explain why undocumented Latino immigrants have come under more intense scrutiny as of late. Yet, aside from the political and public attention, undocumented Latino immigrants remain relatively invisible in society and in the mental health literature. For the purpose of this chapter, the terms *undocumented Latinos* will refer to all individuals from Mexico, Central America, and South America who are not authorized to be in the United States.

Unlike immigrant mental health in general, little attention has been given to the unique stressors that undocumented immigrants encounter living in the United States. With few exceptions, most literature that has focused on the mental health status of immigrants does not differentiate between documented and undocumented Latinos. This may be due, in part, to the population's reluctance to disclose immigration status. Finch and Vega (2003) reported that documentation status was not assessed because researchers were concerned with skewed responses and a loss of trust between the participants and the researchers. As a result, few distinctions have been made between the stressors of documented and undocumented Latino immigrants.

Previous research indicates that Latino immigrants, in general, experience stressors such as cultural dissonance, poverty, discrimination, and language barriers. Zea, Diehl, and Porterfield (1997) indicated that being physically and socially uprooted from their homes was a primary source of stress for these immigrants because the social networks of family and friends were not always easily replaced. Similarly, Cervantes, Padilla, and Salgado de Snyder (1991) stated that Latino immigrants also experienced low educational attainment, low socioeconomic status, and low rates of adaptation, which contributed to mental health problems. Even though documented and undocumented immigrants may share similar stressors with regard to adjustment and adaptation, greater pressure accompanies those of undocumented status.

Of the few studies that have addressed the mental health of undocumented Latinos, that of Pérez and Fortuna (2005) found that undocumented Latinos were more likely to have a diagnosis of anxiety, adjustment, alcohol abuse disorders, and other psychological problems compared to documented immigrant Latinos and U.S.-born Latinos. The specific psychosocial stressors they experienced included occupational problems, legal difficulties, and barriers to health care. Unfortunately, research in the area of circumstances and the emotional experiences of undocumented Latinos is scant. The following section is a review of the unique circumstances, experiences, and stressors that undocumented Latinos may come across in the United States.

STRESSORS OF UNDOCUMENTED LATINOS

The stressors that undocumented Latinos experience can be categorized into four domains: (a) intrafamilial conflict, (b) fear of discovery, (c) limited access to services due to undocumented status, (d) and political policy and public sentiment toward undocumented immigrants.

Intrafamilial Conflict

Falicov (1998a) identified two areas of intrafamilial conflict that may arise for undocumented Latino families: separation and power imbalance. Separation during immigration occurs frequently for many undocumented Latino families and occurs for both practical and economic reasons. Often, the father immigrates to the United States first. The mother and children may immigrate at a later time once the father is established to some degree, or when it is economically feasible. During the time of separation, the mother may reorganize the family so that she functions as the head-of-household, a role not easily relinquished after reunification with the father. Falicov (1998a) indicated that the family might reorganize again once reunification occurs. This is a time when the father may become excessively rigid to reestablish his authority. Another source of stress for the parents is marital conflict, which may arise from prolonged separation from each other or from their children.

In cases where both parents immigrate without the children, the psychological consequences can be quite negative. Children may experience depression, nightmares, eating problems, school failures and other somatic complaints. These symptoms may develop during separation or, conversely, be delayed until reunification. Falicov (1998b) indicated that reincorporating the children into the family could be traumatic, especially if the children have developed a strong attachment to a different caregiver during the time of separation. Overall, this research suggests that reunification and reorganization of the family is stressful and painful for both parents and children.

Another intrafamilial conflict may result from cultural disparity within the family. Falicov (1998a) indicated that leadership positions in the family shift and are often partially assumed by a more acculturated son or daughter. These displacements may lead to anger and vulnerability on the part of the parents as the son/daughter gains status and power within the family. This is further complicated by the stresses of adolescence, where acculturated children strive for greater independence outside of the family, contrary to the family's underlining value of interdependence. The power differential may be exacerbated when the children are U.S.-born citizens while the parents remain undocumented. Furthermore, the parents' fear of discovery may prevent them from seeking counseling or other services that may aid in addressing familial conflict.

Fear of Discovery

One of the primary concerns many undocumented Latinos have is the fear of being caught or discovered by the authorities or by the United States Citizenship and Immigration Services (USCIS). Salgado de Snyder, Cervantes, and Padilla (1990) reported that undocumented immigrants lived in constant fear of being reported to the USCIS and deported back to their country of origin. Thus, it would follow that fear may lead undocumented Latinos to engage in avoidance behaviors to circumvent being asked about their immigration status. For example, they may avoid questions from officials where their children attend school, they may be less willing to seek medical attention and, if victimized, they may be less willing to report the incidents to the authorities. Even though some of these institutions would not generally inquire about legal status, many undocumented individuals may be unwilling to run the risk of discovery.

Another significant psychosocial stressor is fear of discovery in the workplace. Both Heyman (1998) and Pérez and Fortuna (2005) posit that undocumented immigrants are vulnerable to exploitation by employers. A report by the Pew Hispanic Center (2005) indicated that Latinos were underpaid for their services in the agriculture, hospitality, and construction industries. The report specified that undocumented Mexican immigrant wages were amongst the lowest in the United States and were certainly below both the poverty level and minimum wage. Undocumented migrant women were the most vulnerable to substandard wages. Yet, undocumented Latinos have little recourse in combating low unjust wages or being unfairly fired. Furthermore, they cannot report these egregious employment practices because of their status.

The constant withholding of identity information by undocumented Latinos may result in many leading dual lives (an internal vs. external life). Personal information regarding their undocumented status may only be revealed to close friends and family. Heyman (1998) and Porter (2005) reported that many undocumented Latinos obtain fabricated identification in order get a job. The fake documents generally include a green card and a Social Security Card. Therefore, to the outside world, they may give false information such as birthplace and length of residence in the United States to corroborate information provided by the falsified documents.

Even though false documentation is obtained to work, employment status may still be tenuous since the lack of genuine documentation may lead to loss of employment and subsequent deportation. This can certainly contribute to stress experienced by undocumented Latinos. Porter (2005) reported that, in some instances when false documents were used, the Internal Revenue Service sent letters to employers indicating that the identification number did not match the identification number in their system. As a result, employers dismissed the employees affected or the employees quit, fearing authorities were tracking them. It is evident that fear of discovery and deportation has a tremendous impact on how undocumented Latinos live their lives and how they exist in society.

Access to Services

Over the past two decades, proposed legislation and laws have attempted to limit delivery of governmental services and the rights of undocumented Latino immigrants, both in state and nationwide. Many of these laws affected Latino immigrants disproportionately because, as previously stated, Latinos constitute the largest undocumented population. At the state level, the 1994 proposition 187 in California attempted to deny health care and public education to undocumented individuals. More recently in California, anyone unable to provide documentation of legal residence was barred from obtaining a driver's license. This left many Latinos without a means of transportation. Proposition 200 in Arizona required proof of U.S. citizenship or a passport from any person who received basic public services or registered to vote. Similarly, Colorado attempted to amend their state constitution so that all undocumented Latino immigrants were banned from receiving any nonemergency medical services.

At the federal level, the Illegal Immigration Reform and Immigrant Responsibility Act of 1996 limited public benefits to undocumented individuals by requiring proof of citizenship for public benefits and verification of immigrant status for social security and higher education assistance. The Personal Responsibility and Work Opportunity Reconciliation Act of 1996 further disqualified many undocumented immigrants from what it considered entitlement programs such as food stamps, housing assistance, Medicaid, and Medicare-funded hospitalization. Overall, federal, state, and local governments have been effective in impeding the access to services among undocumented Latinos.

Berk and Schur (2001) reported that when California's proposition 187 was passed in 1994, a community health clinic in Los Angeles saw a 60 percent drop in visits a week after the election. The authors went on to report that 39 percent of undocumented Latinos were afraid to obtain health care under the passage of Proposition 187 because of the fear of being reported to the USCIS. The continuous efforts to limit services to undocumented Latinos, coupled with adaptation and adjustment issues, have implications for psychological well-being.

This ongoing barrage of legislation to limit access to governmental services places undue stress on many undocumented Latinos. Whereas most individuals take the ability to visit a doctor or applying for federal assistance for granted, this population has to weigh the risk of whether their actions will expose their immigration status. This constant worrying is only compounded by the fact that they may not be getting adequate health care, wages, or other services they may need for their day-to-day living. Thus, the cumulative impact likely has implications for their daily well-being and for their overall mental health.

Political Policy and Public Sentiment

Bacon (1996) and Michelson (2001) suggest that political actions and events precipitate public sentiment rather than the reverse. Yet, both are powerful forces that may influence attitudes toward undocumented Latinos. Legislation affecting access to services to undocumented immigrants was reviewed earlier. What follows are recent immigration policies that seem to make life more difficult for and affect society's perception of undocumented Latinos.

In the years since September 11, 2001, there has been an emergence of legislation to prevent terrorism in the United States. Most notably, the Border Security Act of 2001 and the USA Patriot Act of 2001 were intended to increase security measures and enhance border patrol of undocumented individuals in an effort to prevent terrorism. The impact of these acts has extended beyond terrorists to affect undocumented Latino immigrants. For example, the Border Protection, Antiterrorism, and Illegal Immigration Control Act of 2005 proposed that undocumented immigrants be automatically deemed criminals and be stripped of many basic rights such as due process. People who aided or employed undocumented immigrants would be considered smugglers, and the provision eased the process of deportation.

The initial accepted goal of protecting the United States from terrorism seems to have come with a human and social cost for undocumented Latinos. Antiterrorist legislation has put unnecessary strain on undocumented Latino immigrants, although this was an unintended effect. This has resulted because measures intended for potential terrorists also implicated undocumented Latinos due to their immigration status. As a result, a greater level of fear has permeated the community. Furthermore, legislation to prevent terrorism has likely had the unintended consequence of negatively impacting public sentiment toward undocumented Latinos. This supposition is supported by previous research that suggests that political actions often precipitate negative public sentiment.

For example, prior to the campaigning and passage of proposition 187 there had not been strong anti-immigrant sentiment since 1986, with the passage of the Immigration and Reform Control Act. After the passage of proposition 187, Hovey, Kain, Rojas, and Magana (2000) reported increased negative attitudes by documented persons toward immigration, corroborating the link between legislation and public sentiment. Similarly, after the passage of the USA Patriot Act, 60 percent of the U.S. public considered current levels of migration to be a critical threat. Jonas and Tactaquin (2004) further stated that equating immigrants with terrorists led to the perception that capturing undocumented Latino immigrants was the same as capturing and deporting terrorists in order to protect the United States. Unfortunately, no empirical research was found that examined public sentiment just prior to the events of September 11, 2001. Nonetheless, research suggests that negative public sentiment becomes widespread because of the language and images used to influence the public via the media.

Researchers have sufficiently documented the connection between the media and public sentiment toward undocumented Latino immigrants. During the campaigning for proposition 187, television footage of Latino undocumented immigrants crossing the border served to influence public attitudes against Latinos in California and increased support for the proposition. Such negative sentiment likely has detrimental effects on how undocumented Latinos are perceived and treated by society.

Since the passage of antiterrorist legislation, reports of mistreatment have increased and have impacted the daily lives of Latino undocumented immigrants. In the media, they have been likened to locusts and bacteria, as well as being characterized as cooks, maids, janitors, and gardeners. Jonas and Tactaquin (2004) found that detentions and deportations for immigrant violations have increased, as has fear of vigilante groups. There has been an increase in raids, more harassment by police, and greater mistreatment in detention facilities.

The impact of public sentiment is further complicated by the lack of understanding and disconnect between endorsement of terrorist (anti-immigrant) legislation and the daily lives of many American citizens. This is most evident in the service industry, where American citizens may directly benefit from the presence of undocumented immigrants working as nannies, housekeepers, or gardeners. Santa Ana (1999) reported that immigrant labor elevated the standard of living for the middle-class by providing them with services they could not otherwise afford at a low cost. Ironically, many American citizens may not perceive that legislation endorsement affects them directly. For example, in Arcadia, California, residents proactively maintained a predominantly white community, even though the community was heavily dependent on Latinos, few of which lived in the community. In essence, U.S. citizens may express negative sentiment toward undocumented Latinos but continue to utilize their services.

Sustained political policy and negative public sentiment can have detrimental effects on the psychological wellbeing of many undocumented Latinos. From the examples mentioned above, one can glean some of the negative psychological effects that result: (1) issues of safety, and (2) not feeling valued. Recipients of this negative sentiment may continually have concerns about their safety and the safety of their families. They may feel unprotected by lawmakers and fearful that negative public sentiment could result in physical harm. Also, many undocumented Latinos feel unwanted in a society where they are contributing valuable work. This may negatively impact undocumented Latinos' self-worth, which may lead to maladaptive behavior and adjustment.

RECOMMENDATIONS FOR PRACTICE

The unique circumstances and experiences of undocumented Latinos have implications for how mental health providers deliver mental health services to this population. In light of the aforementioned stressors that undocumented Latinos encounter daily, it would make sense that these stressors leave many vulnerable to mental health problems. Thus, the issue is not whether this population needs psychological help, but rather: as mental health providers, how do we ensure that they receive the mental health services they need? Principle D: Justice of the APA ethical guidelines states that "Psychologists recognize that fairness and justice entitle all persons to access to and benefit from the contributions of psychology and to equal quality in the processes, procedures, and services being conducted by psychologist" (American Psychological Association [APA], 2002a, p. 4). In this vein, psychologists and mental health professionals in general have a social responsibility to ensure that undocumented Latinos get the psychological help they need, irrespective of their documentation status. What follows are recommendations and suggestions for psychologists and mental health professionals to address issues of access and delivery of psychological services.

Within the counseling process, mental health providers are advised to shift and incorporate a new role into their practice, such as that of a social intermediary. In essence, the mental health provider becomes the link to the outside world, informing the client of the differences that exist in culture, beliefs, expectations, and societal norms between the host and the Latino culture. This aids in the transition and adjustment that many undocumented Latinos experience. Similarly, mental health providers should be familiar with resources relevant to an undocumented population. These include information about social services, means programs, referrals for legal advice on immigration, health care services, ELL courses (English Language Learners), and educational enrollment procedures. In addition, mental health providers should be aware of the different laws that could limit services to undocumented Latinos.

In keeping with the role of a social intermediary, engaging in unconventional methods of mental health service delivery may be necessary. For example, mental health providers may want to help the clients connect with the aforementioned resources and follow up with clients outside the 50-minute counseling session. Also, immigrant Latino clients may need appointments in the evening or on weekends that accommodate their work schedules better. In-home therapy visits would be another way to make services accessible to this population, as long as confidentiality is ensured. Specifically, in-home visits would help to determine the needs of the clients in order to provide effective service delivery.

Whether the therapy relationship is individual, group, or family, mental health providers should consider avoiding questions regarding immigration early in the counseling relationship. It is important to establish a strong therapeutic alliance before asking questions regarding clients' migration. When inquiry occurs too early, undocumented clients may become nervous or withhold information from the mental health provider.

With regard to mental health agencies that deliver services to undocumented Latinos, it is essential that agency staff is sufficiently aware of the psychosocial and legal issues that undocumented Latinos face. Agencies should also recruit more bilingual mental health providers, since many recent immigrants may still be learning English and may not benefit from psychological services in English. Mental health agencies may also want to create an inviting environment where there is a large Spanish-speaking clientele. This would include having magazines and brochures in Spanish, as well as culturally relevant pictures on the walls of the waiting room.

Providing a welcoming environment may encourage help seeking and increase the trust of undocumented Latino immigrants in the therapist.

Greater attempts should be made by mental health professionals to engage in outreach to the communities where undocumented Latinos reside. This would consist of attending church groups or functions and providing information on psychological services available to the community. Mental health providers could address the myths, the process, why someone would seek services, and the benefits of counseling. In this way, the counseling process could be demystified and perhaps become less stigmatizing. Issues of confidentiality could also be addressed during outreach so that undocumented Latinos are assured that their status will not be questioned. In addition, community members would become familiar with mental health providers performing outreach, which could encourage seeking counseling services.

Mental health providers may also want to reconsider how they present themselves to the Latino community where undocumented individuals may reside. Rather than indicating that they are offering therapy, which may be stigmatizing to some Latinos, clinicians should offer support or parenting groups instead. Undocumented Latinos may be more willing to attend psycho-educational groups where they perceive that they are gaining information, in addition to discussing their current problems. Psycho-educational groups such as those addressing parenting strategies, handling migration, and adjusting to a new country are just a few examples of topics that are pertinent to the undocumented Latino population.

In terms of training, it is important for the field of psychology in general to train more mental health providers who are not only culturally competent to work with this population, but who are also linguistically competent. Even though cultural competency can be addressed through educational training, language is still a significant barrier to accessing mental health services for documented and undocumented Latino immigrants. Training programs are encouraged to make greater efforts to recruit bilingual individuals who will return and work with undocumented Latino immigrants and the greater Latino community.

Training programs should also consider offering courses specific to working with the differing Latino populations. Tailoring counseling courses to the Latino psychology is still developing at both the doctoral and master's level. These types of curriculum innovations are necessary if training programs are to produce clinicians who are both linguistically and culturally competent to work with Latinos in general and undocumented Latinos in particular.

CONCLUSION

The sentiment and unique experiences surrounding undocumented immigrants in the United States is hardly new. However, the current landscape has become increasingly hostile and negative toward undocumented immigrants than in years past. The aggressive deportation efforts of today hearken back to the 1950s, when there were systematic attempts to deport Latinos, mainly those of Mexican descent, back to their home country. In fact, the immigration enforcement efforts have become so aggressive that undocumented immigration has dropped and the overall undocumented Latino population has declined. This heightened anti-immigrant sentiment can be attributed to antiterrorist efforts. In the past, undocumented Latino immigrants were used as scapegoats during an economic downturn and for political gain. Now, the war on terrorism has made it easier to persecute undocumented Latino immigrants any time under the auspices of protecting the country.

Based on the stressors outlined in this chapter and their implications for mental health, psychologists and mental health providers in general are encouraged to examine their helping role with undocumented Latino immigrants. The multicultural guidelines set forth by the APA (2002b) encourage psychologists to promote racial equity and social justice. As such, psychologists share in the responsibility to advocate for and work toward social justice for this and all populations that are treated unfairly. Overall, if we are to promote and advance diversity in our profession, we must ally with those populations that are otherwise forgotten.

REFERENCES

American Psychological Association. (2002a). *Ethical principles of psychologists and code of conduct.* Retrieved October 18, 2006, from http://www.apa.org/ethics/code2002.pdf.

American Psychological Association. (2002b). *Guidelines on multicultural education, training, research, practice, and organizational change for psychologists.* Retrieved July 31, 2008, from http://www.apa.org/pi/multiculturalguidelines.pdf.

Bacon, D. (1996). For an immigration policy based on human rights. *Journal of Social Justice, 23,* 137–153.

Berk, M. L., & Schur, C. L. (2001). The effect of fear on access to care among undocumented Latino immigrants. *Journal of Immigrant Health, 3,* 151–156.

Cervantes, R. C., Padilla, A. M., & Salgado de Snyder, N. (1991). The Hispanic stress inventory: A culturally relevant approach to psychosocial assessment. *Psychological Assessment, 3,* 438–447.

Falicov, C. J. (1998a). *Latino families in therapy: A guide to multicultural practice.* New York: Guilford.

Falicov, C. J. (1998b). The cultural meaning of family triangles. In M. McGoldrick (Ed.), *Re-visioning family therapy: Race, culture, and gender in clinical practice* (pp. 37–40). New York: Guilford.

Finch, B. K., & Vega, W. A. (2003). Acculturation stress, social support, and self-rated health among Latinos in California. *Journal of Immigrant Health, 5,* 109–117.

Heyman, J. M. (1998). State effects on labor exploitation: The INS and undocumented immigrants at the Mexico-United States border. *Critique of Anthropology, 18,* 157–180.

Hovey, J. D., Kain, C., Rojas, R. S., & Magana, C. (2000). Proposition 187 reexamined: Attitudes toward immigration among California voters. *Current Psychology, 19,* 159–173.

Jonas, S., & Tactaquin, C., (2004). Latino immigrant rights in the shadow of the national security state: Responses to domestic preemptive strikes. *Social Justice, 31,* 67–91.

Michelson, M. R. (2001). The effect of national mood on Mexican American political opinion. *Hispanic Journal of Behavioral Sciences, 23,* 57–70.

Pérez, M. C., & Fortuna, L. (2005). Psychosocial stressors, psychiatric diagnoses and utilization of mental health services among undocumented immigrant Latinos. *Journal of Immigrant & Refugee Services, 3,* 107–123.

Pew Hispanic Center. (2005, December 6). *Survey of Mexican migrants, part three: The economic transition to America.* Retrieved May 5, 2006, from http://www.pewhispanic.org: Rakesh Kochhar.

Pew Hispanic Center. (2006, March 7). *The size and characteristics of the unauthorized migrant population in the U.S.: Estimates based on the March 2005 current population survey.* Retrieved May 6, 2006, from http://www.pewhispanic.org: Jeffrey S. Passel.

Porter, E. (2005). Not on the radar: Illegal immigrants are bolstering social security. *Generations, 29,* 100–102.

Salgado de Snyder, V. N., Cervantes, C., & Padilla, A. M. (1990). Migración y estrés postraumático: El caso de los Mexicanos y Centroamericanos en los Estados Unidos. [Migration and posttraumatic stress: The case of Mexicans and Central Americans in the United States]. *Acta Psiquiátrica y Psicológica de América Latina, 36,* 137–145.

Santa Ana, O. (1999). "Like an animal I was treated": Anti-immigrant metaphor in US public discourse. *Discourse & Society, 10,* 191–224.

Zea, M. C., Diehl, V. A., & Porterfield, K. S. (1997). Central American youth exposed to war violence. In J. G. García & M. C. Zea (Eds.), *Psychological interventions and research with Latino populations* (pp. 73–93). Boston: Allyn and Bacon.

CHAPTER 9

Resilience and Protective Factors for African American and Latina Girls

Anita Jones Thomas and Caryn R. R. Rodgers

The nation listened in shock as Don Imus called the Rutgers women's basketball team "nappy-headed ho's." Many were surprised at the shock jock's insensitivity, and the furor over the uproar led to his eventual removal from the airwaves. But for many African Americans, the incident was a reminder of the subtle and pervasive forms of racism that exist, and for African American women, the unique form of racism and sexism, gendered racism, that influences the perceptions and image that people have of them. These incidents influence the identity development and psychological functioning of girls, along with interpersonal relationships and other outcomes. Similarly, Latinas have to face issues that influence their identity development and psychological functioning. Whenever the face or portrait of immigration reform is displayed, it includes mostly images of Latinos or Hispanics, despite the fact that many Latino families have lived in the United States for multiple generations. One can argue that African Americans and Latinos are at risk simply on the basis of being ethnic minorities in this country.

Of course, ethnicity is not the only risk marker for African American and Latina girls. There is a continued need for systematic research on African American and Latina girls that characterizes the existing assets and mechanisms that support optimal development in this population. African American and Latina girls face a variety of psychosocial risks, including poverty, living in urban conditions, single parent status, poor academic expectations, and negative stereotypes. Despite the risks that girls face, they also display strength and resilience. Both African American and Latina girls have higher levels of academic achievement and success than their male counterparts. African American girls tend to have a more positive sense of self, as well as a better body image, than white girls. Resilience and strength can be seen in identity development and other protective factors, including self-esteem, racial socialization, and peer support. This chapter will briefly outline the specific risk factors for African American and Latina girls, and then discuss areas of resilience and protective factors. The chapter will discuss the unique identity development of African American and Latina girls and adolescents, the influence of oppression on identity development, self-concept, and psychological functioning, and the role of socialization experiences (armoring) in helping girls cope with oppression and fostering positive identity development.

OPPRESSION AND AFRICAN AMERICAN AND LATINA GIRLS

African American and Latina girls face risk due to the pervasiveness of oppression and negative stereotypical images and perceptions of them. They are viewed according to ethnic minority status and gender, a so-called double jeopardy burden by which society places them in two marginalized categories. There are three stereotypes of African American women stemming from slavery: Mammy, Sapphire, and Jezebel. Mammy is the slave who worked in the owner's house, typically serving as nanny, housekeeper, and cook, and is portrayed as an obese, dark-skinned woman with broad features. She is seen as nurturing, caretaking, selfless, and a good problem-solver. Sapphire, the second image, is strongly associated with the character from the Amos and Andy radio and television show of the 1940s and 1950s. She is perceived as nagging, manipulative and controlling of men, harsh, loud, and argumentative. The third image, Jezebel, is seen as sexy, seductive, and always desirous of sex. African American women are often viewed as promiscuous, loose, immoral, sexually aggressive, and lacking sexual restraint (Mitchell & Herring, 1998).

Similar to African American women, Latinas are often viewed from a negative perspective. The media tends to depict Latinas as passive and submissive, dependent, and emotional. The *marianisma* image is the counterpart to the machismo image of Latino men. Women, particularly mothers, are to behave and function like the Virgin Mary. They are to be pure, asexual, willing to serve others, and submissive to men, and even boys, in families. Marianisma defines the set of cultural expectations for girls that include family commitment, respect for authority, and limitations of girls' mobility (Negy & Woods, 1992). Similar to African American women, Latinas are often portrayed with a focus on their physical attractiveness. They are often seen as promiscuous and sexual, or obese and curvy like the women from the movie *Real Women Have Curves*. The sexuality of young Latinas is seen in the notion of high teenage pregnancy rates and large Latino households with lots of children.

Gendered racial oppression and discrimination influence adolescent girls' identity development and have negative effects on physical and psychological outcomes. Research on adult populations suggests that racism leads to physical and psychiatric symptoms, including high blood pressure, somatic symptoms, anger, paranoia, anxiety, frustration, resentment, helplessness/hopelessness, low self-esteem, and subjective distress (Clark, Anderson, Clark, & Williams, 1999). Experiences with sexism have been linked to premenstrual symptoms, somatization, obsessive-compulsive behaviors, interpersonal sensitivity, depression, and anxiety (Landrine, Klonoff, & Campbell, 2000). Research on African American adolescents indicates that experiences with racism have a significant impact on their mental health, academic achievement, self-esteem, and overall emotional development. Similarly, research on Latina adolescents suggests that they both experience and have anxiety regarding discrimination. Preliminary research on the stereotypical roles of African American women and psychological functioning suggests a relationship between images and symptoms including depression, anxiety, paranoia, and interpersonal sensitivity. Given the significant physical and mental health implications of oppression, more attention needs to be paid to how these experiences influence identity development and functioning and, more importantly, how girls manage to display resilience in the presence of risk.

RESILIENCE

The research and literature on ethnic minority youth has primarily focused on understanding risk factors and developing interventions to reduce risk. Recently, attention to African American and Latina youth has begun to address strengths and resilience. In this chapter, we define resilience as a dynamic process encompassing positive adaptation within the context of significant adversity. This process does not only incorporate individual level processes, but also entails contextual factors including family, community, and environment that contribute to the daily living experience of youth. Resilience helps us to begin to address disparities that exist in the outcomes of children facing similar risks. If two children attend the same lower achieving school in an urban setting beset with violence, what is the process that makes one child thrive and the other succumb to drug dealing and a life of crime? What factors promote healthy lifestyle choices? Models of resilience often include the notion of protective or promotive factors, characteristics, traits, or processes that help individuals to adapt to, become immune to, or overcome risks.

Additionally, models are beginning to address larger contextual and systemic factors including culture, race, and ethnicity. For example, the Phenomenological Variant of Ecological Systems Theory (PVEST) (Spencer et al., 2006) is a model that attempts to account for the race/ethnicity and cultural experiences of African American youth by integrating social, historical, and cultural contexts within the normative developmental process. The model proposes that the perceptions individuals have of their experiences and their self-evaluation throughout the process is critical to functioning, health, and well-being. PVEST includes five components with bidirectional processes that operate in a recursive and cyclical way. Net vulnerability includes risk and protective factors present in the individual's life. Net stress includes challenges and available support systems. The third component, reactive coping processes, includes both maladaptive and adaptive coping styles, and the fourth component, emergent identities, includes positive and negative identity aspects. The final component is stage-specific unproductive or productive coping outcomes. While the model was developed for African Americans, the issues included are similar for Latino youth. Three areas of research on resilience in African American and Latina girls will be highlighted in this chapter: gendered racial identity, self-determination, and gendered racial socialization.

Identity Development

As a part of identity development, youth begin to answer the question "Who am I?," African American and Latino children and adolescents must also answer the question "Who am I as an ethnic minority in the United States?" (Tatum, 1997) as part of the process of developing racial identity. This process is vital because race/ethnicity plays such an important role in our country and is an important part of identity and self-concept. Racial identity is the part of an individual's self-concept or sense of self that is tied to group membership status and the individual's perceptions of that group membership. When examining racial or ethnic identity development for ethnic minority children and adolescents, it is important to remember that racial identity must be developed within the context of an awareness of race and the sociopolitical connotations of race, along with an understanding of minority status within this culture.

Both general and race-specific models of racial/ethnic identity development have been generated. Regardless of the type of model, the process includes individuals beginning with a naïve sense of racial identity, experiencing some type of significant encounter that leads to exploration of culture, and an immersion into culturally specific activities and relationships. The final stages generally include the process of integrating racial or cultural values into identity and self-concept.

Research on racial identity in African Americans suggests that positive racial identity promotes resilience and strength in children and youth in a number of ways for psychological functioning and academic achievement outcomes. First, positive racial identity is related to positive self-esteem. Second, positive racial identity seems to serve as a buffer for acts of racism, discrimination, or prejudice. It is important for children and adolescents to have a healthy sense of their racial group membership to buffer the internalization of negative stereotypes and perceptions. Racial identity seems to promote psychological well-being and reduce psychological symptoms, particularly depression and anxiety. Racial identity has also been studied in its relationship to academic performance. In seminal studies, Fordham and Ogbu (1986) suggested that high-achieving African American students needed to adopt a raceless persona, one that transcended race, as these students often face accusations of "acting white" when they are successful. Subsequent research has contradicted these findings, suggesting that positive racial identity is both directly related to academic performance and indirectly related to achievement, as it serves as a barrier to the negative effects of discrimination. For example, children who endorse Africentric values have more competitive academic attitudes than children who do not endorse such values. When examining children who report experiences of discrimination, those who have a more positive racial identity and feel more connected to their culture have better academic achievement.

The research on racial or ethnic identity development for Latino youth demonstrates similar outcomes to that for African Americans. Findings suggest that ethnic identity in Latinos is related to positive self-esteem, particularly for those living in predominantly Latino areas. Ethnic identity is associated with psychological functioning. Research suggests that identity development is related to worldview value orientations for Latinos, including more collective and less individualistic relationships and perspectives of harmony with nature (Carter, Yeh, & Mazzula, 2008). Research suggests that ethnic identity of Latinos is related to familial socialization. Ethnic identity is also related to developmental outcomes and competencies, including academic achievement, career expectations, and career self-efficacy.

Gendered Racial Identity and Self-Determination

The literature on racial identity is helpful in examining the resilience of African American and Latina girls, but does not capture the essence of gendered racial identity that serves as a protective factor. They have to develop self-concept in light of both gendered and racist forms of oppression, societal images, and stereotypes. For these girls, the question becomes not only "Who am I?" but also "Who am I as an African American and Latina woman?"

When developing an identity, what becomes most important for African American and Latina girls is the ability to determine their own sense of self and to rise above negative stereotypes. Thomas and King (2007) studied socialization practices of African American mothers and daughters, and found that girls cited the importance of self-determination as the most important message conveyed by mothers.

Racial Socialization

Racial socialization is the process of raising children to have a healthy and positive self-concept within an oppressive society. Research has shown that racial socialization enables African American youth to cope with discrimination, making it important to understand the role of racial socialization.

Racial socialization processes have been linked to outcomes in children and adolescents, and research has suggested that practices and messages were related to racial identity attitudes and to self-esteem, depression and anxiety, and anger management, along with school efficacy and achievement in children and adolescents (Hughes et al., 2006). Children socialized to have a sense of cultural pride were less likely to be depressed, and more implicit forms of racial socialization were linked to positive outcomes for African American children and adolescents. Caughy, Nettles, O'Campo, and Lohrfink (2006) found that children had greater cognitive competence with parents whose home included African American culture in the form of magazines, artwork, toys, and clothing. Research on racial socialization has suggested that parental socialization can reduce negative affective experiences, including depression and anger. Specifically, children socialized in an environment of cultural pride were less likely to be depressed, regardless of gender. Stevenson, Herrero-Taylor, Cameron, and Davis (2002) have discussed how cultural socialization can minimize anger and violence in African American youth. Similarly, research on racial/ethnic socialization processes in Latinas has shown a positive relationship between socialization practices and youth outcomes. Racial socialization is associated with a greater knowledge of heritage and identity development.

Research has shown that, while African American teenagers receive racial socialization messages from their parents, those messages are different for boys and for girls. For example, boys tend to receive more messages on overcoming racism, whereas girls receive more messages pertaining to the pursuit of education, premarital sex and relationships with men, independence, and physical beauty. Girls are socialized to be strong, and are provided with so-called armoring, the ability to withstand the double jeopardy status of being African American and female. The emphasis placed on self-determination and assertiveness reflects the image of the strength of black women. Shorter-Gooden and Washington (1996) propose that girls with a sense of strength are psychologically healthier than girls who do not have this sense of strength.

The gender oppression and stereotypic roles for Latinas is often manifested within Latino households. For example, Latina mothers sometimes provide their daughters with mixed messages that simultaneously tell them to become self-reliant and place primary importance on becoming *mujeres de hogar* (women of the home). Girls must struggle with the notion of honoring cultural values of marianismo juxtaposed with dominant or Western values of academic achievement and career success for women.

EXAMPLES OF RESILIENCE

Resilience in African American and Latina girls can be seen through the positive outcomes in self-esteem, body image, and achievement that many experience. This section presents two portraits of girls who display resilience in the face of adversity. Both examples include clinical implications for psychologists and health providers.

Example 1: Proving Them Wrong

Mariana is a 17-year-old college freshman completing her first semester. She describes her struggles in making it to college, and her surprise at the continued discrimination and pressure that she faces. She begins her story by stating that her sole purpose is to prove them wrong by becoming accomplished and established as a pediatrician. She is proud that she will be the first college graduate in her family, and hopefully the first doctor as well. She recognizes that the entire community is watching her progress, and that her achievements and performance will have an influence on younger generations.

Mariana was born and raised in the Bronx. Her parents migrated to the mainland two years before she was born, after the birth of her older brother. Mariana laughs as people assume that they are illegal immigrants attempting to avoid becoming caught and being deported, and that she is Mexican. She experiences frustrations in explaining that as a Puerto Rican, she is still an American citizen with rights and privileges. Mariana's parents both worked in manual labor positions; her father worked in a garment factory and her mother as a maid. Her father often worked double shifts to support the family; both children attended Catholic schools, as he wanted them to have a decent education.

Mariana discusses how her Catholic education seemed to be both a blessing and a curse. The schools she attended were not located in the Bronx, requiring her to travel by subway. When she was in high school and had to wear a school uniform, she thought that people were snickering and laughing at her. She would overhear comments about how her Mexican family must live with at least three families in the home to be able to afford her Catholic education. Her neighborhood friends did not understand why school was so important to her and her family. Many of her neighborhood friends dropped out of high school or became adolescent mothers by age 16. Mariana felt sexual pressure from the boys in the neighborhood, who teased her that the more educated she became, the less physically and sexually desirable she was. At school, she was teased for speaking with a slight accent, and teachers made negative assumptions and comments about her achievement.

Mariana's resilience and school achievement was encouraged by her family. Both her parents and extended family emphasized school achievement and success, and dissuaded dating or sexual experiences. "Like my aunties and stuff, they always just tell me to be successful and to be all that I can be. You know don't settle for lower, don't settle for less, you know be your best. It makes me more focused." Mariana particularly discussed how her father stressed education. He frequently stated that he wanted better opportunities for his children, and that he did not want them to be perceived as "dumb immigrants who come here illegally to take jobs from real Americans." The socialization and care that she received from her family truly served as protective factors for her.

Mariana also struggled with her ethnic identity. She described herself as *Tajino,* a Puerto Rican with a darker complexion and skin tone. Many people assumed that she was Mexican. She felt that she was not accepted by her peers with lighter complexions, who told her that she was not as attractive and would have a hard time dating. (These messages also served to persuade her to underachieve in school.) During the summer between her junior and senior year in high school, Mariana and her family took a trip to Puerto Rico, where she was exposed to people with a variety of skin tones and shades. She took an active interest in learning more about her heritage and history, and left feeling more positively about herself. She entered college identifying as a black Hispanic. Her ability to define herself and become reconciled to oppressive experiences and intragroup judging served as an additional source of resilience for her. Although Mariana still experiences racism and sexism, as well as negative images and roles, she is determined to move forward and succeed. She feels that her success will serve as a model for other Latina girls.

Example 2: Don't Count Me Out

When Alicia graduated high school at the top her class, she did not think of it as resilience, but rather survival. As an African American girl living in a highly segregated city, with two substance abusing parents who been incarcerated for drug-related behavior, many people counted her out. However; school was an escape for her and her way to get out. So, when her name was in the paper as the valedictorian of her class, she was not surprised because she felt as though she had no choice but to succeed. All of her life, she had been used to managing the chaos of having two parents who were drug addicts and living in a family home where she was not accepted or where she was always viewed as the daughter of the drug addict.

Alicia was able to maintain her educational goals by developing a strong sense of self. She had strong teachers who supported her development and were understanding of the difficulties that arose from her family life. She had a supportive grandmother who stepped in when her parents were incarcerated and who took her to church services and programs for youth.

She played basketball in school, and her coach took a special interest in her, often including her in family functions and activities. He also exposed her to successful African American female athletes, which led to a mentorship with one woman. Alicia identifies her as the person who taught her how to cope with discrimination, and those coping skills helped her to deal better with her parents' substance use. She hopes to help other children in the future in the ways that her teachers, coaches, and others supported her.

Implications

These examples demonstrate that, when people judge outcomes of African American or Latina girls based on negative perceptions and stereotypes, they can inhibit their potential. However, African American and Latina girls who develop a positive gendered racial identity and determine their own sense of self tend to show resilience over risks to produce positive outcomes. Racial socialization, including positive messages from parents, extended family, and other caring adults, also helps to promote strength and well-being in children and youth. Given the risks of negative sexual health, substance use, and underachievement, it is imperative for social service professionals to promote resilience in African American and Latina girls.

Psychologists and other health professionals need to help girls to develop a positive gendered racial identity. This includes helping girls to deconstruct negative images and stereotypes. For example, programs that help to promote healthy self-concepts by critically examining media images, from videos to television and movies, can help girls. Providers can also facilitate the racial socialization process by encouraging families to explore their cultural heritage, and to discuss and deconstruct experiences of oppression. Psychologists can help with prevention through establishing mentor programs with successful African American and Latina women.

Consultation needs to be conducted within educational settings to promote resilience. Psychologists can work with teachers regarding teacher expectations, classroom climate, and oppression within school policies and practices. Programs that help with critical consciousness and positive identity development can also be sponsored in schools.

CONCLUSION

When considering the health of African American and Latina girls in the United States, it is challenging to separate race/ethnicity from health and mental health outcomes. Statistics depict deficits and rates of poor outcomes in relation to poverty, lack of high school completion, substance use, pregnancy, HIV/AIDS, and comparisons are made between ethnic minority group outcomes living in socioeconomically disadvantaged urban communities and middle-class suburban white groups. There is often a fatalistic view and limited portrayal of progress and success among African American and Latina girls. However, what is not discussed is the other side of the story: African American and Latina girls who are reaching their optimal potential.

While some resilience researchers have begun to explore how youth in adverse contexts are able to adapt and experience healthy and positive outcomes, there is clearly more needed that focuses on African American and Latina girls. We need to understand more thoroughly how girls process negative images and stereotypes, along with more appropriate portrayals of this population in the media. We need to understand the gendered racial socialization process and armoring for girls, including specific types of messages portrayed, how girls process these messages, and how girls handle conflicting messages from the media and possibly peers. Research needs to be conducted on the relationship between protective factors and behaviors, particularly sexual health behaviors.

This requires shifting the current paradigm of attempting to predict deficits to identifying existing strengths and resources that promote optimal development. In order to approach an understanding of the dynamic interaction that exists between community, family, and individual characteristics, we might begin with asking questions and implementing more mixed method approaches to explore what strengths and resilience exist in many African American and Latina girls' communities. We also may need to ask a different question: instead of asking what factors are predictive or correlate with pregnancy, we can try to understand what girls in similar communities are doing who are not becoming pregnant. Learning from and incorporating members of communities in identifying resilience and strength may have a powerful impact on how we do our work, as well as enhancing the ownership and awareness of health outcomes among African American and Latina girls.

REFERENCES

Carter, R. T., Yeh, C., & Mazzula, S. L. (2008). Cultural values and racial identity statuses among Latino students: An exploratory investigation. *Hispanic Journal of Behavioral Sciences, 30*, 5–23.

Caughy, M. O., Nettles, S. M., O'Campo, P. J., & Lohrfink, K. F. (2006) Neighborhood matters: Racial socialization of African American children. *Child Development, 77*, 1220–1236.

Clark, R., Anderson, N. B., Clark, V. R., & Williams, D. R. (1999). Racism as a stressor for African Americans: A biopsychosocial model. *American Psychologist, 54*, 805–816.

Fordham, S., & Ogbu, J. U. (1986). Black students' school success: Coping with the "burden of acting White." *Urban Review, 18,* 176–206.

Hughes, D., Rodriguez, J., Smith, E. P., Johnson, D. J., Stevenson, H. C., & Spicer, P. (2006). Parents' ethnic-racial socialization practices: A review of research and directions for future study. *Developmental Psychology, 42,* 747–770.

Landrine, H., Klonoff, E. A., & Campbell, R. (2000). Sexist discrimination may account for well-known gender differences in psychiatric symptoms. *Psychology of Women Quarterly, 24,* 93–99.

Mitchell, A., & Herring, K. (1998). *What the blues is: Black women overcoming stress and depression.* New York: Perigee.

Negy, C., & Woods, D. J. (1992). A note on the relationship between acculturation and socioeconomic status. *Hispanic Journal of Behavioral Sciences, 14,* 248–251.

Shorter-Gooden, K., & Washington, N. C. (1996). Young, black, and female: The challenge of weaving an identity. *Journal of Adolescence, 19,* 465–475.

Spencer, M. B., Harpalani, V., Cassidy, E., Jacobs, C. Y., Donde, S., & Goss, T. N. (2006). Understanding vulnerability and resilience from a normative developmental perspective: Implications for racially and ethnically diverse youth. In D. Cicchetti & D. J. Cohen (Eds.), *Developmental psychopathology: Vol. 1. Theory and method* (2nd ed., pp. 627–672). Hoboken, NJ: Wiley.

Stevenson, H. C., Herrero-Taylor, T., Cameron, R., & Davis, G. Y. (2002). "Mitigating instigation": Cultural phenomenological influences of anger and fighting among "big-boned" and "baby-faced" African American youth. *Journal of Youth and Adolescence, 31*(6), 473–485.

Tatum, B. D. (1997). *Why are all the black kids sitting together in the cafeteria?* New York: Basic Books.

Thomas, A. J., & King C. T. (2007). Gendered racial socialization of African American mothers and daughters. *The Family Journal, 15,* 137–142.

CHAPTER 10

Double-Consciousness: A Journey through the Multiplicity of Personal and Social Selves in the Context of Migration

Debora Upegui-Hernández

As I began to work on this project, I was drawn to W.E.B. DuBois's concept of *double-consciousness* for its power to describe a dilemma that I experience in my life day after day as an immigrant in the United States, and that is constantly echoed by my family and friends. Living between two worlds, struggling between two identities are some of the ways that immigrants describe how they feel about their experiences and their different personal and social identities. For this reason, I decided to embark on a journey that would provide a connection between what DuBois called double-consciousness, at the turn of the century, and what today is being called *transnational identity*.[1] One could say that DuBois's double-consciousness became my place of departure, *home*, while transnational identity became my place of arrival, *host*, if we use the metaphor of migration. Selecting the articles that would fill in the space in-between shaped my journey through the multiplicity of personal and social selves.

The notion of multiplicity of personal and social selves, and the understanding of personal and social identities as interconnected processes rather than as separate modes of operating, becomes a thread that unites the articles examined in this paper. These are extremely important concepts that should be part of the psychological study of migration and the identities of immigrants. This chapter presents a review of the chronological legacy of the concept of double-consciousness within the psychological literature, touching on issues of identity important to the understanding of the psychology of migration. At times, this acknowledgement of individuals functioning in terms of interconnected multiple personal and social selves, is more evident (Calkins, 1908; Martín-Baró & Cañas, 1990;

Sorensen, 1998; Timotijevic & Breakwell, 2000) than at others (Allport, 1937/1949, 1954/1979). Sometimes, the object of study is the self and its multiplicity (Calkins, 1908), while at other times the focus has been on one or more specific identities, with the underlying assumption that individuals have multiple identities and selves (Martín-Baró & Cañas, 1990; Sorensen, 1998; Timotijevic & Breakwell, 2000). All of the authors reviewed in this chapter, except for Allport (1937/1949, 1954/1979), co-incide in regarding the person's social and physical context as a major player in their understanding of their identities and in their formation. As Widerman emphatically affirms in his introduction to DuBois's *The Souls of Black Folk:*

DuBois' insights have profoundly alter the way we look at ourselves . . . He locates us, sketches our features, gives us names. *Us* turns out to be most people on the earth, people of color, emigrants, refugees, mixed bloods, exiles, the poor and dispossessed, women and men who didn't count, who were unseen and unheard . . . The color line *raised the issue of identity.* Theirs, Yours, Mine. Will we blend, change, survive, or is the color line one more measure of the limits of our collective imagination, our cultural graveyard of either/or terminal distinctions. (DuBois, 1903/1990, p. xiii, emphasis added)

The space and time allowed for this paper is limited, and therefore I have limited my search to specific areas that talked about the self in terms of identity and in relation to immigration. However, I have not covered the vast amount of literature that echoes DuBois's concept of double-consciousness. The themes embodied by double-consciousness also emerge in the work on diasporic communities, biculturalism, language identity and sexuality, bilingualism, in the psychiatric literature, and in the literature on crossing borders, to name a few.

Double-Consciousness in *The Souls of Black Folk*

The Souls of Black Folk was published in 1903 and represents a recompilation of individual articles written by W.E.B. DuBois, most of which had previously appeared in the *Atlantic Monthly*. During his Harvard years (1888–1892), DuBois was especially influenced by the teachings of William James. This influence would later be evidenced in his development of the concept of double-consciousness. The book portrays a psychological, social, economical, historical, and political picture of the dilemma that African Americans are forced to live with on American soil, in hopes to bring about social justice for his people.

DuBois uses the notion of multiplicity of selves to analyze the reality of oppression that constituted the lives of African Americans in his time. For him, it is extremely important to re-represent the social image that white Americans have of African Americans in a society that not too long ago "classed the black man and the ox together" (1903/1990, p. 27).

Thus, a first step was to argue the psychological depth of the African American psyche and expose the economic, historical, and political realities that contributed to subduing and veiling them. The choice of words in the title shows a clear effort to humanize a group of people that, in the eyes of white Americans, had been mere possessions. DuBois opens up his book with a psychological analysis of identity among African Americans. "Of Our Spiritual Strivings," the first chapter of the book, provides a psychological analysis, while other chapters are filled with short stories, autobiographical accounts, and economic and political analyses. It is here that he introduces the concept of double-consciousness and the metaphor of the veil. According to DuBois, African Americans are:

Born with a veil, and gifted with second-sight in this American World—a world that yields him no true self-consciousness, but only lets him see himself through the revelation of the other world. It is a peculiar sensation, this double consciousness, this sense of always looking at one's self through the eyes of others, of measuring one's soul by the tape of a world that looks on in amused contempt and pity. One ever feels his two-ness—an American, a Negro; two souls, two thoughts, two unreconciled strivings; two warring ideals in one dark body. (1903/1990, p. 9)

This feeling of existing in a two-fold reality lived by African Americans gives rise to the idea that African Americans possess the "gift of second-sight" whereby they can see themselves from the point of view of their own community and of white Americans. Even though this process is seen as positive and implies the possession of a critical consciousness of the world, their place in it, and oppression, it nonetheless carries with it pain, sometimes anger, and even hate. "From the double life every American Negro must live, as a Negro and an American . . . *from this must arise a painful self-consciousness, an almost morbid sense of personality and moral hesitancy which is fatal to self-confidence*" (DuBois, 1903/1990, p. 146, emphasis added).

The veil represents a metaphor for the division between the world of African Americans and the world of white Americans, where the world of African Americans is almost invisible to white Americans. In contrast, African Americans are aware of both worlds simultaneously, giving rise to this feeling of two-ness. The "veil" is a painful reminder of the barriers and discrimination that lie between the striving and desire for self-fulfillment and achievement of African Americans, and the possibility of actualizing them; it is "the Veil that [hangs] between us and Opportunity" (DuBois, 1903/1990, p. 54). But not everyone is fully conscious and aware of the existence of the veil. It seems that participating in social relations with whites and others stimulates the process of developing a critical consciousness and discovering what lies behind the veil. This characterization of the experience of double-consciousness resonates with the experiences of many immigrants and their children. Unfortunately, the American culture of

DuBois's time was not ready to embrace diversity, and so he felt he could not exist anymore within the duality of being either a Negro or an American; he was neither anymore, he was somewhere in-between. He explains:

The History of the American Negro [which] is the history of this strife—longing to attain self-conscious manhood, to merge his double self into a better and truer self. In this merging he wishes neither of the older selves to be lost. He would not Africanize America, for America has too much to teach the world of Africa. He would not bleach his Negro soul in a flood of white Americanism, for he knows that Negro blood has a message for the world. He simply wishes to make it possible for a man to be both a Negro and an American, without being cursed and spit upon by his fellows, without having the doors of Opportunity closed roughly in his face. (DuBois, 1903/1990, p. 9)

DuBois calls for recognition of the multiplicity of selves that a person can have, and for a social reality that allows their expression. He believes that both African-American and white-American culture have much to offer "in order that some day in American soil two world-races may give each other to each those characteristics both so sadly lack" (1903/1990, p. 14). To this end, he highlights the many things Negroes have to offer America and finds that "through all the Sorrow Songs there breathes a hope—a faith in the ultimate justice of things . . . But whichever it is, the meaning is clear; that sometime, somewhere, men will judge men by their *souls* and not by their *skins*" (1903/1990, p. 188, emphasis added).

Self-consciousness is understood by DuBois as the way in which one perceives oneself in the world; in other words, it defines the identity of the person. By acknowledging that the African-American and white-American worlds are "two great streams: they ripple on in the same sunshine, they approach and mingle their waters in seeming carelessness—then they divide and flow wide apart" (1903/1990, p. 132), DuBois describes how a double-consciousness arises among African Americans. In other words, African Americans perceive themselves to be in two different worlds, one Negro and one American; they have two different selves. Given the pain that feeling this two-ness provokes, he strives to reconcile both selves without losing either one. DuBois builds on James's concept of multiplicity of selves by introducing an analysis of social, economical, and political oppression to it. His focus is reduced to exploring only two possible selves of the African American, and he doesn't embark on exploring other aspects of multiplicity, such as gender and class.

Methodologically, it is an interesting book. It is a testimony to his interdisciplinary, humanistic scholarly intellect and his commitment to social change. It represents a mixture of economical, historical, social, and psychological analysis, fiction, autobiography, and so on. These elements may seem unrelated, but they are all parts of a puzzle. They all fit together under the umbrella of the veil, and are used to exemplify what is like to live behind it from many different perspectives and places in the lives of African Americans. The economical and historical chapters are essential in placing his arguments in context, and the short stories, like that of "black John," put faces and personalities to the numbers and policies presented in the economical and historical analyses in order to counteract the abundant genetic arguments that asserted that blacks were genetically inferior. As Rampersad puts it:

DuBois sought, wherever possible, to codify or enumerate; where this was impossible, he moved to reduce apparent chaos or flux to duality, dilemma or paradox . . . From this long history he sought to extract the meaning of the years, with emphasis sometimes on individual character, on national trait, or on the vicissitudes of black fate . . . He relied on fact but added fiction in short-story form. He placed scholarly objectivity beside personal passion and autobiography. The result is one of the more curious books in American literature, a diverse mixture of styles and genres. (1976/1990, p. 69)

He created a complex and multifaceted picture of the African American community at the turn of the century. His account was complex and complete; this is partly why it has endured as one of the most influential works within the African American, psychological, and immigration literature. His description of the dilemma of multiplicity of selves is echoed in immigrants' accounts of their experiences as they adapt to their new contexts.

Double-Consciousness and Self-Psychology

In 1895, Mary W. Calkins could have become the first woman to ever receive a doctorate in psychology at Harvard, but it never happened although she was one of Royce, Munsterberg, and James's most brilliant students (Dykeman, 1993). Under the premise that Harvard did not award degrees to women, Calkins was denied a doctorate after she finished her studies. She would be denied her right to a Harvard degree yet two more times during her lifetime. Like DuBois, Calkins was intrigued by James's ideas regarding the self and its psychological characteristics. She devoted her career as a psychologist to establishing a place for self-psychology within academia. She was perhaps the first female American psychologist, and was the only woman ever to sit as president in the American Philosophical Society and the American Psychological Association. Only two other scholars ever had the privilege of heading both associations: William James and Hugo Munsterberg. The fact that she headed both organizations evidences the closeness between psychology and philosophy during her lifetime, and serves as background to her efforts to explore the differences between philosophy and psychology in the study of the self.

DuBois and Calkins were both at Harvard in 1890–1891, and they both studied with James while there. Therefore, it is not by chance that Calkins's understanding of self-consciousness is related to DuBois's conception of double-consciousness. In her 1908 article, "Psychology as Science of Self II: The Nature of the Self," Calkins delineates her understanding of the "Conscious Self" and her belief that all consciousness represents consciousness of self. Her goal was to rescue the self from philosophy and make it the most important subject of study for psychology.

The self, as posited by Calkins, has four positive characteristics that distinguish it from either idea or function. The four principles that characterize the self are as follows: (1) it is permanent or persistent, (2) it is inclusive, (3) it is unique, and (4) it is related. She contends that these characteristics distinguish the self from the idea or the function and, taken together, support the essential character of self for psychology. The *permanence* and *persistence* of the self allow Calkins to have "consciousness of myself as 'the same ego then as now,' . . . essential to recognition" (1908, p. 65). In other words, the conscious self sees itself as essentially the same self it was yesterday, and will be tomorrow. For example, if I think I am my mother's daughter, I think that tomorrow I will still be my mother's daughter and not someone else's daughter. The second character of the self is *inclusiveness*, by which Calkins means that the self includes ideas, functions, and experiences, which are all parts of the self. A third aspect is *uniqueness*, which "may be described . . . as a consciousness of a this-which-could-not-be-replace-by-another" and may also be "described as individualizing consciousness" (1908, p. 66). The fourth and perhaps most interesting aspect of the self is its *relatedness*, by which the person thinks of him or herself as "a this-in-relation-with-another" (1908, p. 66). The *relatedness* of self as described by Calkins holds much resemblance to James's social self and relates to DuBois's argument that, in the social relations between African-Americans and white Americans, a second self-concept emerges, developing into a double-consciousness of self. That is, African Americans perceive themselves in relation to African Americans and also in relation to white Americans. Within the context of migration, this would entail the perception of immigrants among other immigrants and members of their host society. Calkins adds:

I am always conscious of something-other-than-myself to which I stand in some relation, receptive or assertive; and according as I am more emphatically conscious of myself or of this "other" . . . I can not, indeed, describe or distinguish myself except in terms of my relatedness to other selves [other individuals]: If I drop out of my conception of myself the consciousness of being child, brother, friend, and citizen, *I simply lose myself.* (1908, p. 66, emphasis added)

Calkins emphasizes that losing or leaving behind any of the consciousness she has of herself in-relation-to-others will mean losing herself. In other words, her self-consciousness in relation to others is essential to the core of her self and to her existence. This assertion gives more power and meaning to DuBois's resistance to losing either his Negro or his American self. Each one of those selves holds an essential part of her/himself and leaving it behind would be losing her/himself. Therefore, a society that does not allow people to express and embrace all of their selves (i.e., self as immigrant, self as American citizen, self as ethnic minority), is an oppressive and socially unjust society that precludes its citizens from actualizing their selves. Such a society undermines the very essence of their humanity and compromises their ability to have a consciousness of self. Even though Calkins does not engage in any discussions of power or oppression, her elaboration of the concept of self and self-consciousness as essential to the psychology of the individual gives strength to DuBois's arguments. It presents the dilemma of two-ness as undermining the psychological essence of a person's humanity, his or her sense of self.

One of the reasons why Calkins's position was contested and did not enlist many followers may have been her choice of methodology. In a time when behaviorism was rising, her methodology of introspection was viewed with skepticism. She affirms that her assertions regarding the self were the result of her own introspection. Introspection was, for her, the only way for the self to be realized and understood. Calkins (1908) firmly believed that any objections to her theory should only be achieved through introspection. Many rejected this methodology on the basis that it was unreliable and could not be validated. Titchener believed that "awareness of the self could not be taken for granted in introspective psychology" (Hillgard, 1987, p. 506), even though he used introspective accounts of his students to theorize about the self.

Double-Consciousness and Personal and Social Selves

The consciousness of self as a subject of inquiry in psychology is taken up again by Gordon W. Allport almost 30 years after Calkins's self-psychology. Behaviorism was a very productive field in psychology, displacing the self as the most important subject. Although Allport is mostly remembered for his contributions to personality psychology, he has been called by Kenneth B. Clark "one of America's preeminent social psychologists" (Allport, 1954/1979, p. ix). In his foreword to the twenty-fifth anniversary edition of Allport's book, *The Nature of Prejudice*, Thomas M. Pettigrew affirms:

[Allport's] honored place in psychology had been achieved years prior to his undertaking the writing of this volume [*The Nature of Prejudice*]; *Personality: A Psychological Interpretation*, published in 1937, had firmly established him as one of the world's leading personality theorists. But it was Allport's book on intergroup prejudice that most directly expressed his deepest concerns and values, that translated his more abstract work into concrete ideas for reform and social change. (Allport, 1954/1978, p. xiv)

Allport the personality psychologist should not be divorced from Allport the social psychologist. Even though the self had almost disappeared from the field of psychology since Calkins, it remained alive within Gestalt psychology and psychoanalysis under the term *ego*. Allport equated Freud's ego with *"Emotional Impulse, Conscience,* and cognitive *Self-consciousness"* (1937/1949, p. 182). Based on these assumptions, he uses the term *self* interchangeably with the term *ego*. Allport does not necessarily negate multiplicity in the study of selfhood, but he strives to provide a structure that would serve to unify the multiple notions of self presented by James. "True, each of us is in some sense not one self, but a multiple system of selves. Yet how closely those selves are united and integrated to one personality!" (Sherrington quoted by Allport, 1937/1949, p. 343). In doing so, he makes a strategic move. His theory strives to accommodate both James and Koffka's notions of self, "whether the self is regarded as the innermost nucleus of all conscious ego-systems (Koffka) or as the interplay of all conscious states (James), does not greatly matter. In either case the self is the subjective moderator of whatever unity the personality may have" (Allport, 1937/1949, p. 345).

Allport understands James' selves—Material, Social, Spiritual and Pure Ego—as existing within a hierarchy. The spiritual self and the pure ego self are understood by Allport to equate with the personality principle. Personality is defined as "the *dynamic* organization within the individual of those psychophysical systems that determine his unique adjustment" (Allport, 1937/1949, p. 48, emphasis added). Consciousness is essential to our personal existence and identity. Allport does not believe that all consciousness is self-consciousness as Calkins does. Yet, he explains that it doesn't take a lot to transform any consciousness into consciousness of self, as long as the person views the experiences as related to *his* interests, *his* memories, and *his* personal life. Martín-Baró and Cañas (1990) make a similar distinction in their description of the process of national identity, which will be addressed in a subsequent section of this paper. By considering consciousness as an essential part of human existence and identity, Allport reinforces Calkins's emphasis on the importance of self-consciousness to the essence of a person and gives much weight to DuBois's struggle to create a society that allows the full expression of a person's selves. How this is achieved after all might highlight the differences between DuBois and Allport. While DuBois lobbies for a society that provides a space for the expression of all of the selves a person may have, Allport sees, in the development of a unifying principle of the personality, the structure capable of bringing order to the chaos produced by the painful experience of DuBois's double-consciousness.

Much like Calkins's principle of the persistence/permanence of the self, Allport's personality exhibits what he calls a "sense of *similarity"* where the recurrence of experiences that appear to be similar in some sense provides the person with a sense of temporal reference of him or herself as being the same *then* and *now*. Another important aspect of the personality as described by Allport is its capacity for *extension of the self*. This occurs in relation to one's possessions, friends, one's own children, other children, cultural interests, abstract ideas, politics, hobbies, recreation, or work. These interests that existed as separate from the self become part of the self, thereby extending it. "What one loves becomes a part of him. And anything one can admire, feel sympathy for, appreciate, revere, deliberately imitate, or become unconsciously identified with, may become *introspected* into the personality, and remain ever after a vital part of it" (Allport, 1937/1949, p. 217). By *introspection*, Allport means a process of adopting cultural standards or the interests of others as part of one's personal set of interests and standards. This process of extension of the self resembles Calkins's principle of *relatedness* where the self recognizes itself as a self-in-relation-to-others, where social and personal identities merge. A third aspect of Allport's personality is that it possesses symbols that act as *anchorage points*, which are strategic points of contact between the self and its social context. They mediate the person's sense of self among others and their position in the social hierarchy by providing points of reference in relationships. This aspect of the personality is tied to his theorizing about prejudice as a subject of social psychology. At the level of the personality, a person's proper name (given name at birth) provides the only label capable of describing his or her uniqueness; therefore, it is the most important anchorage point for the person. Building on his theory of personality and the existence of anchorage points to describe a person, Allport (1937/1949) discusses how the use of labels can have a negative effect in perpetuating stereotypes. Labels and nouns, according to Allport, function to describe a person's social place in society by defining attributes of the person's social groups. He adds:

Most people are unaware of this basic law of language—that every label applied to a given person refers properly only to one aspect of his nature. You may correctly say that a certain man is *human, a philanthropist, a Chinese, a physician, an athlete*. A given person may be all of these . . . Yet neither this nor any other classificatory label can refer to the whole of a man's nature (Only his proper name can do so). (Allport, 1954/1979, p. 179)

Again, he acknowledges the multiplicity of social and personal identities possible within a person, but subverts them in relation to the unifying principle of the personality, which is represented by the proper name.

Another important aspect of Allport's conception of self-consciousness related to DuBois's double-consciousness and to Timotijevic and Breakwell's (2000) concept of threat to identity is the understanding that there is such a thing as too much self-consciousness. According to Roback, self-consciousness could reach a point of hypertrophy where "the natural awareness of the self [is] intensified by frequent failure and consequent experiences of shame" (Allport, 1937/1949, p. 164). Allport suggested that a person feels at home (less self-conscious) when he or she feels comfortable with his or her surroundings, where he feels familiarity with his role within the social group, or where he or she can be safely anonymous. But if the person feels uncomfortable with his or her surroundings:

Finally, all experiences of pain, frustration, and especially of social ridicule engender acute states of self-consciousness that leave permanent effects. Whenever one is unable to achieve, or to continue in a condition of friendly relation with the environment, he must perforce pay attention to his own shortcomings, and thereby become acutely aware of the incompatibility between himself and the physical and social world outside, and of his isolation. (Allport, 1937/1949, p. 164)

This passage provides a psychological explanation of the effects of the oppression and pain experienced by African-Americans as they venture beyond the veil described by DuBois. The pain resulting from this feeling of two-ness among African-Americans results from their understanding of the so-called incompatibility between themselves and the world of white Americans. Although DuBois presents a social critique of oppression, Allport stops short at attributing the feeling of isolation to a person's own shortcomings. Therefore, for Allport, the problem rests with the individual's lack of certain characteristics that would allow him or her to overcome this incompatibility, rather than on the society for producing the conditions that create the incompatibility. Allport's description of the painful experience of becoming aware of how the self is incompatible with its environment, and the feeling of isolation it produces, resembles the way Timotijevic and Breakwell (2000) describe experiences of threat to the identity of immigrants as they arrive to new environments.

Double-Consciousness as National Identity

Martín-Baró and Cañas (1990), like DuBois, used social-psychological research to bring about social change and denunciate oppression, be it psychological, social, economical, or political. It is not surprising then, that in their article about national identity, Martín-Baró and Cañas investigate the role of power and oppression in the formation of a national identity. According to the authors, the process of creating a national identity in El Salvador is an alienating process where the ruling classes, those in power and belonging to the upper socio-economic classes, distort reality to their benefit. Under these conditions, a national identity develops that is not based on the reality of all the groups within the country, and serves to perpetuate oppression. The groups that don't see themselves represented in the so-called national identity created by the ruling class could be said to hold a double-consciousness of national identity. In 1903, DuBois described an American society where white Americans defined what American national identity was and African-Americans felt excluded from that description of Americanness. In 1990, Martín-Baró and Cañas (1990) described a Salvadorian society where the ruling class defines Salvadorian identity and the working poor, indigenous groups, peasants, and displaced peoples of El Salvador felt excluded from it. The authors conceive national identity, ideally, as an exercise in nation-building whereby the objective is to unite and enable a population to work as a group towards a common inclusive goal.

There are two types of factors that make up a national identity: *objective* factors, which are the common characteristics of a given group (e.g., ethnic, economic, political, cultural); and *subjective* factors, which allow a person to assume the national identity and to feel part of the group. There are two aspects related to the subjective factors of a national identity. First, each person has a *consciousness* of the identity; secondly, there is a *normative acceptance* of the identity. This distinction between consciousness of the identity and its acceptance is important, because a person may have consciousness that there is a national identity but may not have accepted it as part of his or her identity. Furthermore, such distinction leaves space for a person to consider him or herself Salvadorian (in this case) without taking on all the characteristics associated with a Salvadorian national identity. The existence of common characteristics does not presuppose the existence of a consciousness of a national identity, nor does the existence of a consciousness of a national identity presuppose the acceptance of that national identity as one's own. Montero (1984, cited by Martín-Baró & Cañas, 1990, p. 2) defines national identity as:

el conjunto de significaciones y representaciones relativamente permanentes a través del tiempo que permiten a los miembros de un grupo social que comparten una *historia* y un *territorio común*, así como otros elementos socioculturales, tales como el lenguaje, una religión, costumbres e instituciones sociales, reconocerse como relacionados los unos con los otros biográficamente.

the group of meanings and representations relatively permanent through time that allow members of a social group that share a *history* and a *common territory*, as well as other sociocultural elements, such as language, religion, customs, and social institutions, to recognize themselves as related to each other biographically. (translation and emphasis are mine)

The history of a people and a common territory are essential in this definition of national identity and sets it apart from a definition of ethnic identity.[2] In an earlier article, Martín-Baró and Cañas (1990) posited that Salvadorians understand themselves as Salvadorians to the extent that they assume the Salvadorian national identity as images that are related to their social group such as family, friends, neighbors, and so on, their specific natural context, their customs, and their lifestyle. This conception of national identity resonates with Calkins's principle of relatedness and with

Allport's extension of the self. It also sets the background for understanding how the image of national identity produced by ruling classes may be different from that of working-class, indigenous, displaced, and peasant Salvadorians. Their realities and the social groups they interact with are bound to be different in terms of class, ethnicity, and so on. Martín-Baró and Cañas are not the commonalities that create a Salvadorian identity, but they are questioning how inclusive a Salvadorian identity created by the ruling class will be. This, in turn, highlights the existence of double/ multiple consciousnesses operating in the negotiation of personal and social identities for Salvadorians, including that of national identity.

They used a number of methodologies to investigate the self-images that Salvadorians had of themselves as Salvadorians nationals/citizens, and to examine whether their national self-identity matched their reality or was the result of an ideological distortion of the Salvadorian national identity. They used both surveys and focus groups to identify what characteristics make up the Salvadorian national identity and to explore what different groups thought it meant to be Salvadorian. The national sample was the only one to mention *alienated* and *exploited* as characteristics of the Salvadorian national identity. This difference is more apparent in the analysis of the focus groups, where the labor workers, peasants, and displaced persons discussed *suffering* and *exploitation* as part of their reality as Salvadorians. On the other hand, professionals, students, and teachers emphasized being a good worker and industriousness as the most common characteristics of being a Salvadorian. Based on these results, Martín-Baró and Cañas argue that middle- and upper-class Salvadorians are unaware of the reality of oppression, alienation, and exploitation that is present in the lives of other Salvadorians.

Salvadorians of a lower socioeconomic status were quick to name the oppression they face, much like African Americans named their oppression, because, according to DuBois, they possess "the gift of second-sight." They experienced DuBois's double-consciousness, although not necessarily on the grounds of race. Therefore, the task of constructing a national identity should be a new national project where all the different social realities merge and are heard, and where *"el trabajo no suponga explotación y la alegría no se funde en la inconsciencia sobre la propia realidad histórica* (where work does not suppose exploitation and happiness does not forge itself in the lack of consciousness of one's own historical reality)" (Martín-Baró & Cañas, 1990, p. 23). In this framework, national identity regains a place of importance in the study of social identity, especially as it relates to the experiences of immigrants and globalization. Typically, United States' psychologists and researchers have studied the social identities of immigrants using the category of ethnic identity; however, with ever increasing globalization and migration flows, it is necessary to reconsider what national identities continue to mean for immigrants in their hosts countries before treating them as ethnic identities.

Double-Consciousness as Transnational Identity

Following the legacy of DuBois (1903/1990), and Martín-Baró and Cañas (1990), Sorensen (1998) challenges the tradition of thinking in terms of fixed entities, dichotomies, and categories. She is pushing open the categories of ethnic, national, social, and personal identity; the definitions of home and host countries as spaces that define identities. Her task is to explore the complexity inherent in the relationship between migration and identity by focusing on the case of the Dominican migration experience. In her own words, "in this world, the Dominican cultural identity space is occupied by transnationals and locals whose lives and experiences are interweaved with the questions of *aquí?* or *allá?*, of here? and there?" (Sorensen, 1998, p. 243). The study of transnationalism is not new. In 1906, Gino Speranza, secretary of the Society for the Protection of Italian Immigrants, affirmed that "the conception of citizenship itself is rapidly changing and we may have to recognize a sort of world or international citizenship as more logical than the present peripatetic kind, which makes a man an American while here, and an Italian while in Italy . . . The old barriers are everywhere breaking down" (cited by Foner, 2001, p. 35). A contemporary of DuBois, Speranza recognized in the experiences of Italian immigrants what DuBois called double-consciousness. They too experienced the sense of two-ness, of two unreconciled strivings, two warring ideals in one body. As we shall see, Sorensen describes this feeling of two-ness as present in the experiences of Dominican immigrants as well.

Although the dilemmas encountered by immigrants since the early 1900s are still alive, the perspectives from which they have been understood have changed. The social context within which migration occurs has gone from a vision of assimilation during the early part of the twentieth century, through to acculturation, melting pot, and finally pluralism. These views all rest on fixed definitions of *home* and *host* countries that serve as points of departure or arrival for the development of identity among immigrants. Sorensen (1998) challenges those definitions, arguing the existence of a transnational space that "encompasses the whole of what individual migrants have lived through and therefore bears the potential for bringing experiences from different times and different locations into one single field of analysis" (p. 244). Sharing this transnational space serves as a common characteristic that allows migrants to view themselves as a group of transnationals that share a social identity: "They are here and there and in between" (Guarnizo, 1994, cited by Sorensen, 1998, p. 244).

Based on the understanding that individuals possess multiple identities that interact with each other, Sorensen adds an analysis of the intersection between gender and transnational identity among Dominican immigrants. Her methodology is reminiscent of the interdisciplinary nature of DuBois's in constructing *The Souls of Black Folk*. She understands that people not only "speak, tell stories, dance, pray, or sing. Informants also *consume* different types of products" (Sorensen, 1998, p. 250). Sorensen directs her attention to the products that are produced and consumed within the transnational space shared by Dominican immigrants, be it literature written from the margins of hybridity and "in-between-ness," television commercials, or public spaces. Her fieldwork dives into the everyday life of Dominican migrants and looks for identity in their day-to-day experiences, which rings truer to what it might be like to share that transnational space. To this end, she analyzes two novels by Julia Alvarez, a known Dominican writer who migrated to New York City early in her life, and two commercials: one used to market cigarettes in Dominican Republic using New York icons, and a second that presents a mini *telenovela* (mini soap opera) of transnational migration in order to market a brand of Dominican rum. Finally, she gives a small ethnographic description of the Dominicanization of a public plaza in Madrid, Spain, as a transnational space. Like DuBois, Sorensen presents us with slices of transnational experiences in the lives of Dominican migrants. The first of Julia Alvarez's novels is an autobiographical account of her life and that of her sisters, *How the Garcia Girls Lost their Accent.* This is a perfect example of what a life narrative of a transnational Dominican woman might look like. In Sorensen's (1998) words:

The Garcia girls—the story of them—is a story of the clash between two worlds—the incompatibility of being an emancipated young woman from New York in the Dominican Republic and the hardships and losses of being a Dominican woman in New York City . . . Back "home" on a holiday visit one of the sisters considers that return would be the solution to her *split* identity. She never returns, though, and the story about the Garcia girls concludes as follows: The girls' struggle toward womanhood is inseparable from their struggle to understand their own multifaceted identity, and to come to terms with it. *This identity is neither Dominican nor American, but both and in-between.* (p. 252, emphasis added)

The dilemma the Garcia girls lived through could not be closer to the African American dilemma DuBois narrates for us. Perhaps the merging of selves DuBois calls for could realize itself somewhere in this transnational space, this in-between space to which Sorensen refers. Others have also articulated the existence of an in-between space as a challenge to traditional fixed identity categories (Anzaldúa, 1987/1999). In the above passage, we can also discover Allport's theorizing about the effects of painful self-consciousness and the realization of incompatibilities between the personal reality and the social reality around the self conceptualized as a threat to identity in Timotijevic and Breakwell's (2000) work.

Double-Consciousness and Migration and the Threat to the Identity Concept

The experience of migration serves as the backdrop for the discussion of identity and multiplicity of personal and social selves. Timotijevic and Breakwell (2000) explore how migration might represent a threat to identity, and more broadly how sociopolitical contexts might create threats to identity. They based their argument on *Identity Process Theory*, where identity represents a dynamic social product that influences the social context by affecting its social processes. It results from the interaction of the capacities for memory, consciousness, and biological characteristics with physical and societal structures. The researchers assume that people actively monitor their identity, are self-aware, and at the same time renovate, replace, revise, and remove elements of their identity as they see fit; in other words, they are *self-constructors* of their identities. Breakwell's identity process theory recognizes that there is continuity of self-identity across time and space, but that this continuity is subject to the person's own reflexive interpretation. This continuity also appeared in Calkins's definition of the self as permanent/persistent across time, and in Allport's sense of similarity in the recurrence of experiences. A most important aspect of identity process theory that Timotijevic and Breakwell (2000) point out, is that "the distinction between social and personal identity is abandoned. Seen across the biography, social identity is seen to become personal identity: the dichotomy is purely a temporal artifact" (p. 356). This expands the interconnectedness between social and personal identities implicit in Allport's writings (1937/1949, 1954/1979). It also resonates with the process that Martín-Baró and Cañas (1990) describe, whereby aspects of the social identity of a group are evaluated and incorporated as part of an individual's social and personal identity according to their fit with his or her own values and cultural standards.

The structure of the identity described by Breakwell (1986) possesses two dimensions: *content* and *value/affect*. The content dimension could easily be understood according to Calkins's principles of uniqueness and inclusiveness, for it includes the characteristics that, taken together, make the individual unique. The content dimension includes properties usually believed to belong to the social identity of the individual, such as group membership, roles, social category labels, and so on, and those usually seen as the content of personal identities, such as values, attitudes, cognitive style, and so on. The value/affect dimension of identity allows the individual to assign positive or negative value/affect to a specific characteristic. Based on the value/affect assigned to the elements that make up the identity, the individual modifies, revises, or removes elements from his or her identity as needed in order to accommodate changes in the social context. The process by which one revises one's identity is called *evaluation* and serves to regulate the identity process, as well as the process of *assimilation/accommodation,* by which one either absorbs new components into one's identity or reorganizes the existing identity in order to create a place for new elements. The desirable states for the structure of identity are called guidance principles, and they may be temporally and culturally specific. Therefore, one society may desire continuity, distinctiveness, self-efficacy, and self-esteem (i.e., Western industrialized societies) while another may hold other aspects of identity as desirable. This can change with time and across situations, as well as across the lifetime of the person. Changes in identity can occur as a result of changes in social context according to:

  i. Their personal relevance
  ii. The immediacy of involvement in them
  iii. The amount of change demanded
  iv. How negative the change is deemed to be. (Timotijevic & Breakwell, 2000, p. 357)

If the processes of assimilation-accommodation are not able to provide the basis of maintaining the guidance principles of the identity (i.e. continuity, distinctiveness, self-efficacy, and self-esteem in Western industrialized societies), then a threat to the identity is experienced. "For a threat to evoke action, it must gain access to consciousness" (Timotijevic & Breakwell, 2000, p. 357). Migration can represent a threat to identity if it results in changes in the social context where the bases for continuity, distinctiveness, self-esteem, or self-efficacy are no longer available to the individual. This experiencing of threat is likely to trigger changes in identity. Just as DuBois (1903/1990), Calkins (1908), Martín-Baró and Cañas (1990), and Sorensen (1998) explore the multiplicity of selves and identities, Timotijevic and Breakwell (2000) recognized that:

it is questionable to what extent people indeed act only in terms of just one identity . . . Any social identity does not necessarily function in isolation from other identities within the overall identity-structure—it exists in a specific position relative to other aspects of identity as well as the overall identity-structure. (p. 359)

Exploring how migration and radical sociopolitical upheaval might pose a threat to identity and how immigrants cope with such threat, Timotijevic and Breakwell (2000) chose to examine life-narratives of former Yugoslavian migrants. Given the exploratory nature of the subject and the highly sensitive nature of the issue of inquiry, they interviewed migrants from the former Yugoslavia in-depth. They used Interpretative Phenomenological Analysis to discern important recurrent themes; that involved three steps: an initial close reading of each transcript, identifying shared themes, and exploring links and possible conflicts between the themes that emerged. They concluded that:

Being an immigrant, a refugee, a foreigner, a stranger or a guest, are the new labels and categories that one has to deal with . . . For our respondents, being an immigrant requires dealing with two opposing, but equally derogating representations—that of an intruder (in relation to the host-country) and of a traitor (in relation to the home-culture) . . . They both reflect distinctiveness based on exclusion. (Timotijevic & Breakwell, 2000, p. 366)

These words echo a feeling of being in-between worlds; one is no longer from here or there, as Sorensen puts it, but rather finds oneself in a social and psychological space between the home and the host country. According to Timotijevic and Breakwell (2000), each individual would revise, renovate, replace, or remove some elements of his identity in order to accommodate this new reality. They still understand identity within the dichotomy of home and host country. It may well be that a third "transnational space," as Sorensen calls it, will come to play an important role in how this reconstruction of identities occurs or perhaps in determining how much reconstruction is needed.

CRITICAL TURNS IN THE JOURNEY THROUGH MULTIPLICITY OF PERSONAL AND SOCIAL SELVES

The concept of double-consciousness, as described in DuBois's book *The Souls of Black Folk* (1903/1990) has taken many turns and detours throughout its intellectual life within psychology. I will now mention a few turns and detours going from double-consciousness to multiple consciousness, multiple, national, and transnational social identities. One of the most important turns occurs with respect to how the study of identity is split into the theoretical dichotomy between personal identity and social identity, whereby the former related to the domain of personality psychology and the latter to the domain of social psychology. This theoretical dichotomy was not there in DuBois' definition of double-consciousness, where self-perception was the result of the social relations between African Americans and white Americans, nor was it there in Calkins and James's concept of the self or selves. On the contrary, that which is considered social identity was part of the self and the personal identity as well. Allport talks about social and personal identities as separate processes where the principle of *anchorage points* (from his personality theory) and *social labels* (from his work on prejudice) name different social identities that are unified by the *proper name* (label that represents the *Personality* structure). Later in 1985, Martín-Baró challenges this dichotomy and Timotijevic and Breakwell (2000) write it off in stating that "the distinction between social and personal identity is abandoned" (p. 356) in Breakwell's (1986) model of identity process theory. This view is shared by Sorensen, which further invites us to consider social relations across international borders as worthy of study as well.

A recurrent theme in the evolution of DuBois's double-consciousness as a concept has to do with his account of pain associated with its development.

He further elaborates on the effects of such pain and isolation on the psychological well-being of African Americans. Calkins (1908) addresses the effects of not being able to express all of one's selves, whereby losing one of one's multiple selves means losing oneself entirely. However, she does not explore the pain or stress that may result from having to live in between social worlds that are or seem incompatible. A discussion of this pain reappears in Allport's theorizing of the personality; he posits that unfamiliar and uncomfortable contexts and surroundings elicit a painful self-consciousness where the person recognizes an incompatibility between him or herself and the context. However, while DuBois denounces social, economical, and political oppression as the cause of such pain, Allport believes that the pain develops from realizing one's own shortcomings and seems to let society off the hook. The incompatibility is a result of the individual being unfit for the society rather than the society not providing a space for the person's self-realization. Martín-Baró and Cañas (1990) discuss the pain that develops when one becomes conscious of the social injustices and oppression, and does not feel represented in the national identity ideologized by the ruling classes. The pain is a result of invisibility and exclusion from the process of national identity construction. Sorensen (1998) acknowledges and discusses the pain that lacking a complete sense of belonging either in the host or the home country creates, which in many respects echoes Timotijevic and Breakwell's (2000) concept of *threat to identity*, that undermines people's sense of continuity (essential to the self) and creates a feeling of isolation.

The authors differ in their opinion regarding what they consider an ideal situation for the self or selves. While DuBois (1903/1990), Calkins (1908), Sorensen (1998), Martín-Baró and Cañas (1990) and Timotijevic and Breakwell (2000) agree that all identities, social or personal, should be able to coexist and be expressed, Allport believes that the *personality* should serve the function of providing organization and a hierarchy for the sake of achieving the unity every personality strives for. On the other hand, Sorensen (1998) suggests that a *transnational* or *in-between* space would allow the merging of selves that DuBois calls for to occur, perhaps necessitating fewer revisions of identity than those described by Timotijevic and Breakwell (2000), and occurring in a less oppressive and stressful way. Martín-Baró and Cañas (1990) understand that, in an ideal situation, a national identity would be an inclusive national project that unites and facilitates citizens of the same nation-state working together towards a common goal. One way in which oppression can be fought is therefore by allowing the expression of a person's social and personal selves. This will not win the war, but is one more battle towards victory.

However narrow or complex the authors' definitions of their particular concepts are, they coincide in reminding their readers that people's lives and experiences are complex and multiple and should not be reduced to fixed categories or theoretically, socially, psychologically, or politically superficial dichotomies. People's experiences will always push theoretical dichotomies and boundaries (i.e., DuBois's double-consciousness, Calkins's self, Allport's discussion of social labels, Martín-Baró and Cañas's national identity, Sorensen's transnational space, and Timotijevic and Breakwell's migrants' identity). The recognition of multiplicity in people's lives becomes essential to counteracting oppression and the invisibility of groups that are oppressed in different ways.

WHAT LIES AHEAD?

I began to work on this chapter with the understanding that the process of immigration and transnationalism are areas that merit the attention of personality and social psychologists. As I reach the conclusion of this task, I leave with a stronger conviction that transnational identity should be explored more intensively from a psychological perspective. As Deaux (2000) points out: "Not only is it timely and important as a social issue, but it is wonderfully rich in possibilities for theory and research" (p. 429). It seems urgent that we bring awareness and make visible the many ways in which gender, class, and race inequality manifests itself within circles of transnational migration.

It is clear that transnational migration represents a difficult choice for migrants and a source of trauma, loss, and violence for some. But at the same time, it can represent a space for rupture, resistance, and possibility. Feminist psychologists have reminded us of the importance of highlighting and giving voice to those moments of resistance, agency, and resilience in order to recognize the full value and dignity of people's lives as a whole (Fine, 2007; Lykes & Coquillon, 2007). And it is here, in the social and psychological study of transnational migration, such as mothering across borders; transnational nickels—how women send money home; trafficking of bodies; undocumented women laborers in the United States; domestic violence among undocumented women who can't seek help; and undocumented children who are growing up in prison cells away from family and friends, where the most important lessons can be learned and where action is most needed.

NOTES

1. Transnational identity as such doesn't seem to be articulated within psychology yet, although the term has begun to be used within anthropology, sociology, and migration studies. It is my belief that the study of transnational identity within psychology merits consideration. I hope to provide foundations for those links in this chapter.

2. In reality, these identities are sometimes harder to pull apart and differentiate. In many instances, ethnic identity is taken to stand for national identities when the person doesn't live in the country of nationality. Still, many immigrants understand their identities as national identities and not as ethnic identities.

REFERENCES

Allport, G. W. (1937/1949). *Personality: A psychological interpretation.* New York: Henry Holt and Company.

Allport, G. W. (1954/1979). *The nature of prejudice.* New York: Addison-Wesley Publishing Company, Inc.

Anzaldúa, G. (1987/1999). *Borderlands: The New Mestiza = La Frontera* (2nd ed.). San Francisco: Aunt Lute Books.

Breakwell, G. M. (1986). *Coping with threatened identities.* London: Methuen.

Calkins, M. W. (1908, January 30). Psychology as science of self II: The nature of the self. *The Journal of Philosophy, Psychology and Scientific Methods, 5*(3), 64–68.

Deaux, K. (2000). Surveying the landscape of immigration: Social psychological perspectives. *Journal of Community & Applied Social Psychology, 10,* 421–431.

DuBois, W.E.B. (1903/1990). *The souls of black folk.* New York: Vintage Books/The Library of America Edition.

Dykeman, T. B. (1993). *American women philosophers 1650–1930: Six exemplary thinkers.* Lewiston, NY: The Edwin Mellen Press.

Fine, M. (2007). Feminist designs for difference. In S. N. Hesse-Biber (Ed.), *Handbook of feminist research: Theory and praxis* (pp. 613–620). Thousand Oaks, CA: Sage.

Foner, N. (2001). Transnationalism then and now: New York Immigrants today and at the turn of the twentieth century. In H. R. Cordero-Guzmán, R. C. Smith, & R. Grosfoguel (Eds.), *Migration, transnationalization, and race in a changing New York* (pp. 35–57). Philadelphia: Temple University Press.

Hillgard, E. (1987). *Psychology in America: A historical survey.* San Diego, CA: Harcourt Brace Jovanovich.

Lykes, M. B., & Coquillon, E. (2007). Participatory and action research and feminisms: Toward transformative praxis. In S. N. Hesse-Biber (Ed.), *Handbook of feministh research: Theory and praxis* (pp. 297–326). Thousand Oaks, CA: Sage.

Martín-Baró, I., & Cañas, J. S. (1990). ¿Trabajador alegre o trabajador explotado? La identidad nacional del Salvadoreño (Happy Worker or Exploited Worker? The National Identity of Salvadoreans). *Revista Interamericana de Psicología/ Interamerican Journal of Psychology, 24*(1), 1–24.

Rampersad, A. (1976/1990). *The art and the imagination of W.E.B. DuBois.* New York: Schocken Books Inc.

Sorensen, N. N. (1998). Narrating identity across Dominican worlds. In M. P. Smith & L. E. Guarnizo (Eds.), *Transnationalism from below* (pp. 241–269). New Brunswick, NJ: Transaction Publishers.

Timotijevic, L., & Breakwell, G. M. (2000). Migration and threat to identity. *Journal of Community & Applied Social Psychology, 10,* 355–372.

Appendix: Key Questions

CHAPTER 1

What can I do to contribute to an accepting and positive atmosphere for the identity formation and psychosocial development of multiracial persons?

CHAPTER 2

The shift from unilinear to bilinear models of acculturation provided the theoretical and empirical foundation for the study of bicultural identity. In what direction is the field of biculturalism heading? What will likely be the focus of future research on biculturalism?

CHAPTER 3

How does your racial identity and sexual orientation impact your work with this population?

CHAPTER 4

What are the social and psychological implications of the increasing numbers of interracial marriages?

CHAPTER 5

How are the effects of the glass ceiling on female academics of color similar and different from others (e.g., nonethnic minority women, men of color)?

CHAPTER 6

How can narratives be useful in psychotherapy in terms of helping clients to heal?

CHAPTER 7

How can our society increase and improve culturally competent mental health services for Asian American immigrants?

CHAPTER 8

As mental health providers, how can we advocate for (undocumented) Latino immigrants so that they receive the necessary mental health services?

CHAPTER 9

What are the factors that promote or contribute to resiliency in African American and Latina girls?

CHAPTER 10

How does the concept of double consciousness, experienced by African Americans at the early twentieth century, relate to the experience of immigrants in the United States today?

About the Editor and Contributors

JEAN LAU CHIN, EdD, ABPP, is professor and dean of the Derner Institute for Advanced Psychological Studies at Adelphi University in Garden City, New York. Prior to her current position, she held executive management positions as Systemwide Dean of the California School of Professional Psychology at Alliant International University; president, CEO Services; regional director, Massachusetts Behavioral Health Partnership; executive director, South Cove Community Health Center; and co-director, Thom Child Guidance Clinic. She is a licensed psychologist with over 35 years of experience in education, health, and mental health services. Her prior faculty appointments included: associate professor at Boston University School of Medicine and assistant professor at Tufts University School of Medicine. Dr. Chin is an educator, administrator, clinician, and scholar. She has published extensively, with 10 books, many chapters and articles, and over 200 presentations in the areas of diversity and cultural competence; ethnic minority, Asian American, and women's issues in health and mental health; and leadership. Her most recent books are: *Women and Leadership: Transforming Visions and Diverse Voices* (2007) and *Learning from My Mother's Voice: Family Legend and the Chinese American Experience* (2005). She serves on many national and local boards including: the Advisory Committee for Women's Services and the Eliminating Mental Health Disparities Committee for Substance Abuse Mental Health Services Administration, U.S. Dept of Health and Human Services; Board for the Advancement of Psychology in the Public Interest of the American Psychological Association; board member of the National Asian Pacific American Families Against Substance Abuse; and president of the National Council of Schools and Programs of Professional Psychology.

ANABEL BEJARANO, PhD, is assistant professor in the clinical psychology PsyD program at the California School of Professional Psychology at Alliant International University in San Diego; she also maintains a private practice. Dr. Bejarano's areas of interest are Latino mental health, with a focus on interpersonal violence and trauma, migration and acculturation, and ethnic identity and child development. She has presented nationally on these issues. Her research interests included suicidality among young Latinas. She is actively involved in the leadership of the American Psychological Association, the California Psychological Association, and the San Diego Psychological Association, with a focus on diversity issues. Dr. Bejarano was born in Bogotá, Colombia, and migrated to the United States in early childhood.

VERÓNICA BENET-MARTÍNEZ is an associate professor of psychology at the University of California, Riverside. After receiving her BS in psychology from the Universitat Autonoma de Barcelona, she pursued a PhD in social-personality psychology at the University of California, Davis, and later was a postdoctoral researcher at the University of California, Berkeley. She was on the faculty at the University of Michigan until 2003, when she returned to California to join the faculty at University of California, Riverside, where she heads the Culture and Personality laboratory. Her main research interests are (1) biculturalism: contextual and individual processes involved in the integration of two or more cultural identities; and (2) culture and personality: identification and measurement of indigenous and universal personality constructs and cultural influences on personality.

STEPHEN CHEUNG is associate professor of the Department of Graduate Psychology at Azusa Pacific University in Azusa, California. He has taught various therapy courses, including group therapy and family psychology and therapy. Before he started full-time teaching in 2004, Dr. Cheung had been a program director and clinical psychologist at Asian Pacific Counseling and Treatment Centers (APCTC) in Los Angeles, coordinating and supervising their adult and children programs for twelve years. While serving at APCTC, he taught part-time at California State University at Los Angeles and Pepperdine University. For over three decades, he has been providing short-term and longer-term psychotherapy to a wide range of clients. Consequently, he has specialized in: immigrant mental health; therapy for eating, substance-related, personality, mood, anxiety, and attention-deficit hyperactivity disorders; and childhood maltreatment and grief. Dr. Cheung has been a founding member of the Consortium on Asian American Mental Health Training in Los Angeles that has been providing annual training conferences for mental health professionals since 1994. Moreover, he has served in various capacities in Division 43 (Society for Family Psychology) of the American Psychology Association (APA), the Asian American Psychological Association (AAPA), and the First 5 California.

ALICIA M. DEL PRADO is an assistant professor at the Wright Institute in Berkeley, CA. She has a PhD in counseling psychology from Washington State University and a BS in psychology from Santa Clara University. She completed her predoctoral internship and postdoctoral fellowship at University of California, Berkeley, where she provided individual and group counseling to multiculturally diverse clientele in the university's counseling center. Dr. del Prado has taught undergraduate and graduate courses on psychopathology, cross-cultural psychology, psychological and educational assessment, and career development at Santa Clara University, Sonoma State University, and Washington State University. Dr. del Prado has a professional and personal commitment to multiculturalism. She was born and raised in the San Francisco Bay area in an Italian and Filipino family. For her dissertation, she developed and validated an enculturation scale for Filipino Americans. She has conducted and published cross-cultural research studies on personality with participants in Australia, Japan, Malaysia, Mexico, the Philippines, and the United States. A multiracial woman, she is especially dedicated to working toward the actualization of full visibility and voice of multiracial persons.

MARIA L. DITTRICH is a licensed psychologist in private practice in McLean, VA, just outside Washington, DC. She is also an assistant clinical professor of psychology at George Washington University. She earned her PhD in clinical psychology from George Washington University in 2005 and was formerly associated with South Florida State Hospital in Pembroke Pines, FL. Dr. Dittrich spends the majority of her professional time in private practice, but also teaches undergraduate courses in clinical psychology, abnormal psychology, psychological tests, and research methods. Her clinical and research interests include the process of coming out to selves, families, and others, as well as negotiating one's new identities along the way. She works mainly with adults, couples, and sexual minority youth. Dr. Dittrich is a member of the American Psychological Association (Divisions 12 and 44) and Virginia Psychological Association, and is listed in the National Register of Health Service Providers in Psychology.

JONATHAN R. FLOJO is a staff psychologist at the University of California at Irvine Counseling Center. He received his PhD in counseling psychology from the University of Oregon. His professional work centers on access and equity. His specialty areas include multicultural mental health, cultural competence, healthcare policy, educational development and academic persistence, program evaluation, and policy analysis. He has provided consultation and technical assistance to nonprofit agencies in education, healthcare, and mental health. He has been a behavior analyst, early interventionist, therapist, career counselor, and program evaluator. He has taught in a variety of settings including preschool, elementary, university undergraduate, and university master's and doctoral level programs.

LISA E. HARRIS is a PhD candidate in clinical psychology at The Derner Institute of Advanced Psychological Studies at Adelphi University. She holds a master's degree in social work from the School of Social Work at New York University, and she is a Licensed Master Social Worker in New York State. Ms. Harris has been working in the mental health field with culturally, racially, and socioeconomically diverse populations in a variety of settings for over ten years, addressing numerous clinical issues that include substance addiction, sexual orientation, and minority disenfranchisement. Besides her studies, Ms. Harris continues to see clients at the Washington Square Institute in Greenwich Village, New York City.

QUE-LAM HUYNH is a doctoral candidate in social/personality psychology at the University of California, Riverside. Her research lies at the intersection of cultural, social, and personality psychology. Specifically, her interests include acculturation/enculturation theory and measurement, biculturalism, multiple identity negotiation, bicultural identity development, and cultural essentialism. She received a BA in psychology from the University of San Diego and an MA in research psychology from California State University, Long Beach.

ANITA JONES THOMAS, PhD, is a counseling psychologist with specializations in multicultural counseling and family therapy. Dr. Thomas received her bachelor's degree in human development and social policy from Northwestern University, and a master's degree in community counseling from Loyola University Chicago. Her doctorate in counseling psychology was received from Loyola University Chicago. Dr. Thomas is assistant professor at Loyola University Chicago where she teaches courses in school counseling, theories, multicultural issues, and family therapy. She has also served as professor at Northeastern Illinois University. Her research interests include racial identity, racial socialization, and parenting issues for African Americans. She has also conducted training seminars and workshops on multicultural issues for state and national professional organizations in counseling and psychology, and in hospitals and corporations, as well as serving as a consultant for human service organizations. Dr. Thomas has served as governor for the Illinois Counseling Association, president of the Illinois Association for Couples and Family Counseling, and corresponding secretary for the Association of Black Psychologists, Chicago chapter. She is currently a member of the American Psychological Association's Task Force on Resilience and Strength in Black Children and Adolescents.

DEBRA M. KAWAHARA is an associate professor in the clinical psychology PsyD program at the California School of Professional Psychology at Alliant International Psychology. She also maintains a private practice in San Diego, CA. Her research and professional interests include multicultural and community psychology, Asian American mental health, women's issues, and cultural competency in mental health services and supervision. Dr. Kawahara has numerous publications and presentations in these areas. Her most recent publication is the book *Feminist Reflections on Growth and Transformation: Asian American Women in Therapy*, focusing on the integration of multicultural and feminist principles in psychotherapy when working with women of Asian ancestry. She also has been an active member and officer for several professional organizations, including the American Psychological Association and the Asian American Psychological Association.

GIDEON S. KIM, MA, is a candidate for a PhD in clinical psychology at The Derner Institute for Advanced Psychology. He received a master's degree in counseling from the Alliance Graduate School of Counseling and is a licensed mental health practitioner in New York State. Mr. Kim was also a Medicaid service coordinator working with the Office of Mental Retardation and Developmental Disability through the Jewish Guild for the Blind.

JAMES LYDA is currently a staff psychologist at University of California, Berkeley, Counseling and Psychological Services. He earned his PhD in counseling psychology from the University of Oregon in 2008. Dr. Lyda was awarded an APA Minority Fellowship in Mental Health and Substance Abuse Services in 2003. Over the past seven years, he has worked in college counseling centers at the University of Oregon, University of Minnesota, Twin Cities, and UC Berkeley, serving a diverse group of traditional and non-traditional undergraduate, graduate, and professional students. He has also held clinical positions in community mental health and child and family service agencies. His clinical interests have focused on psychosocial development in young adulthood, and multicultural counseling. Specifically, Dr. Lyda's research has focused on racial identity development and psychosocial aspects of mixed race identity, particularly in traditional age college students. Dr. Lyda is, himself, of mixed African American and European American heritage. He and his partner reside in San Francisco.

NADINE NAKAMURA is a postdoctoral research fellow at the University of California, San Diego. She graduated from George Washington University in 2007 with a PhD in clinical psychology. Dr. Nakamura's research interests include HIV risk taking behaviors with ethnic/racial and sexual minorities, HIV prevention intervention development, and negotiating multiple identities. Her clinical experience is primarily with LGB and college student populations. Dr. Nakamura has taught a variety of undergraduate courses, including Asian American Psychology. She is a member of the American Psychological Association and serves on Division 44's Committee on Racial and Ethnic Diversity.

ANGELA-MINHTU D. NGUYEN's research lies within the areas of cultural, social/personality, and industrial/organizational psychology. She is specifically interested in acculturation, biculturalism, bilingualism, cultural frame-switching, and cultural intelligence training. She holds a BA in psychology from the University of San Diego and an MA in industrial/organizational psychology from California State University, Long Beach. She is currently pursuing a PhD in social/personality psychology from the University of California, Riverside.

KIRSTEN PETERSEN is a doctoral candidate at the Derner Institute of Advanced Psychological Studies. She received her BFA in animation from the School of Visual Arts in 1999 and worked as a freelance animator and comic book artist for several years before deciding to return to school to become a psychologist. At the time of this publication, Ms. Petersen will have completed an externship at Rikers Island, a New York City correctional facility, where she saw patients and ran an art group. Ms. Petersen's current research interest is looking at experiences of intimacy among bisexual individuals in same-sex and cross-sex relationships and how those experiences may relate to adult attachment style.

LUCILA RAMOS-SÁNCHEZ was born in Mexico and raised in Northern California. She received her BA and MA in psychology from California State University, Chico. She received a master's degree and doctorate from the University of California, Santa Barbara in counseling/clinical/school psychology, with an emphasis on counseling psychology. Lucila is currently an associate professor in the Department of Counseling Psychology at Santa Clara University. She developed and is currently coordinator of the Latino Counseling Emphasis, a concentration of courses aimed at working the Latino population. Lucila has published numerous articles in the area of Latino mental health, with particular interest in variables that affect counselor credibility, the effects of bilingualism in the counseling process, and stress associated with acculturation issues. Her research also includes the examination of the relationship between self-efficacy and academic achievement of Latino students and Latino immigrant mental health. Lucila lives in Santa Clara with her husband and her children. Her interests include spending time with family, running, and reading.

CARYN R. R. RODGERS earned her doctorate in clinical psychology from St. John's University in Jamaica, NY. Upon achieving her doctorate, Dr. Rodgers completed the Leadership and Education in Adolescent Health (LEAH) fellowship in adolescent medicine through Harvard Medical School at Children's Hospital Boston. Subsequently, she completed a fellowship in Community-Based Participatory Research (CBPR) through the W. K. Kellogg Community Health Scholar program at Johns Hopkins University Bloomberg School of Public Health. She currently serves as a faculty member in the Prevention Intervention Research Center in the Department of Pediatrics at Albert Einstein College of Medicine in the Bronx, NY. Dr. Rodgers focuses on adolescent health promotion in low-income urban communities of color. Her research examines the dynamic interaction between protective and risk factors of adolescent problem behaviors (i.e., substance use and sexually risky behavior). Through the employment of CBPR as a research approach, Dr. Rodgers works with communities, families, and youth to further understand factors that promote resilience, strength, and adaptive functioning among economically disadvantaged urban youth of color. Through the identification and promotion of resilience within communities, she intends to develop and promote effective prevention and intervention programs to increase adaptive and successful life outcomes for low-income urban youth and families of color.

ALLISON M. ROTHMAN, currently entering her fourth year of doctoral training, is a PhD candidate at the Derner Institute. She completed her undergraduate degree at the University of Pennsylvania. Ms. Rothman has presented her research at the 2007 APA Convention and has previously published a co-authored article in the Journal of Consulting and Clinical Psychology. Her research experience and interests include socioeconomic status and adolescent well-being, with particular focus on relationships with parents and identity. Ms. Rothman has also contributed to research involving entitlement and work sharing in contemporary relationships. She currently sees patients at the Center for Psychological Services at Derner, as well as through the New York Psychoanalytic Society and Institute. Her patients are from a community population and include young children, adolescents, and adults, with family therapy as her current clinical focus.

JESSICA SHIMBERG, MA, is a doctoral student in clinical psychology at Adelphi University's Derner Institute for Advanced Psychological Studies. She completed her undergraduate degree at New York University. Ms. Shimberg has presented her research at the New York State Psychological Association's 2007 annual convention. She is currently working on her dissertation, which focuses on personality, romantic relationships and infidelity. Of particular interest to her is how gender differences in attitudes toward cheating are mediated by aspects of personality, such as attachment style and empathy.

JANICE M. STEIL was trained as an experimental social psychologist with special interests in the psychology of justice and gender. Her early work focused on the conditions that differentiate when those who are disadvantaged by a discriminatory system will deny their own disadvantagement as compared to when they will protest and seek change; as well as the conditions under which the advantaged will act on behalf of the disadvantaged. In 1979, after receiving her PhD from Columbia, she became a faculty member at the Derner Institute at Adelphi University where she began to apply her interests in gender and social justice to the area of work and family and dual earner relationships. Her book, *Marital Equality: Its*

Relationship to the Well-Being of Husbands and Wives, was published in 1997. Consistent with her interests, she was an associate editor of *Psychology of Women Quarterly* and is a Division 35 fellow of the American Psychological Association.

JUSTIN P. STEIL is pursuing a JD/PhD in law and urban planning at Columbia University. He is an editor of *Searching for the Just City: Debates in Urban Theory and Practice,* forthcoming from Routledge, and author of the chapter in that volume, "Can the Just City Be Built from Below?" His work on racial and economic justice has included positions as advocacy director for a financial justice nonprofit fighting predatory lending, program manager for an environmental justice organization focusing on brownfield redevelopment, program manager for a project bringing youth and prisoners into critical dialogues about just responses to violence, and trainer with a domestic violence crisis center instructing police in the support of survivors of sexual assault. Broadly interested in issues of difference, power, and justice, his dissertation focuses on local government responses to immigration. He received an MSc in city design from the London School of Economics and an AB in African-American Studies from Harvard University.

JOSEPH E. TRIMBLE (PhD, University of Oklahoma, Institute of Group Relations, 1969), formerly a fellow at Harvard University's Radcliffe Institute for Advanced Study, is professor of psychology at Western Washington University, a senior scholar at the Tri-Ethnic Center for Prevention Research at Colorado State University, and a research associate for the National Center for American Indian and Alaska Native Mental Health Research at the University of Colorado Health Sciences Center. He has held numerous offices in the International Association for Cross-Cultural Psychology and the American Psychological Association (APA). He holds fellow status in three APA divisions: 9, 27, and 45. He is past-president of the Society for the Psychological Study of Ethnic Minority Issues and a former council member for the Society for the Psychological Study of Social Issues. Since 1972, he has served as a member of scientific review committees and research panels for the following federal agencies: NIAAA; NIDA; NIA; NIMH; National Heart, Lung and Blood Institute; NICHD; NCI; National Center for Research Resources; Risk, Prevention, and Health Behavior, NIH; Center for Substance Abuse Prevention; National Academy of Sciences; NSF; NIDA's Subcommittee on Epidemiology and Prevention Research; and NIDA's Risk, Prevention, and Health Behavior Initial Review Group. Currently, he is a member of NIDA's Health Services Research Subcommittee. Dr. Trimble has generated over 130 publications on cross-cultural and ethnic topics in psychology, including 16 edited, co-edited, and co-authored books; his co-edited *Handbook of Racial and Ethnic Minority Psychology* was selected as one of *CHOICE* magazine's Outstanding Academic Titles for 2004. His recent books include (with Celia

Fisher) the *Handbook of Ethical Research with Ethnocultural Populations and Communities*, and (with Paul Pedersen, Juris Draguns, and Walt Lonner) *Counseling Across Cultures, 6ᵗʰ Edition*. He has received numerous excellence in teaching and mentoring awards for his work in the field of ethnic and cultural psychology, including: the Excellence in Teaching Award and the Paul J. Olscamp Outstanding Faculty Research Award from Western Washington University; APA's Division 45 Lifetime Achievement Award; the Janet E. Helms Award for Mentoring and Scholarship in Professional Psychology at Teachers College, Columbia University; the Washington State Psychological Association Distinguished Psychologist Award for 2002; the Peace and Social Justice Award from APA's Division 48; and the Distinguished Elder Award from the National Multicultural Conference and Summit in 2007.

DEBORA UPEGUI-HERNÁNDEZ is a doctoral candidate in the Social-Personality Psychology Program at the CUNY Graduate Center. She is currently working on her dissertation, titled: *Colombian and Dominican Second Generation Immigrants Negotiating Multiple Identities: A Multiple Methods Secondary Analysis*. Her research interests include: identity negotiation, multiplicity of identities, national/racial/ethnic identity, transnational identity, immigration, displacement, education, and social justice research. She has recently presented papers related to conceptualizing and operationalizing a transnational research agenda within psychology at The Border is Everywhere: "New" Spaces and Actors in Transnational Migration between Latin America and the United States symposium at the Latin American Studies Association in Montreal, Canada (September, 2007) and at the Rethinking Latin America and the Caribbean, Latin America and Caribbean Studies conference at Stony Brook University, Manhattan, NY (April, 2007).

Index